KASHMIR AND SINDH

NATION-BUILDING, ETHNICITY AND REGIONAL POLITICS IN SOUTH ASIA

Suranjan Das

T0346441

Anthem Press

KASHMIR AND SINDH

by Suranjan Das

ISBN   1 89885 587 0 (hardback)
         1 89885 569 2 (paperback)

Printed in Hungary by Interpress

Anthem Press

Anthem Press is an imprint of the Wimbledon Publishing Company
P.O. Box 9779, London SW19 7QA Fax: +44 (20) 8944 0825

**To my mother
who remains a source of my strength
to meet the challenge of life**

Contents

Preface

This volume owes its origin to a Volkswagen Stiftung-funded research project on 'Foreign Affairs as Home Affairs: A Comparative Analysis of Inter-State Relations in the Arab East and South Asia', which was jointly undertaken by me and Dr Eberhard Kienle of the School of Oriental and African Studies, University of London. The generous Volkswagen grant provided me with preliminary research support and enabled me to undertake research trips to the UK and USA. Subsequent Visiting Fellowships at the University of Illinois at Urbana-Champaign, USA, and the Maison des Sciences de l'Homme, Paris, offered me ideal facilities to collate the data and plan this monograph. But the present study would have remained incomplete if in the concluding part of my research I had not received financial assistance from a Ford Foundation grant to the Peace Studies Group, Department of History, University of Calcutta.

In the course of writing this monograph I incurred many a debt which can hardly be repaid. To Professor Barun De I am grateful for providing me with the entry points to address the 'ethnic question' in south Asia. The analytical framework for the present monograph, however, developed from the lengthy and critical discussions I had with Eberhard on the literature of ethnicity and nation-building. In fact Dr Kienle's book on *Ba'th vs. Ba'th: the conflict between Syria and Iraq 1968–1989* (London: 1990) provided me with theoretical insights to explore in a comparative context the relationships between the politics of ethnicity and nation-building. I have been fortunate to receive constructive comments from Professor Tapan Raychaudhuri, Professor Stephen Cohen, Professor Jean Racine, Professor Richard Herrmann, Dr Raj Chandravarkar, Dr Crispin Bates, Dr Gowher Rizvi and Professor Sumit Ganguly that helped me to sharpen or modify my arguments. I would also like to recall my rewarding interactions with Dr Moonis Ahmar, Dr Mohammed Waseem and Dr Iftikhar Malik. The challenging questions that were posed to me at the seminars in Oxford and Cambridge universities and at Maison des Sciences de l'Homme in Paris made me rethink some of my initial formulations on the nature of the Kashmir and Sindh questions. Thanks

1

are due to the staff of India Office Library and Records (London), the Indian Institute Library (Oxford), the Centre for South Asian Studies (Cambridge), Library of Congress (Washington DC), Nehru Memorial Library and Museum (New Delhi) and National Library (Calcutta) for rendering me all possible assistance. Professor Bireswar Banerjee very kindly prepared the maps. My colleague Hari Vasudevan ungrudgingly read the entire manuscript and spent long hours suggesting various stylistic changes. Professor Bharati Ray, Professor Jayanta Ray, Professor Basudeb Chattopadhyay, Bhaskar Chakrabarti and Professor Arun Bandopadhyay of my Department in Calcutta University have kept me intellectually alert, without which I would not have been able to undertake new research ventures. I should also put on record the unalloyed support I have received from my family – my mother, parents-in-law and brother. My wife Suparna – herself a historian – has been a source of sustenance, both intellectually and emotionally. Suhasini provided me with pleasant breaks between computer sessions. Unfortunately, however, my father who had a keen interest in this work could not see the finished product. Finally, I am most grateful to the Department of History, University of Calcutta, for sponsoring the publication of this monograph under its UGC Special Assistance Programme. Sincere thanks are also due to Shri Kanak Bagchi for supervising the production of this volume with considerable care and rigour.

Recent scholarship has highlighted the need to develop a comparative approach for unfolding the common dilemmas in South Asian political processes. In this work an attempt has been made to explore the Kashmir and Sindh questions within the two common subcontinental parameters of nation-building and ethnic assertions. While the book was in press Navnita Chadha-Behera's much awaited *State, Identity and Violence: Jammu, Kashmir and Ladakh* (Delhi: 2000) was published. It will remain a matter of regret that I was unable to use this work which could have enriched my thesis on the Kashmir question in Indian federalism. If the arguments in my monograph appear unconvincing, or suffer from inaccuracies, the responsibility remains mine alone.

Suranjan Das
Department of History
University of Calcutta

Introduction

A state can be defined as an organization invested with the monopoly of means of coercion over a given territory and population. By contrast, a nation is a grouping of individuals who, on the basis of whatever criteria and in contradistinction to other such groupings, owe each other feelings of loyalty and solidarity. States *per se* claim to represent nations. For a state exercises its authority in the name of the people. But there could be a situation where a state fails to be coextensive with nation, leading groups of individuals living within the frontier of that particular state to imagine themselves as members of a loyalty group whose identity does not coincide with the borders of that state.[1] In such circumstances, possibilities of cross-border loyalties may also exist. Such potentials are especially strong in the Third World where the process of artificial decolonization has caused non-convergence of state borders with cultural and ethnic frontiers. Faced with this lack of congruence between state and nation, a successor state in the former colonized world has recourse to a nation-building project. This involves an attempt to forge a domestic political and social consensus for creating a nation, so that the state and nation become coterminous.

In each nation-building process, identity politics constitutes a mediating force between state and society. A crucial aspect of identity assertions in multi-ethnic post-colonial states has been ethnic politics. While in the industrialized world of the North ethnic politics is usually played out within existing state structures, and ethnic identities tend to get subsumed by more encompassing identities emanating from socio-politico-economic processes, ethnic assertions in the Third World states – particularly where nation-building strategies betray gross distortions – usually assume separatist and irredentist tendencies, challenging the format of nation-state created in the wake of decolonization. Not surprisingly, the implicit assumption in traditional political science literature that states correspond to nations and nations to states has been exploded by continuing doses of ethnic secessionism, especially in the Third World. Methodologically, the present explication of the Kashmir question in India and the Sindh issue in Pakistan draws upon the insights provided by this analytical model which relates ethnic politics to the non-convergence of state and nation.

1. NATION-BUILDING IN INDIA AND PAKISTAN

1.1. The Indian Scene[2]

The Transfer of Power to the two successor states in the subcontinent represented – to borrow a term from Antonio Gramsci – 'a passive revolution', passive not in the sense that the people were inactive, but passive because there was no telescoping of political and social revolution. The political transformation was not accompanied by a fundamental socio-economic transformation. That was the historical context of future distortions in the nation-building processes in India and Pakistan which have generated ethnic secessionism in both countries.

Despite certain obvious outward changes in forms of governance or employment of new political hyperboles, the Indian government under Jawaharlal Nehru largely represented a continuation of British attitudes both in form and substance. Hamza Alavi has shown that, like many other post-colonial regimes, the successor states in South Asia were 'overdeveloped'.[3] The British Raj had reared a repressive state apparatus which exceeded the needs of an 'underdeveloped and poor post-colonial state'. The Congress government after 1947 unfortunately chose not to 'develop an alternative state structure', but to maintain the police and paramilitary organizations inherited from the British.[4] As Betelheim contends, the administrative system in independent India thus retained many of the colonial system's imperfections.[5] The Indian people generally confronted the same civil servants and police personnel who had treated them with 'scorn and brutality' during British rule. N.K. Bose, by no means a leftist critic of the Indian polity, thus summarized the situation in the late 1950s:

> ...by virtue of the circumstances of peaceful transfer of power, the Congress inherited an administrative structure which it tried to use for a new purpose. Its idea became, not to disrupt the status quo, but to build up its 'socialistic pattern' of economy on the foundation of the existing order without a violent disturbance. In this prosaic task of reformation, the Congress party...had tried to convert every problem of national reconstruction into an

administrative problem… The identification of the Congress with the status quo, even if the ultimate intention may be of using it as a spring-board for reform…has made the organization unpopular… The loss of ethical quality in the contemporary endeavours of the Congress in the reorganization of its party machinery, or in the matter of running an old administrative machinery without sufficient proof of desire or capability of reforming the latter, has created a kind of frustration, and even of cynicism amongst those who had made the attainment of political freedom synonymous with the advent of social revolution or moral regeneration.[6]

The relationship that the Congress government in independent India developed with the police and military signified a shift from the party's 'ostensible antagonism until 1947 to increasing interdependence…in the post-colonial period'.[7] Between 1949 and 1950 the Congress regime in New Delhi used about 12,000 armed police personnel to curb the Telengana peasant upsurge; in the first decade of independence as many as 800 recorded deaths resulted directly from police actions; the police expenditure of the Indian government increased from Rs. 9 million in 1951–2 to Rs. 800 million in 1970–71; the army assisted the civil authorities to restore order on 476 occasions between 1961 and 1970 and 250 times between 1980 and 1983.[8]

The economic policy of the first government in independent India was one of compromise. Despite his 'leftist' pretensions, Jawaharlal opted in the Industrial Policy Resolution of 1956 for a 'socialistic' and not a 'socialist' pattern of society. Although a system of mixed economy and Five Year Plans was adopted in principle, what actually occurred was 'a move towards state capitalism' with considerable participation by the private sector. The following table demonstrates the importance of the private sector during Nehru's stewardship of the country:

(*Crores* – tens of millions, or 100 *lakhs* – of rupees in current prices)[9]

	First Five Year Plan	Second Five Year Plan
Public	55	938
Private	283	850

At the close of the Third Plan period, the public sector's share increased by only four per cent, while about nine-tenths of the total domestic product came from the private sector during the same period.[10] The few top business houses with a strong communal and regional character – 20 according to the Mahalanobis estimate and 75 according to the Monopolies Inquiry Commission Report of 1965 – retained a controlling voice in the economy.[11] Besides, the volume of direct foreign investment rose from Rs. 2,176 million in 1948 to Rs. 6,185 million in 1964 and the share of foreign companies in gross profits of the Indian corporate sector increased from 29.8 per cent in 1959–60 to 33.3 per cent in 1962–3.[12] An inevitable upshot of such developments was a substantial rise in the absolute number of people below the poverty line and an increasing concentration of wealth. There were reasons to fear that the number of the poor by the turn of the century would exceed the total population of the country at the time of independence.[13]

The political system that developed under Nehru also betrayed a particular contradiction. On the one hand, the country had one of the world's broadest spectra of political formations. On the other, the establishment of Congress hegemony resulted in one-party political order. The Congress party won impressive majorities in parliamentary elections and maintained organizational strength outside legislatures. Opposition groups, except the Communists and Jana Sangh (now the BJP), were mostly formed by rebels from the Congress itself, many of whom either rejoined the parent body or became champions of local interests. Since the opposition failed to present a united national front, the Congress under Nehru could win 60–80 per cent of parliamentary seats without securing 50 per cent of the votes cast. Congress dominance came to coexist with 'competition but without a trace of alternation'.[14]

In such circumstances Nehru tended to accept opposition until it remained 'diffused and articulated within the orbit of the Congress system'.[15] Each non-Congress provincial regime thus fell victim to the hegemonic drive of the Congress party. Between 1952 and 1964 Nehru imposed President's Rule (a constitutional term for central rule) on federal units at least five times either to dislodge non-Congress Chief Ministers or to offset the collapse of merger moves between Congress and non-Congress groups. This one-party domination distorted the functioning of Indian federalism. Undue political, administrative and financial centralization under Congress guidance became the hallmark of the Indian polity. 'The most important state leaders were attracted to the centre, and the centre had enough prestige to bring local party leaders and legislators into line.'[16] State governors were inevitably 'hand-picked' by the centre; efforts were always undertaken to have 'malleable' Chief Ministers even at the cost of elevating personalities with no local base, as was the case with the installation of Dr Katju in Madhya Pradesh by Nehru in 1963. The Planning Commission that formulated the Five Year Plans, the Finance Commission that allocated financial resources for the states, the University Grants Commission that oversaw higher education, the All India Radio that ran the broadcasting network – all these were and are still controlled by the central government. The imposition of the Emergency in 1975 and the populist authoritarianism of Mrs Gandhi were logical corollaries to this centralized state structure and one-party democracy. This distorted centre-state relation has tended to create serious regional economic imbalances. For instance, in terms of economic progress, the eastern and north-eastern areas of the country have fallen far behind the western and southern parts, thanks to 'discriminatory interventionism' of the central government. A recent study of the Associated Chambers of Commerce and Industry showed that even in the sphere of external financial assistance for developmental projects, the richer provinces of the country cornered more than 37 per cent of the total grant in 1997–8, as against 22 per cent in 1990–91.[17] In the words of the veteran Indian Marxist leader B.T. Ranadive, the centrist posture of Indian federations has led to:

> distortions in the functioning of the constitution and concentration of all powers in the hands of the Centre, leading to inequalities in economic advance.[18]

Big business, urban professionals and bureaucracy – civil and military – provide the sustaining force for this centralized political structure.[19] This centrist process, smacking of the Viceregal style, has been called 'the dominance of gubernatorial politics'.[20] Such unitary features of Indian federalism undoubtedly bred 'corrosive regional dissensions' that have often tended to gain expression in the form of 'sectarian violence and political anomie, undermining the very basis of national unity that

7

centralization is supposed to achieve'.[21] In a multi-ethnic state with uneven economic and political growth under a centrist bourgeois-landlord rule any ethnic or linguistic dissension acquired an anti-Delhi character.[22] Indian federalism has recently experienced the healthy sign of coalition politics resulting in a coexistence of central and provincial governments with different political orientations. But the country now faces a new challenge – the attack on secular credentials of the constitution from the Sangh Parivar-led Hindu sectarian forces.

1.2 The Pakistan Experience[23]

At the time of Independence, Pakistan had no viable party organization to sustain the political structure of the new nation. Unlike the Indian National Congress, which had an enduring presence in 'the local structures of politics in Hindu-majority provinces', the Muslim League was a patchy body with practically 'no organizational presence in the Muslim-majority provinces'.[24] Jinnah was the sole spokesperson of Muslim politics in British India only at the national level; he had little command over local politicians.[25] In such circumstances the Muslim League after August 1947 had to fall back upon regional political networks among locally powerful landed magnates who were, however, not subjected to any rigorous party control. The tenuous political hold of Jinnah and the central government over local politics was further complicated by both the ethnic diversity in Pakistan and the fact that the new state was a geographically splintered territory with the western wing separated from the eastern wing by a thousand miles and an intermediate Indian territory.

The political void created by the absence of an effective party machinery of the League was filled by a centralized political structure under the aegis of a Punjabi-dominated military-bureaucracy combine. Inevitably, whenever the generally fractious politicians agreed on the adoption of a constitution to govern the country, this axis stepped in to assume political power. Pakistan thus remained under military or quasi-military rule for nearly 21 years of its existence, being governed under six different constitutions, most of which were eyewashes for military domination over the political system.[26] The pre-eminence of this military-bureaucratic grouping was bolstered up by the US-led Western bloc, which sought to use Pakistan as an outpost in the Cold War confrontation with the erstwhile Soviet Union. The Western patrons of Pakistan felt that the brittle state of the country's economy required a depoliticized military regime to facilitate economic growth, of course, in neoclassical terms having little regard for social equity.[27]

The martial rule of Ayub Khan (1958–68) was apparently a period of unprecedented economic growth for Pakistan. Throughout the 1960s the gross national product (GNP) of Pakistan rose by 5.5 per cent and the per capita GNP by three per cent. In the first half of the same decade a 17 per cent expansion was registered in the large-scale industrial sector.[28] Towards the end of the 1960s the adoption of Green Revolution technology also caused a substantial agricultural growth. Besides, the pursuit of pro-Western foreign policy enabled Pakistan to receive a liberal dose of foreign aid that constituted 42 per cent of the total investment in the industrial sector even in the 1980s.[29] Nevertheless, this economic boom brought little benefit to the masses. Instead, it accentuated a deep class polarization in Pakistani society. New industrialization accrued benefits to 22 families – mostly Punjabis – who exercised control over nearly 66 per cent of industry, 97 per cent of insurance and 80 per cent of banking. Amongst the Asian countries Pakistan's investment in education tended to be the lowest. Moreover, wages of industrial workers fell by nearly 12 per cent in West Pakistan between 1954 and 1967.[30] Small traders were ruined by Ayub's preference for large industrial houses and big businesses. Inflation seriously eroded the income of students and minor government employees.[31]

Agrarian policies of the Ayub regime undermined the economic position of small and poor peasants too. The 1959 land reforms proved to be cosmetic. A Land Ceiling Law was introduced. But nearly 57 per cent of the resumed land belonged to the uncultivated category, although the government paid Rs. 89.2 million as 'compensation' for this barren land. Besides, a large part of this resumed land was given to military and civilian officials at throwaway prices.[32] Not surprisingly, during the Ayub days the increasing percentage of large-size farms was associated with a corresponding decline of small- and medium-size farms. At the same time the manipulative practices of big landlords and other intermediaries deprived the small peasants of access to markets. In the absence of land reforms, the introduction of new production technologies accordingly led to a shrinkage of employment opportunities in the rural areas.

The other corrosive aspect of the nation-building process in Pakistan was the regional imbalance within the country. Punjabi hegemony over the military-bureaucratic state apparatus and imposition of a pan-Pakistani Urduized culture resulted in the marginalization of other ethnic groups like Bengalis, Pathans, Baluchis and Sindhis. None of the constitutions of 1956, 1962 or 1973 contained effective provisions for the reflection of provincial interests. The 1973 constitution did exhibit some federal principles, but when there was an attempt to implement them they proved to be more apparent than real. Regional discriminations were thus inbuilt in the Pak polity.

Immediately after the creation of Pakistan, the Bengalis in the eastern wing of the country represented just over half of the nation's population, but even at the end of the 1950s they represented only five per cent of the officer corps of the army, 15 per cent of the air force, 20 per cent of the navy and a bare presence in the civil service.[33] At the other end of the spectrum Baluchistan – the largest province of Pakistan – remains the most poverty-stricken and least populated. Compared to the national average of 30 per cent, only 8.5 per cent of the Baluch population is literate. This has severely restricted their presence in the civil and military administration. The Sindhis – as the present volume indicates – have been similarly discriminated against in the matter of government employment. Not surprisingly, in 1985, while the Punjabis occupied 56 per cent of the federal posts, the respective shares of rural Sindh, urban Sindh, the NWFP and Baluchistan were 3.5 per cent, 25 per cent, 11 per cent and 2.5 per cent.[34] In the same year the Punjabi presence in middle and senior level jobs of the public sector was to the tune of 41 per cent, while the shares of rural Sindh, NWFP and Baluchistan was respectively 3.5 per cent, 6 per cent and 1 per cent.[35]

Lack of integrated economic development caused this regional imbalance, resulting in growth conclaves juxtaposed by backward zones. It resulted in a form of internal colonization. Punjab emerged as the chief supplier of finished products and the main purchaser of raw materials in the Pakistani market. The erstwhile East Pakistan was worst hit by this arrangement. With 'its lower per capita income [it] became a handy dumping ground for over-priced and generally poor quality West

Pakistani manufactures'.[36] Again, although Baluchistan produced 80 per cent of the country's gas requirements[37], a paltry sum of Rs. 25 million was earmarked for development planning of that province during the first three Five Year Plans.[38] Similar evidence of economic discrimination against Sindhis has been cited in this work, and need not be detailed here. What is more, this policy of economic centralization, and the consequent lack of uniformity in economic progress, was capped by the imposition of a state-sponsored Urduized Islamic pan-Pakistani identity. This threatened the linguistic identities of East Bengalis, Sindhis, Baluchis and numerous ethnic groups in the North-West Frontier Province. To quote a pertinent remark:

> In an apparent inversion of the Indian example where concessions to language were countered by continued central controls on the constituent units, the Pakistani state opted to stump linguistic regionalism…[39]

The rise of Zulfiqar Ali Bhutto at the end of the 1960s with his slogan of Islamic socialism and a promise of social justice for the underprivileged generated new hopes for rectifying the structural imbalance in Pakistan's federal polity. But a considerable gap soon became manifest between the rhetoric and actual political practice of Bhutto. When parliamentary elections were held in 1970, Bhutto's Pakistan People's Party (PPP) won a majority of seats in the western wing of the country. But during the actual process of the transfer of power from a military to a civilian government, Bhutto demonstrated scant respect for the Awami League, which had swept the poll in the eastern part of Pakistan.[40] What followed was the secession of East Bengal from Pakistan and its christening as the sovereign state of Bangladesh. The failure of the PPP to respect the democratic wish of East Bengalis can be explained by the hegemony within the PPP of the landed aristocracy, which remained committed to the country's military bureaucratic establishment and a centralized political structure.[41] The dominance of propertied elites within the PPP also impeded the implementation of Bhutto's promised 'socio-democratic' reforms in Pakistan.[42]

To sustain his position Bhutto now had recourse to Mrs Gandhi-type populist authoritarianism. Opposition-controlled elected provincial governments were dismissed. Civil liberties were severely restricted. Constantly haunted by a fear of Bangladesh-style secessionist war, Bhutto accused all political opponents of disrupting the national unity and integrity of the country. He even went so far as to rig the parliamentary election of 1977. This instantly caused a massive political agitation under the leadership of the very urban middle class who had once helped Bhutto to capture political power. The movement against 'civilian dictatorship' forced Bhutto to announce a second election in Pakistan. But by then the army had intervened. Bhutto was hanged in a judicial murder plotted by General Zia-ul-Haq who now imposed on Pakistan a regime marked by a blend of military dictatorship and theocracy. It was only after the General's death in a plane crash in 1988 that formal democracy was restored in Pakistan. Yet the army retained a controlling voice and a centralized polity under Punjabi hegemony remained the order of the day. Few commentators were thus surprised when General Pervez Musharraf ousted the civilian government on 12 October 1999, once again jeopardizing Pakistan's march to democracy. In the words of a leading Pakistani commentator:

> The Quaid-I-Azam was a towering figure but like the banyan tree nothing grew under its shadow. And so the Pakistan dream was left to those who lacked vision and in due course started to interpret it to suit their own agenda. The present generation has no real idea of what Pakistan was meant to be. It sees what it is, torn by sectarian strife, with no comprehension of our…[national] purpose[43].

Reviewing the political structures in India and Pakistan, Jalal makes an interesting analytical distinction between formal and substantive democracy.[44] While the former 'is a genuine democracy insofar as it guarantees, among other things, the right to vote and the freedom of expression', the latter entails 'empowerment of the people, not as abstract legal citizens but as concrete and active agents capable of pursuing their interests with a measure of autonomy from entrenched structures of dominance and privilege'.[45] Jalal also points out that the degree of authoritarianism in the sense of 'organized power embedded in the institutional structure of the state' depends upon the strength of

12

'formal, much less substantive, democracy'.[46] In Jalal's perception both India and Pakistan have been subjected to authoritarianism. Although India technically adopted a parliamentary form of government, contends Jalal, in reality what prevails is not substantive but only formal democracy which has created conditions for 'a partnership between the political leadership and the non-elected institutions of the state' to subordinate the people to 'democratic authoritarianism'. On the other hand, the people of Pakistan – and later Bangladesh – were subjected to the supremacy of non-elected state institutions and became victims of 'military-bureaucratic authoritarianism'.

Such an interpretation of subcontinental politics, however, tends to ignore the role played by different social forces in shaping the politics of a state. It is undoubtedly true that the Congress, as the ruling party in New Delhi, had constantly accommodated the bureaucracy, the police and the military within the political structure of the Indian state to ensure its political domination, sometimes even at the cost of undermining the democratic spirit of the constitution. However, to reduce the entire process of democratic political formation in India to a mere game of manipulation for personal gain by politicians is possibly an exaggeration. Even a formal and rudimentary process of political transaction through periodic elections ensures a gradual opening up of political space to several disadvantaged social groups and widens the opportunity to influence the process of economic reforms by these groups. After all, India is perhaps the only nascent democratic state where ruling parties or coalitions have repeatedly lost elections both at national and provincial levels. This certainly testifies to the increasing political consciousness of the Indian electorate. Moreover, the Left Front governments in West Bengal, Kerala and Tripura are successfully experimenting with alternative styles of governance within the national polity to ameliorate the conditions of the rural and urban poor.[47] In Pakistan and Bangladesh, too, there has been strengthening of civil societies. But the radical potential of democratic transformations becomes clearly more visible in the twists and turns of Indian electoral politics. The Indian political process cannot thus be considered within the generalized paradigm of 'authoritarianism'.

Nevertheless, a common denominator of Indian and Pakistani federalism has been the hegemonic drive of central governments to subsume regio-local aspirations and sentiments. Failure to adequately

13

accommodate provincial feelings within the broader national agenda has been a singular drawback of nation-building processes in both these multi-ethnic states. This dichotomy has generated ethnic dissensions within the two nation-states, and such ethnic outbursts have tended to develop cross-border ramifications, creating inter-state tensions in regional politics. Herein lies the connection between nation-building, ethnicity and regional politics in contemporary South Asia. The Kashmir question in India and the Sindh problem in Pakistan clearly demonstrate this co-relationship. In examining these two issues the politics of the nation-state obviously cannot be the only focus of attention. But both the Kashmir and Sindh questions are inextricably connected with the problem of ethnicity. In such circumstances we need to establish some sense of the theoretical proposition that ethnic politics has raised in the South Asian context in general, and in Kashmir and Sindh in particular. In developing the argument of this book attempts have thus been made to come to terms with these aspects of nation-building.

2. ETHNICITY IN SOCIAL SCIENCE LITERATURE

Derived from the ancient Greek word *ethnos* (nation), the term ethnicity today is like a hat which has been hung on various pegs. Originally used to categorize mankind along racial lines, it is now employed by social scientists in a much broader sense to imply self-consciousness of a group of people united, or closely related, by shared experiences such as language, religious belief, common heritage or political institutions.[48] While race is usually used to denote the attributions of a group, ethnic identity typifies the creative responses of a group of people who consider themselves marginal to the societal mainstream. Banton feels that if race reflects positive tendencies of identification and inclusion, ethnicity embodies negative tendencies of dissociation and exclusion.[49] It was with the Black Power movement in the USA during the 1960s – which sought to emphasize Black Americans as a distinct social group – that such juxtapositions as residential segregation and integration, and cultural segmentation and assimilation, became the central concern of ethnic studies. Barth pushed the ball further with his emphasis on the notion of 'boundary' as the main criterion for the self-definition of ethnic

14

groups.[50] Anderson completed the circle with his thesis of 'Imagined Communities'.[51] Ethnic identity now developed in the hands of social scientists as a 'form of role attribution, both internal and external'.[52] An ethnic group has come to be viewed as

> a collectivity existing within a larger society, having real or fictional common ancestry, memories of a shared historical past, and a cultural focus on one or more symbolic elements defused as the epitome of their peoplehood. Examples of such symbolic contiguity (as in localism or sectionalism)… [are] religious affiliation, language or dialect forms, tribal affiliation, nationality, phenotypical features or any combination of these.[53]

In this context a number of Western scholars and their recent Russian counterparts, have been propounding the idea of 'The Ethnic Revival'. To quote a leading proponent of this school:

> The dissolution of ethnicity. The transcendence of nationalism. The internationalization of culture. These have been the dreams, and expectations of liberals and rationalists in practically every country, and in practically in every country [have been] disappointed… Today the cosmopolitan ideals are in decline and rationalist expectations have withered… I have called this trend 'The Ethnic Revival'.[54]

It is argued that 'the so-called nation-state is rarely a true appellation since very few states have an ethnically homogeneous population'.[55] Increasing preoccupation with ethnic pluralism has also made ethnic studies focus on such aspects of national development as cultural integration, frequency and intensity of ethnic conflicts, and procreation of ethnic movements. Such works stress patterns of national identities based on ethnic myths, symbols and memories.[56] Fukuyama's notion of the 'End of History', too, appears to have coincided with the age of ethnicity.

Methodologically, most of the scholastic works on ethnicity have had recourse to either of two frameworks: the primordialist model, which emphasizes historical 'continuity of the ethnic community as a determining factor for personal identity', or the instrumentalist approach where ethnicity is viewed primarily as a kind of political organization.[57] The former considers ethnicity as 'involuntary', based as it is on kinship, descent and symbolic qualities.[58] But its critics contend that mere cultural exclusion or distinctiveness cannot be sufficient indicators of ethnic boundaries.[59] For ethnic assertion essentially depends upon the articulation of differences between 'us' and 'them' through such tangible determinants as language, religion, history or territorial boundaries. The instrumentalist approach to ethnic studies accordingly stresses the 'formation of ethnic identity as a conscious, utilitarian action designed to achieve specific political and economic goals'.[60] Without delving deep into the merits of either of the two approaches, it is perhaps reasonable to argue, as Eriksen does, that ethnicity has both a strong emotional appeal and an equally strong politically mobilizing potential.[61] As has been aptly remarked:

> there is an ethnographic question about the way in which the various groups in a situation perceive each other… There is also a political economy question about how particular forms of ethnic consciousness arise… Ethnicity and the generation of a sense of 'them' and 'us' takes place within a wide historical and sociological framework and therefore their presentation of self is related to the repertoire of ethnicity open to them.[62]

Ethnicity today has thus gained recognition as an important principle for political organization, and as a focus for individual identity. In specific historical conjunctures a combination of these two variables, as the present explication of Kashmir and Sindh issues will demonstrate, can be extremely powerful and volatile.

There is nothing wrong *per se* in studying ethnic diversities within a nation-state. To quote an Indian commentator: '…ethnicity can be a useful technical term, for in contemporary usage, it connotes, above all else, the signification of the primordially constituted "other" as an outsider.'[63]

But a problem arises when ethnicity is viewed as the central point of social contradictions and treated, in the words of Glazer and Moynihan, as a 'more fundamental source of stratification'.[64] For it is doubtful if ethnicity can be necessarily linked to an objective criteria. Instead, the relevance of ethnicity, as Ardener reiterates, depends upon being made socially relevant.[65] In the words of Eriksen, ethnicity is 'ideologically constituted; indeed, many ethnic groups contain members who do not perceive ethnicity as important, but who would rather attach themselves to a political organization based on a different ideology – for example, class membership'.[66] What is emphasized here is the 'segmentary character of identities' at the level of the individual citizen. An individual needs to be considered not only as a member of an ethnic group, but also as a member of various other non-ethnically constituted social formations. For instance, a Sikh in the Punjab may be a member of his/her religious community, but he/she can also belong to the fraternity of Indian lawyers, have Hindu and Muslim friends and even be attached to an international communist movement. In fact, there can be significant interrelationships between class and ethnicity,[67] although they need to be analytically distinguished from one another. What we should, therefore, recognize is that ethnicity is the result of a contact, not of isolation. It is not natural, external or unambiguous, but is dynamic in nature.

2.1 Studying Ethnicity in Subcontinental Politics

In the subcontinental context ethnic movements have been distinguished from other forms of ascriptive mobilization like communalism.[68] While in ethnic politics the 'other' is inevitably presented as anti-national or secessionist, in communal conflict the involved groups are internal to the system, each demanding favours from the ruling authority. Ethnic assertions in South Asia have tended to assume the form of 'ethnonationalism' where members of an ethnic group get involved in politics for the preservation of cultural values, self-identity and group consciousness.[69] Recent studies emphasize the cruciality of the state as a factor in such ethnic politics. The growing incidence of ethnic assertion in the country has thus been linked either to the Indian state's centralizing drive, or to an intensified competition for power in centre, provinces and localities.[70] Marxist scholars have demonstrated how the ruling class in post-1947 India imposed national unity from the top by reducing regional and cultural divergences to a common national identity to create a national market in the interests of a rising indigenous bourgeoisie. Ethnic politics in India has largely developed against the backdrop of this stifling of local

17

and ethnic aspirations by a centrist bourgeois-landlord rule. In such circumstances ethnic assertions in India usually acquire an anti-Delhi character. The current Kashmir imbroglio, as the present volume indicates, and the Punjab crisis, as demonstrated elsewhere,[71] need to be viewed in this perspective. The insurgency in Kashmir has strong domestic roots, and cannot be brushed aside merely as the product of an external game to dismember India.[72] George Fernandes, once a member of the Indian cabinet in charge of Kashmir, himself admitted: 'I do not believe any foreign hand created the Kashmir problem. The problem was created by us... others took advantage of it.'[73] Farooq Abdullah, the current Chief Minister of Jammu and Kashmir, also remarked in the same breath: 'It is India that is responsible for what has happened in Kashmir... they betrayed my father in '53... they betrayed me in '84...'[74]

Similarly, in multi-ethnic Pakistan the overtly centrist nation-building agenda of a pre-eminently Punjabi ruling class provoked outbursts from other ethnic groups seeking to sustain their self-identities. The Sindh question essentially developed as a response to the distorted nation-building process in Pakistan.

Scholarly attention has recently been focused on how internal conflicts in the Third World transcend national borders to become a crucial ingredient in regional security politics.[75] The subcontinent represents a classic case where the departing colonial ruler constructed national frontiers for its two successor states which did not represent a convergence between nation and state, or between ethnic and state identities. Consequently, cross-border loyalties amongst sections of the population survived the boundaries imposed between the two successor states. When in the context of centralizing nation-building strategies ethnic political assertions occur in outlying or frontier areas of these nation-states, the distinction between domestic and external affairs, or between home and foreign politics, loses its significance in the traditional sense. Political actors from across the borders of neighbouring states could then deny the marks of their different objective nationalities and treat themselves as members of a single 'loyalty group'. This makes ethnic politics transcend its domestic contours and foment regional tensions, reinforcing Buzan's notion of 'regional security subsystems and security complexes' where ethnic assertions constitute vital local or domestic ingredients to define national security priorities within a particular region.[76] The present insurrection in Kashmir and the current turmoil in Sindh, as the present work unfolds, represent this pattern, although while Kashmir remains a site of conflict between India and Pakistan, Sindh's incorporation in Pakistan is not questioned. The 1971 Bangladeshi ethnic assertion, the insurgency politics in North-East India, the Tamil question in Sri Lanka and the Pan-Arabism of the late 1950s and 1960s in the Middle East are yet other obvious indicators of this particular facet of Third World politics.

3. SOURCE MATERIAL

Gaining access to official sources of information, whether in India or Pakistan, on either Kashmir or Sindh was extremely difficult. While visa restrictions denied me research trips to Pakistan, many of the Indian official papers on Kashmir still belong to the 'classified' category, and hence could not be consulted. Fieldwork in Jammu and Kashmir itself was impeded by frequent outbreaks of violence. Although I consulted the Indian newspapers and the sizeable non-official Indian and Western literature on Kashmir, I could hardly find the Pakistani publications on Kashmir or Sindh in India because of the restrictive nature of the 'book trade' between the two neighbours. Fortunately, however, I was able to consult the rich deposits on South Asian politics in the India Office Library (London), Indian Institute (Oxford), Centre for South Asian Studies (Cambridge), Library of Congress (Washington), National Archives of the USA (Washington), University of Illinois at Urbana Champaign (USA) and the India Centre of the Maison des Sciences de l'Homme (Paris). In fact, the research for this volume has been largely based on materials available in these non-South Asian repositories. I am aware of the limitation in the database for the present work. But this was due to reasons beyond my control. Practitioners of contemporary history, especially for regions plagued by political instabilities, are bound to be handicapped in the matter of source materials. I, too, have been constrained by this problem. What I have tried to do is to make the best of a difficult job.

NOTES

1. Commentators like Uri Raan have emphasized non-'Nation-State Fallacy', arguing that 'in well over 90 per cent of the independent countries existing today, the state either is considerably larger or much smaller than the area inhabited by the corresponding nation or staatsvolk'. See U. Raan, 'The Nation State Fallacy', in Joseph V. Montville ed., *Conflict and Peacekeeping in Multiethnic Societies* (Lexington: 1990).
2. This section is based on S. Das, 'The Indian National Congress and the Dynamics of Nation-Building: Aspects of Continuity and Change' in T.V. Sathyamurthy ed., *State and Nation in the Context of Social Change* (Delhi: 1994).
3. H. Alavi, 'The State in Post-colonial Societies: Pakistan and Bangladesh',*New Left Review* (July/August 1974), pp. 59–81.
4. See M. Shepperdson and C. Simmons eds., *The Indian National Congress and the Political Economy of India 1885–1947* (Aldershot: 1988).
5. C. Bettleheim,*India Independent* (tr. W.A. Caswell, London: 1968).
6. N.K. Bose, 'Social and Cultural Life in Calcutta',*Geographical Review of India*, 20 December 1958.
7. D. Arnold,*Police Power and Colonial Rule: Madras 1859–1947* (New Delhi: 1986).
8. M. Shepperdson and C. Simmons eds., *The Indian National Congress*, p. 16.
9. A. Chaudhuri, *Private Economic Power in India: A Study in Genesis and Concentration* (Delhi: 1975), p. 160.
10. ibid. p. 161.
11. A.K. Bagchi, 'Public Sector Industry and Quest for Self-reliance in India',*Economic and Political Weekly*, 17, 14–16 April 1982, pp. 615–28.
12. N.K. Chandra, 'Role of Foreign Capital in India', *Social Scientist*, no. 57, 1977, pp. 3–20; G.K. Shirokov, *Industrialisation of India* (Moscow: 1973).
13. A. Maddison, 'The Historical Origins of Indian Poverty', *Banca Nazionale Del Lavoro Quarterly Review*, 23, 92, 1970, pp. 31–81; T. Raychaudhuri, 'Historical Roots of Mass Poverty in South Asia: A hypothesis', *Economic and Political Weekly*, 20, 18, 4 May 1985, pp. 801–6; R. Krishna, 'Growth, Investment and Poverty in Mid-term Appraisal of Sixth Plan', *Economic and Political Weekly*, 18, 47, 19 November 1983, pp. 1972–82.
14. W.H. Morris-Jones, 'Dominance and Dissent: Their Inter-relations in the Indian Party System' in his *Politics Mainly Indian* (Madras: 1978), pp. 213–32.
15. B.P. Dua, 'Indian Congress Dominance Revisited' in P. Brass and F. Robinson eds., *The Indian National Congress and Indian Society 1885–1985: Ideology, Social Structure and Political Dominance* (Delhi: 1989); L.W. Pye, 'Party Systems and National Development in Asia' in J. La Palmobara and M. Weiner eds., *Political Parties and Political Development* (Princeton: 1966).
16. G. Rosen, *Democracy and Economic Change in India* (Berkeley: 1967), p. 70.
17. *The Statesman* (Calcutta), 5 September 1999.
18. B.T. Ranadive, 'National Problems and the Role of Working Class' in *National Problems and the Working Class in India* (Calcutta: 1989).
19. P. Bardhan, 'Dominant Proprietary Classes and India's Democracy' in A Kohli ed., *India's Democracy: an Analysis of Changing State-Society Relations* (Princeton: 1988).
20. P.B. Mayer, 'Development and Deviance: The Congress as the Raj' in J. Masselos ed.,*Struggling and Ruling: The Indian National Congress 1885–1985* (Delhi: 1987).

21. P. Bardhan, 'Dominant Proprietory Classes', p. 224.
22. B. De and S. Das, 'Ethnic Revivalism – Problems in the Indian Union' in K.S. Singh ed., *Ethnicity, Caste and People: India and the Soviet Union* (New Delhi: 1992).
23. This section is based on S. Basu and S. Das, 'Introduction' in S. Basu and S. Das eds., *Electoral Politics in South Asia* (Calcutta: 2000).
24. A. Jalal, *Democracy and authoritarianism in South Asia: A comparative and historical perspective* (Cambridge: 1995), p. 5.
25. A. Jalal, The *Sole Spokesman: Jinnah, the Muslim League and the Demand for Pakistan* (Cambridge: 1985).
26. A. Jalal, *The State of Martial Rule: The origins of Pakistan's political economy of defence* (Cambridge: 1990), p. 1.
27. Noman provides a detailed analysis of the political strategy of economic development in Pakistan in this period. See O. Noman, *The Political Economy of Pakistan 1947–85* (London: 1988), pp. 27–32.
28. ibid. pp. 35–43.
29. ibid.
30. ibid.
31. See the contributions on Pakistan in K. Gough and H.P. Sharma eds., *Imperialism and Revolution in South Asia* (New York: 1973).
32. *Land Reform in West Pakistan*, vol III, Appendix 18, (Government of Pakistan 1967). Quoted in A. Hussain, 'Land Reforms in Pakistan: A Reconsideration' in I. Khan, *Fresh Perspectives on India and Pakistan* (Oxford: 1985), p. 208.
33. R. Islam, *Pakistan: Failure in National Integration* (Dhaka: 1977).
34. Urban Sindhis consist of Urdu-speaking Muhajirs and Punjabis. See S. Kardar, *The Political Economy of Pakistan* (Lahore: 1987), p. 11; A. Jalal, *Democracy and authoritarianism in South Asia*, p. 190.
35. ibid.
36. A. Jalal, *Democracy and Authoritarianism in South Asia*, p. 187.
37. ibid. p. 192.
38. ibid. p. 191.
39. ibid. p. 188.
40. See F. Ahmed's contribution in K. Gough and H.P. Sharma eds., *Imperialism and Revolution in South Asia*.
41. See S. Basu and S. Das eds., 'Introduction' in *Electoral Politics in South Asia*.
42. For details see ibid.
43. O. Kureishi, 'The country that got derailed on its way to nationhood', *The Asian Age* (Calcutta), 12 September 1999.
44. A. Jalal, *Democracy and Authoritarianism in South Asia*, p. 3.
45. ibid.
46. ibid.
47. See the works of T.J. Nossiter, *Marxist State Governments in India* (London: 1988); A. Kohli, *The State and Poverty: The Politics of Reform* (Cambridge: 1989); G. Lieten *Continuity and Change in Rural West Bengal* (New Delhi: 1992); K. Westergaard, *People's Participation: Local Government and Rural Development – The Case of West Bengal* (Copenhagen: 1986); N. Webster, *Panchayati Raj and the Decentralisation of Development Planning in West Bengal: A Case Study* (Copenhagen: 1990); J. Basu et al. eds., *People's Power in Practice: 20 Years of Left Front in West Bengal* (Calcutta: 1997).
48. See B. De and S. Das, 'Ethnic Revivalism: Problems in the Indian Union', for a discussion along these lines.

49. M. Banton, 'Modelling Ethnic and National Relations', *Ethnic and Racial Studies*, 17:1, 1994. Also see his *Racial and Ethnic Competition* (Cambridge: 1983).
50. F. Barth ed., *Ethnic Groups and Boundaries: The Social Organisation of Cultural Difference* (London: 1969). See the Introduction.
51. B. Anderson, *Imagined Communities: Reflections on the Origin and Spread of Nationalism* (London: 1983).
52. G. DeVos and L. Romanucci-Ross eds., *Ethnic Identity: Cultural Continuities and Change* (Chicago: 1982).
53. R.A. Schermerhorn, *Ethnic Plurality in India* (Arizona: 1987).
54. A.D. Smith, *The Ethnic Revival* (Cambridge: 1981), p. 1.
55. ibid. p. 9. In 1971 only 12 out of 132 independent states were found to be ethnically homogeneous.
56. See A.D. Smith, 'Chosen People: Why Ethnic Groups Survive', *Ethnic and Racial Studies*, 15:3 (1992), pp. 440–49; C. Enloe, 'Religion and Ethnicity' in P. Sugar ed., *Ethnic Diversity and Conflicts in Eastern Europe* (Santa Barbara: 1980); P. Kitromildes, 'Imagined Communities and the Origin of the National Question in the Balkans', *European History Quarterly* 19: 2 (1982); J. Edwards, *Language, Society and Identity* (Oxford: 1985).
57. For an analysis of various analytical approaches to the study of ethnicity see John Hutchinson and A.D. Smith eds., *Ethnicity* (Oxford: 1996).
58. For a representation of this school see C. Geertz, 'The New Integration Revolution: Primordialist Sentiments and Civil Politics in New States' in C. Geertz ed., *Old Societies and New States* (Glencow: 1968) and H. Isaacs, *Ideas of the Tribe* (New York: 1975).
59. See W.A. Douglass, 'A Critique of Recent Trends in the Analysis of Ethnonationalism', *Ethnic and Racial Studies*, vol. III, no. 2, April 1988.
60. See F. Barth, *Ethnic Groups and Boundaries* and Ernest Gellner, *Nations and Nationalism* (Ithaca: 1983).
61. T.H. Eriksen, 'Ethnicity and Nationalism: Definitions and Critical Reflections', *Bulletin of Peace Proposals*, vol. 23 (2) 1992, 219–24.
62. J.A. Vincent, 'Differentiation and Resistance: ethnicity in Valle d'Aosta and Kashmir', *Ethnic and Racial Studies*, vol. 5, no. 3, July 1982, p. 314.
63. D. Gupta, *The Context of Ethnicity: Sikh Identity in a Comparative Perspective* (Delhi: 1997), p. 6.
64. N. Glazer and D.P. Moynihan, *Ethnicity* (Harvard: 1975).
65. E. Ardener, *The Voice of Prophecy and other Essays* (Oxford: 1989).
66. T.H. Eriksen, 'Ethnicity', op. cit., p. 21.
67. T.H. Eriksen, *Ethnicity and Nationalism* (London: 1993).
68. For instance, see D. Gupta, *The Context of Ethnicity*, pp. 6–10.
69. See J. Rotschild, *Ethnopolitics: A Conceptual Framework* (New York: 1981).
70. P. Brass, *The Politics of India after Independence*, New Cambridge History of India, vol. IV: 1 (Cambridge: 1990). Both Horowitz and Brass stress the role of new, urbanized, indigenous elites in the Third World in using ethnic constituencies and symbols as bases of mass support. See D. Horowitz, *Ethnic Groups in Conflict* (Berkeley: 1985) and Paul Brass *Ethnicity and Nationalism* (New Delhi: 1991).
71. D. Gupta, *The Context of Ethnicity*.
72. S. Bose thus calls the Kashmir crisis a 'crisis of Indian Democracy'. See his *The Challenge in Kashmir: Democracy, Self-Determination and a Just Peace* (New Delhi: 1997). p. 51.
73. G. Fernandes, 'India's Policies in Kashmir: An Assessment and Discourse' in R. Thomas ed., *Perspectives on Kashmir* (Boulder: 1992).

74. Cited in S. Bose, *The Challenge in Kashmir*, p. 51.

75. Pioneering research in this context was done by M. Weiner. See his 'The Macedonian Syndrome: An Historical Model of International Relations and Political Development', *World Politics*, vol. XXIII, no. 4, July 1973. The analytical framework was further developed in A. Suhrke and L. Garner Noble eds., *Ethnic Groups in International Relations* (New York: 1977); Fredrick L. Shiels ed., *Ethnic Separatism and World Politics* (New York: 1984); M. Ayoob ed., *Regional Security in the Third World: Case Studies from South-East Asia and the Middle East* (Kent: 1986); A. Said and L.R. Simmons eds., *Ethnicity in an International Context* (New Brunswick: 1976) and J.F. Stack, Jr. ed., *Ethnic Identities in a Transnational World* (Connecticut: 1981).

76. See B. Buzan, 'Regional Security (1)', *Arbejdspapirer* no. 28 (Copenhagen: 1989). Also see A.D. Smith, 'Ethnic Myths and Ethnic Revivals' *Archives Europeenes De Sociologie*, 24 March 1984, for an argument that ethnicity is responsive to both external and subjective circumstances. The best attempt to view South Asian ethnic politics in the context of regional security is found in K. Khory, 'Separatism in South Asia: Politics of Ethnic Conflict and Regional Security' (Unpublished Ph.D. thesis, University of Illinois at Urbana Champaign: 1991).

Chapter 1

The Kashmir Imbroglio

On a rubble-strewn lot in downtown Srinagar, two women wade dazedly in the ruins of a mosque while a dozen men hack at mounds of broken brick and blackened plaster, carrying off basket-loads of debris on their heads. Ghulam Quadir, a local bank manager, surveys the slow-moving cleanup from the only clear space for miles around – a 10-foot square of cement that used to be his kitchen floor. The rest of Quadir's four-storey house went up in smoke last month, along with 125 buildings. This conflagration in the capital of India's half of divided Kashmir [is] like at least a dozen similar incidents in the once idyllic valley.[1]

This is an apt description of a regular happening in Jammu and Kashmir where insurgency politics challenges the authority of the Indian state. The Kashmir problem – as it is dubbed in official discourse – has certainly attracted the attention of scholars, journalists and political commentators. It has been seen as the outcome of a distorted decolonizing process in the subcontinent, or of incompatible ethnic identities in Jammu and Kashmir, or of regional economic backwardness. A recent work documents 'the asymmetry between mobilization and accommodation [that] caused disaffected Kashmiris to take an ethnic and violent turn'.[2] While modernization opened up for Kashmiris new 'possibilities of alternative futures', the undermining of democratic content in the region's political process is believed to have stultified the potentials of such options, which created conditions for the generation of violent and separatist politics.[3] Another thesis, however, considers neither economic resentment of the people of Jammu and Kashmir nor threats to Kashmiri cultural identity to be a crucial factor behind the current politics of violence in that province. Instead, the present outburst has been related to the nature of mobilization and deinstitutionalization of politics in Jammu and Kashmir.[4] In this literature the beginnings of the current imbroglio in Jammu and Kashmir are related to disputes between provincial political elites and the central government in New Delhi 'over power in a weak institutional setting'.[5] Yet another recent dissertation links the political turbulence in Kashmir to the most powerful collective urges of our times: the struggle for democratic government, and the quest for 'national self-determination'.[6] Others have reconciled themselves with a pessimistic view of the Kashmir issue as an insoluble irritant in Indo-Pak relations, and an unavoidable ingredient in South Asian regional instability. One finds in such works a feeling of remorse that one of nature's most beautiful gifts has become a 'place of ugly politics'. Ayesha Jalal aptly sums up this helplessness amongst such strategic analysts: 'A glittering prize, a tantalizing dream, a festering sore, Kashmir is the fairy tale that tortures the South Asian psyche.'[7]

The present exercise, however, seeks to go beyond the received paradigms and proposes to look at the Kashmir question from the 'bottom up', considering it essentially as an aspect of a general trend in Third World politics where ethnic assertion tends to become a part of regional inter-state tensions. This argument is consonant with the school of thought in international relations which sees post-1945 Third World conflicts as 'endogenous and not exogenous in origin', where threats to national security come either from ethnic strife or 'weak legitimacy of ruling elites'.[8] The overlap between the population of neighbouring countries in terms of ethnic and religious criteria and the impossibility of preventing the mobility of population across borders often make the line dividing 'the interstate dimension of regional conflict from its intra-state dimension' extremely 'thin'.[9] What results in such circumstances is a blurring of traditional distinctions between external and domestic conflicts.[10] The crux of the Kashmir question lies in an attempt on the part of a significant section amongst the Kashmiris to differentiate themselves from the interests of the wider Indian nation.[11]

1. THE KASHMIR QUESTION: HISTORICAL SETTING

Kashmir lies in the heart of Asia, having age-old links with both South and Central Asia, and surrounded by Pakistan, Afghanistan, China and India. Since 1947 it has been a contested site between India and Pakistan. While 67 per cent of the once unified domain inhabited by seven million people is under Indian administration, the remaining 33 per cent, comprising two and a half million people, continues to be under Pakistani control. Events leading to the present scenario are fairly well known. But they need to be retold in order to initiate any worthwhile discussion of the Kashmir problem.

Kashmir was one of the 560-odd princely states in the subcontinent which accepted British paramountcy, but were not subjected to direct British administration. During the process of decolonization such princi-palities – ruled by their hereditary Maharajas or Nawabs – were granted the options of either joining any of the successor states of India and Pakistan or staying independent. The native princes were, however, tacitly advised by the Raj to judge the question of accession to either India or Pakistan on the basis of geographical contiguity and the religion of the majority community in the principalities.[12] But the Maharaja of Kashmir did not have a ready answer. This presaged the future crisis that tore the kingdom apart.

The kingdom of Kashmir had an overall Muslim majority of 78 per cent, but was ruled by the Hindu Maharaja Hari Singh.[13] Its demographic distribution along religious lines was also uneven, the Kashmir Valley being predominantly Muslim, the Jammu region overtly Hindu, and the Ladakh area distinctly Buddhist. Besides, since the 1930s the Indian National Congress and the Muslim League were ranged on opposite sides in Kashmir's political landscape. The triggering point for this politi-cal polarization was a popular secular movement led by Sheikh Abdullah of the National Conference against the Maharaja's autocratic misrule.[14] While Mahatma Gandhi and Jawaharlal Nehru were enthusiastic supporters of the National Conference, Jinnah and the Muslim League opposed it. In the context of such contradictory pulls the Maharaja of Kashmir initially preferred to join neither India nor Pakistan, and chose to sign a Standstill Agreement with both. But the matter was 'overtaken by events' when an uprising occurred in October 1947 in support of the demand for *Azad Kashmir* (Independent Kashmir) in the predominantly Muslim area of Poonch. The Maharaja instantly despatched his troops to crush it. This invited an infiltration of Pathan tribesmen from across the Pakistan border, ostensibly to rescue their Muslim brethren from Hindu persecution. The Maharaja now forsook his ambivalence and appealed to India for help, which was granted on condition of his accession to the

27

Indian Republic. Signed by the Maharaja in this context, the Treaty of Accession to India was accepted by the British Governor-General Lord Mountbatten.[15] Indian troops were then flown into Kashmir and the tribal intruders advancing towards the capital city of Srinagar were driven back. The Pakistan army formally intervened on behalf of the tribesmen, which occasioned the first Indo-Pak war.[16] The war was terminated by the cease-fire of January 1949, leaving Pakistan with one-third of the old Kashmir kingdom, while the rest became the province of Jammu and Kashmir of the Indian federation. That cease-fire line, adjusted later after the 1972 Shimla Pact, continues to be the Line of Control between the Indian and Pakistani parts of Kashmir.[17] India internationalized the Kashmir issue when Nehru referred it to the United Nations Organization in a bid to expose Pakistan's violation of international norms. But the UNO's mediatory role in Kashmir has been largely unsuccessful. As with any regional conflict in the Third World, the Kashmir issue has also been complicated by big-power intervention. But this aspect has been kept outside the ambit of this book.[18]

It is generally admitted that Pakistan's intervention on behalf of the tribesmen provoked anger amongst the Kashmiris, which significantly contributed to India's success in beating off the Pakistani challenge to the Treaty of Accession.[19] Kashmir's integration with India was thus marked by the Kashmiris' disapproval of Pakistan and gratitude towards India. The Indian Prime Minister Jawaharlal Nehru was so confident of popular approval for the Maharaja's Accession to India that he proposed with much fanfare the holding of a plebiscite to legitimize Kashmir's joining of the Indian Union. A special clause was also inserted in the Indian constitution in the form of Article 370 to ensure a fundamental autonomy in the internal administration of Jammu and Kashmir. But today a predominant section of Kashmiris is involved in a secessionist insurgency against the Indian state, which reached a climactic point in 1990. The erosion of the 'Indian psyche' amongst a sizeable section of Kashmiris cannot be explained merely by a Pakistani or even an international conspiracy to 'Balkanize' the Indian federation. No other than J.N. Dixit, the former Foreign Secretary of India, admitted 'The disturbances in Kashmir were not entirely due to Pakistani activities alone but were also due to the alienation of some segments of the Jammu and Kashmir population.'[20]

The roots of Kashmiri intransigence towards the Indian state largely lie, as the present study argues, in contradictions within the nation-building strategy adopted by the Indian ruling class.

Kashmiri society had been always multi-religious – 78 per cent Muslims cohabiting with Hindus (generally known as Pundits), Sikhs, Punjabis and Buddhists. In the Indian part of Kashmir the religious composition of the population is as follows: 65 per cent Muslims (predominantly of the Sunni persuasion) primarily inhabiting the Kashmir valley; 28 per cent Hindu and two per cent Sikh living mostly in the Jammu region; and one per cent Buddhist concentrated in the sparsely populated Ladakh area.[21] Archaeological discoveries at Baoursahama have pushed back Kashmir's antiquity to 3000 BC, almost contemporaneous to the Mohenjadaro civilization. Kashmir has also over the years retained a distinct cultural identity. Most Kashmiris speak Kashur – one of the oldest spoken and most literary languages of modern India.[22] Interactions between Kashmiri, Vedic and Buddhist traditions gave birth to a syncretic school of philosophy in Kashmir, the two best exponents of which were Vasugupta (9th century AD) and Abhinav Gupta (10th century AD). Subsequently, Kashmir accepted Islam, although not as 'a negation but as a culmination of a proud spiritual heritage'.[23] Islam in Kashmir, accordingly, has a character of its own, retaining many pre-Islamic practices.[24] Mysticism and Sufism flourished in Kashmir; Kashmiri lyrics on life and nature brought together the best of Saivite and Sufi traditions.[25] In the words of G.M.D. Sufi: '...the cult of Buddha, the teachings of Vedanta, the mysticism of Islam have one after another found a congenial home in Kashmir.'[26]

Shah-i-Hamdan Lalishari, a Hindu woman sage, and Sheikh Nur-ud-in, the founder of the Rishi order in Kashmir, appealed to both Saivism and Sufism to preach the brotherhood of man through their mystic poems.[27] Until recently, shrines like Charar-i-Sharif were frequented by Hindus and Muslims alike. Some sacred spots like the Shah-i-Hamdam mosque, Baha-ud-din shrine and Akhum Shah mosque are still used by both Hindus and Muslims.[28] Such Kashmiri surnames as Bhatt and Pandit are common to Hindus and Muslims. Not unnaturally, Kashmir was also relatively free of communal disturbances before 1947. The Kashmiri dress, food and drink, too, are perceived to have a distinct character. Traditionally, Kashmiri dress comprises a white skull-cap and a long sleeveless coat (*phakran*), while the *katgir* (charcoal burning pot) carried under the coat to keep one warm during winter is a 'Kashmiri artefact'. Kashmiris themselves usually take salt tea, but offer green tea to visitors. Tea is invariably served from a *samovar*. Dishes such as *haq* (local spinach) and *gostaba* (meat balls) are typically Kashmiri.[29]

The Kashmiris – cutting across religious faiths – have thus preserved an overarching 'identity as distinct and separate within the subcontinent'.[30] A broad cultural homogeneity and the geographical compactness of the region encouraged people settling in Kashmir from ancient times to merge 'their individual identities into one whole'.[31] But instead of ensuring the full flowering of this *Kashmiriyat* (the feeling of being Kashmiri) the Indian state sought to integrate it with Pan-Indianism. The present Kashmir imbroglio is essentially an assertion of the threatened *Kashmiriyat*.

2. KASHMIR IN INDIAN POLITICAL DISCOURSE

Organized political opinion in India – conservative, liberal or progressive – has consistently advocated Kashmir's integration with the Indian federal structure, although from different ideological standpoints. The *Organiser*, a mouthpiece initially of the Hindu revivalist Bharatiya Jana Sangh and then its successor the Bharatiya Janata Party, proclaimed on 15 January 1948: 'Historically Kashmir has been a part of India. By India, we mean the Hindu India.'[32] The Bharatiya Jana Sangh opposed Nehru's idea of a plebiscite in Kashmir and in 1952 launched the 'Integrate Kashmir Movement'. Rejecting Article 370 of the Indian constitution that had guaranteed certain special rights for the Kashmiris, Shyama Prasad Mookherjee, the party's parliamentary spokesman, asked on 20 June 1952: 'Is Kashmir going to be a republic within a republic? Are we thinking of another sovereign parliament within the four corners of India?'[33] Golwalkar, the Rashtriya Swayamsevak Sangh (RSS)[34] chief, declared on 24 August 1953 that the solution of the Kashmir question: '...should not be left to the people of Kashmir. The opinion of the entire country should be taken in deciding the future of Kashmir.'[35] By April 1957, the Bharatiya Jana Sangh had explained its stand on Kashmir: '[Kashmir's] accession to India ...was final and irrevocable... The real problem...[is to] liberate the territory still held by Pakistan.'[36]

In 1964 the Party further hardened its stand when it resolved:

If 14 *lakhs* [1 *lakh* = 100,000] of Muslims of Kashmir valley loathe to live in secular India in spite of all that India has done for their material and political advancement during the last 17 years, then nationalist India will be forced to rethink over its entire policy in regard to Indian Muslims, 93 per cent of whom had voted for Pakistan in 1946 elections...[37]

During the 1980s the Bharaitya Janata Party demanded not only the scrapping of Article 370 from the country's constitution, but also the splitting of the province into three parts: the Muslim-majority Kashmir valley, the Hindu-dominated Jammu and the Buddhist-majority Ladakh.[38] To make a public demonstration of Kashmir's oneness with India the BJP launched in early 1992 a 'unity pilgrimage' from the southern tip of the country, which was to end with the hoisting of the tricolour in Srinagar on 26 January. The then President Murli Manohar Joshi did unfurl the national flag in Srinagar, although not with promised pomp and show, but amidst local protests and tight security cover by the Indian army.[39] Currently holding the reins of power in New Delhi, the BJP seems determined to pursue a state-centric approach to the Kashmir issue.

The ideological mainspring of the Bharatiya Jana Sangh/Bharatiya Janata Party's rigidity on the Kashmir question stems from its refusal to reconcile itself with the Partition of the subcontinent. The *Organiser* of 29 January 1948 had remarked: '...the Muslim League and its creation of Pakistan are based on untruth, brute force, violence and aggression.' Balraj Madhok, the Party's leading think-tank member, prophesied: 'It is [as] unrealistic to think this partition is going to stay as to think that Germany is going to remain divided for all time to come.'[40] As late as 1990, the RSS theoretician K.R. Malkani was fondly predicting: '...in 25 years, or in five years, Pakistan will not exist. Two or three Pakistani states...will be in...India.'[41]

At the other end of the Indian political spectrum the liberals and socialists found in Kashmir's integration with India the *sine qua non* of secularism. Nehru expressed this feeling best when he used his Presidential Address to the 1951 Delhi session of the Indian National Congress to assert: 'Kashmir has become the living symbol of that non-communal and secular State which will have no truck with the two-nation theory on which Pakistan has based itself.'[42]

On another occasion Panditji remarked: 'Kashmir is symbolic as it illustrates that we are a secular state, that Kashmir with a...large majority of Muslims nevertheless of its own free will wished to be associated with India.'[43] Even two years before his death Nehru had not changed his stance, as is revealed from his letter of 26 July 1962 to Premier Nath Bazaz: 'Kashmir affects the whole of India because secularism in India also has not got such firm foundations as I would like it to have.'[44]

Likewise, the socialist leader Ram Manohar Lohia pleaded for stronger unity between India and Kashmir, rejecting the idea of a plebiscite on the grounds that '...if democracy created difficulty in the task of...[creating] a common nationality of Hindus and Muslims, then I attach more importance to that task.'[45] Supporting this argument, the Praja Socialist Party leader H.V. Kamath strongly felt that steps should be taken for recovering Pakistani-occupied Kashmir.[46] The undivided Communist Party of India (CPI) agreed too: '...the best interests of the people of Kashmir lay in their union with India. That would help strengthen the democratic movement in both countries.'[47]

The Party dubbed the UNO as an Anglo-American imperialist agency, which was to be debarred from Kashmir.[48] Revising its earlier thesis of the 'right of self-determination for national minorities',[49] the CPI asserted '...any move for separation or secession [of Kashmir from] the Indian Union would be a reactionary move which would be a God-sent opportunity to imperialists [to] make that state a pawn in their hands.'[50]

In the aftermath of Independence most of the Muslim political leaders in India had also endorsed the Indian government's stand on Kashmir, as the March 1958 national convention of Muslim legislators testifies.[51] In the same spirit Arif Mohammad Khan, a former member of the Indian cabinet, reiterated in 1990: 'If Kashmir goes, Indian Muslims for generations to come will have to suffer the consequences'.[52]

It should be admitted, however, that not all colleagues of Nehru viewed the Kashmir issue in the context of a clash between secularism and communalism. For instance, Acharya Kripalani, the Congress President during those fateful days of 1947, nursed the Hindu revivalist hope of undoing the Partition when he remarked: 'neither Congress nor the Indian nation has given up its claim of a united India.'[53] Sardar Vallabhai

Patel, the first Home Minister in independent India, was more candid: 'sooner or later, we (the people of India and Pakistan) shall again be united in common allegiance to our country'.[54] In fact, Patel preferred to view the Kashmir problem as a part of his overall concern of integrating the princely states within the Indian Union. That Patel's stand on Kashmir was bereft of Nehru's high idealism was revealed when he warned the Muslims in India:

It is your [Indian Muslims] duty now to sail in the same boat and sink or swim together. I want to tell you very frankly that you cannot ride on two horses. Select one horse, whichever you like best. Those who want to go Pakistan can go there and live in peace! Let us live here in peace to work for ourselves.[55]

On another occasion Patel remarked:

Appeasement of the Muslims prompted the assassination of Gandhi… what will happen if we weaken [our hold] over Kashmir or if a plebiscite is decided against us, and one million Hindus are driven? Not only the assassination of Nehru, but also reprisals against…Muslims in India.[56]

One feels in such statements the reverberation of the BJP's current Hindutva discourse. Vallabhbhai candidly stated that peace with Pakistan could not be purchased at the expense of Kashmir[57] and warned: 'Come what may, we will not give up Kashmir and we shall certainly see this business through.'[58]

Such strong notions for Kashmir's integration with India were partly coloured by India's security considerations. Although strategically important for both India and Pakistan, India's control over Kashmir appeared to be particularly crucial in view of the perceived threat from China. As early as 26 October 1947 when a confrontation with China was beyond the pale of imagination, Nehru had telegraphed the British Prime Minister:

Kashmir's northern frontiers…run in common with those of three countries, Afghanistan, the USSR and China. Security of

Kashmir, which must depend upon its internal tranquillity and existence of stable government is vital to [the] security of India, especially since part of southern boundary of Kashmir and India are common. Helping Kashmir, therefore, is an obligation of national interest to India.[59]

Kashmir's security connection with India was succinctly explained by an Indian commentator:

[Kashmir gives] us direct gateways to the North-Western Province of Pakistan and Northern Punjab. It is India's only window to the Central Asian Republics of the USSR in the north, China on the east and to Afghanistan on the west. Out of the five gateways opening into the geographic entity called India – Quetta, Gumal and Kurram Valleys, Khyber and Chitral – the last one, in Kashmir, is the most easily accessible and at the lowest altitude.[60]

Pakistan's joining of the US-sponsored military pact brought Cold War politics to Indian doorsteps, which further increased the strategic significance of Kashmir for India. Nehru wrote to the Pakistani Prime Minister on 5 March 1954: '...the acceptance of military aid by Pakistan from the US has given an entirely new turn to the Kashmir dispute as well as to events in Asia.'[61] The subsequent construction of the 537-mile Karakoram highway between the Indus valley of Pakistan and Sinkiang in China convinced New Delhi that any weakening of her hold over Jammu and Kashmir might encourage Chinese expansion in that region. For India, Kashmir became a 'strategic bowl', which could not to be dispensed with.[62] As M.C. Chagla told the UN Security Council: 'Kashmir is an integral part of India...no country can be a party to giving up part of itself.'[63]

3. KASHMIR AND NATION-BUILDING IN INDIA

3.1 The Nehru Years

In the context of the Indian discourse on Kashmir outlined above, it was not unnatural for New Delhi to adopt a centralizing posture towards Kashmir. Once the Maharaja acceded to India, he was made to abdicate in favour of Sheikh Abdullah. The November 1951 elections for the Jammu and Kashmir Constituent Assembly returned the Sheikh's National Conference with a massive majority. But it was this election which betrayed the seeds of present discord in Kashmir. First, the 'election' itself was dubious. Most of the Assembly members were elected unopposed, not due to a dearth of opposition candidates but either because the nomination papers of the opponents of the National Conference were rejected on 'technical' grounds, or because the opposition groups boycotted the poll. Such electoral incongruities certainly created ripples of political discord in Jammu and Kashmir. Secondly, Abdullah's ministry suffered from a narrow localist basis, four out of five members coming from the Muslim-dominated Kashmir Valley, and the remaining one belonging to the Hindu-majority Jammu. This had a communal implication. Thirdly, Sheikh Abdullah's program to build a *Naya Duniya* (New Kashmir)[64] – admirable as it was – which aimed to undo the feudal relations of production unfortunately generated dissensions along communal lines. Land Ceiling Laws were imposed; surplus land was distributed amongst the landless; a moratorium on peasants' debt was introduced.[65] According to a Kashmir government estimate 188,775 acres of land were 'transferred' to 153,399 tillers by March 1953.[66] Sheikh Abdullah also proposed schemes for nationalizing the core sectors in the economy. But this radical blueprint for socio-economic reconstruction provoked a convergence of conservative and Hindu reaction. Most of the landlords in Kashmir were Hindus who usually operated as absentee *zamindars* from Jammu, and Abdullah's land reforms meant their expropriation in favour of Muslim smallholders. Again, the policy of nationalization primarily hurt the trading class, still predominantly Hindu. The Kashmir Chamber of Commerce thus submitted a memorandum to the Sheikh in 1953 urging abolition of state trading, introduction of free competition in trade and abolition of restrictions on private transport.[67] A class antagonism thus came to be overlaid with communal overtones.[68]

Hindu revivalist organizations readily exploited this new situation by developing a movement against the anti-Dogra pro-communist National Conference.[69] Initially organized under the aegis of the Praja Parishad, and subsequently led by the erstwhile Jana Sangh and Hindu Mahasabha, the agitation aimed 'to achieve full integration of Jammu and Kashmir state with the rest of India like other acceding states, and safeguard the legitimate democratic rights of the people of Jammu (i.e. Hindus).'[70] The slogan raised was: 'One Prime Minister, one flag and one constitution' (*Ek Pradhan, Ek Nishan aur Ek Vidhan*).[71] By mid-1952 this Hindu resurgence assumed violent overtones. Encouraged by the Hindu protest in Jammu, the Buddhists in Ladakh also started demanding 'autonomy'. A crisis was precipitated when the Jana Sangh leader Shyama Prasad Mookherjee defied a government ban and entered Kashmir to 'boost' the integration movement. Shyama Prasad was arrested and later died in custody. This instantly incited Hindu anger across the country, Abdullah being widely accused of causing Shyama Prasad's death.

The Hindu outburst naturally unnerved the Kashmiri Muslim mind, which was now haunted by a fear of Hindu domination. An enraged Sheikh Abdullah exclaimed: '[the Praja Parishad agitation] literally poured cold water on the efforts of the National Conference to rally Muslim support for India all these years.'[72] In his address to a National Conference rally Sheikh Abdullah regretted in no uncertain terms: 'The confidence created by the National Conference in the people here (concerning Accession to India) has been shaken by the Jana Sangh and other communal organizations in India.'[73] Consequently, Abdullah reportedly became increasingly disillusioned about Jammu and Kashmir's integration with the Indian federation and allegedly toyed with the idea of Jammu and Kashmir as an independent state.[74] The Indian authorities even suspected 'secret negotiations' between the Sheikh and US officials in support of this move.[75] Faced with the growing independent stance of Abdullah and confronted by a Hindu affront, Nehru reconsidered his earlier premise that 'No satisfactory way can be found in Kashmir except through him [Abdullah].'[76] Jawaharlal now felt that a total union between Jammu and Kashmir and the Indian state was the only option left to him. B.N. Mullik, who worked closely with Nehru during those years, remarked: 'If anything accelerated the final break between Sheikh Abdullah and India it was the Praja Parishad agitation.'[77]

Fortunately for Jawaharlal, his integrationist moves in Kashmir were facilitated by dissensions within the National Conference itself. Led by Bakshi Ghulam Mohammad, three of his own cabinet colleagues charged Abdullah with having 'lost the confidence of the people' by intentionally delaying the 'implementation of the [New Delhi] Agreement'.[78] Abdullah, however, refused to resign. But in August 1953 his ministry was dissolved and he was put behind bars. Bakshi Ghulam Mohammad, a keen supporter of Kashmir's complete union with India, assumed power.[79] These moves certainly could not have been undertaken without Nehru's tacit approval. Besides, they indicated the assertion of conservatives within the Congress who had been always suspicious of Sheikh Abdullah.[80]

Henceforth, the story of Indian state's relations with Jammu and Kashmir became one of steady intrusion of New Delhi's authority. A Presidential proclamation of 1954 substantially curtailed the functions of the Kashmir legislature and the Indian President Rajendra Prasad during his visit to Kashmir in April of that year proclaimed: '...history and mutual understanding had cemented the ancient ties between Kashmir and India to such an extent that any break in the relationship was inconceivable.'[81]

In early 1956 the Jammu and Kashmir Constituent Assembly ratified the state's 'merger' with India. On 29 March Nehru formally abandoned his earlier proposal of a plebiscite in Kashmir[82] and veered around to the idea that 'facts [about Kashmir] had to be recognized as they are'.[83] Speaking before the Security Council on 3 May 1962 V.K. Krishna Menon explained the Indian position:

> ...we are not prepared to do anything in any part of India that will shake the stability of our country, undermine our economy or create conditions of trouble in South-East Asia. There is no provision in our Constitution for the secession of any State.[84]

By 1963 the offices of the *Sadar-i-riyasat* and Prime Minister in Kashmir were redesignated in conformity with the Indian constitution respectively as the Governor and Chief Minister. The jurisdiction of such crucial agencies of the Indian state as the Audit, Customs and Finance Departments, the Supreme Court and the Election Commission were also extended to Jammu and Kashmir. On 27 November 1963 Nehru informed Parliament about the progress in 'the gradual erosion of the special status of Jammu and Kashmir'.[85] In December 1964 the territorial limits of Articles 356 and 357 of the Indian constitution were expanded to enable the central government to proclaim Presidential rule[86] in Kashmir and allow the Indian parliament to legislate laws for Kashmir.[87] The authority of the Indian state was thus firmly clamped on Jammu and Kashmir. This process was buttressed by Bakshi Ghulam Mohammad's coercive regime.[88] Public order apparently prevailed. But it was deceptive normalcy. *Kashmiriyat* had been insulted and the dissolution of Sheikh Abdullah's ministry in August 1953 marked the first turning point in the emotional rupture between a predominant section of Kashmiri Muslims and the Indian state.[89] Sheikh Abdullah could justly recall: 'Since 1953, I have felt that the people of Kashmir do not enjoy the confidence of Indian leaders.'[90]

Recent studies have shown that towards the end of his life Nehru appeared to have realized how his 'integrationist' steps concerning Kashmir had alienated the Muslims of the province.[91] Even Sheikh Abdullah acknowledged this transformation in Nehru: 'I found him a very different man. He had realized that there was a wide gap between the problems of the people and his ability to solve them.'[92]

Jawaharlal is believed to have become favourably disposed to the idea of a confederation between India, Pakistan and their smaller neighbors. To quote Nehru:

> Confederation remains our ultimate goal. Look at Europe, at the Common Market. This is the urge everywhere. There are no two peoples anywhere nearer than those of India and Pakistan, though if we say it, they [the Pakistanis] are alarmed and think we want to swallow them.[93]

On 8 April 1964 Jawaharlal released the Sheikh from imprisonment and persuaded him to meet the Pak President Ayub Khan with the 'federation proposal'. But the Pakistan President 'dismissed Abdullah, partly because...he suspected Nehru's sinister hand but, more importantly, because it might also give the Bengalis in East Bengal autonomy'.[94] Nevertheless, Jawaharlal suggested a personal meeting with Ayub. But unfortunately he breathed his last on 27 May 1964 and hopes for a reopening of the Kashmir question from the Indian side have ever since been buried.

3.2 Post-Nehruvian period and accentuation of political crisis in Jammu and Kashmir

Kashmiri Muslim antagonism against the Indian state was not, however, to become absolute. This was amply revealed during the 1965 Indo-Pak war. The 1963 December Muslim uprising in Jammu and Kashmir to protest the alleged theft of a holy relic from the Hazratbal mosque had been viewed by the Pakistani ruling elites as 'the defiant struggle of Kashmir's four million Moslems to be free'.[95] Besides, India's military humiliation at Chinese hands in 1962, and Nehru's death two years later, made Pakistan feel that the time was now most opportune to make India undo its Kashmir mission. In this context Pakistan initiated, in the spring of 1965, 'Operation Gibraltar'. Mujahedin and commandos were sent across the border to incite a revolt in Kashmir in a bid to prepare the ground for the entry of Pakistani soldiers into the Indian province as 'liberators'.[96] But 'Operation Gibraltar' backfired because Kashmiri Muslims generally collaborated with the Indian security forces to confront Pakistani mujahedin. It is well known how the scope of the war was subsequently expanded and Pakistan was forced to retreat and accept a Soviet-mediated cease-fire in September 1965.

Unfortunately, the Indian state failed to reward Kashmiri loyalty. Instead of recognizing the *Kashmiriyat*, New Delhi – emboldened by a military victory against Pakistan – fell back upon its traditional dictum of Kashmir's integration with India. This mood was confirmed by the Prime Minister, Mrs Gandhi, in New York on 31 March 1966:

> The second invasion of Kashmir by Pakistan last autumn has destroyed whatever marginal or academic value the old UN Resolutions might have had [on Plebiscite]. Kashmir is also vital to the defence of India in Ladakh against China. Any

plebiscite today would by definition amount to questioning the integrity of India.[97]

Henceforth, Delhi's primary concern was to ensure a puppet government in Jammu and Kashmir, thus frustrating the ethnic aspirations of the majority of Kashmiris. Sheikh Abdullah was rearrested on charges of being 'anti-Indian' and the province was deprived of such fundamental rights as freedom of speech, association, assembly and protection against arbitrary arrest, which were technically enjoyed in other parts of the country.[98] To quote Sheikh Abdullah:

> ...the democratic process [of India] stops somewhere near Pathankot. Between Pathankot and the Banihal Pass you find only a shadow of these rights and after Banihal you do not find even semblance of them![99]

The year 1971 marked yet another landmark in New Delhi's centralizing drive against Kashmir. The third consecutive military triumph over Pakistan, the bifurcation of Pakistan and the emergence of Bangladesh, and the Pakistani Prime Minister Zulfiqar Ali Bhutto's visit to India to sign the Shimla Pact – all these epitomized the height of India's success in South Asian regional politics. Mrs Indira Gandhi now bluntly declared that Kashmiris 'are Indian citizens and share its common goals and aspirations'.[100] In a letter to Sheikh Abdullah Mrs Gandhi stated more candidly:

> ...the clock cannot be put back and we have to take note of the relations of the situation.[101]

Realist that he was, Sheikh Abdullah also appreciated the changed circumstances and signed an agreement with the Indian government in February 1975. Jammu and Kashmir was now recognized as a constituent unit of India and no proposal for any change in the provincial constitution was to be effective without the consent of the President of India. The 1975 agreement also forced the serving Congress Chief Minister of Kashmir to step down in favour of Sheikh Abdullah. Abdullah's reassumption of power was legitimized by his remarkable success in the 1977 legislative elections, widely acknowledged as the first fair poll in the state. A working equation between Delhi and Srinagar survived till Abdullah's death in September 1982. The new political spirit was reflected during the Sheikh's funeral when his body was draped with the Indian tricolour and mourners chanted: *Sher-e-Kashmir ka kya irsad? Hindu, Muslim, Sikh Itehad* ('What was the message of the Lion of Kashmir? Friendship between Hindus, Muslims and Sikhs').[102] A distinguished Indian journalist, M.J. Akbar, summed up the atmosphere: 'Sheikh Abdullah had died an Indian... The Government of Pakistan had no comment to offer on the death of Sheikh Mohammad Abdullah.'[103]

The apparent peace in Jammu and Kashmir was, however, a lull before the storm. The Sheikh's son Farooq won the contest for succession with Mrs Gandhi's blessing, becoming both the leader of the National Conference and the interim Chief Minister of the province. But once in the saddle, Farooq Abdullah realized that he lacked the charisma of his father, which had artificially subsumed the dichotomy between *Kashmiriyat* and authority of the Indian state. If he was to survive in Kashmiri politics he needed to 'absorb' this dissent and contradication.[104] Not unnaturally, Farooq increasingly adopted an anti-Delhi stance and when elections were held to the Jammu and Kashmir Assembly in 1983 the National Conference and Mrs Gandhi's Congress Party were ranged on opposite sides. Riyaz Punjabi expressed the popular Muslim reaction in Kashmir:

> The ego of the people was satisfied in as much as Farooq Abdullah had refused to be subdued by the very same might of the Congress Party who had dismissed the National Conference government in 1953, and had imposed successive unrepresentative governments on the people.[105]

Matters got complicated when Mrs Gandhi adopted the 'Hindu card' to contain Farooq.[106] The Congress(I) was now replaying the Praja Parishad game of the 1950s. Mrs Gandhi's slogan of 'Hindu minorities of Kashmir in danger' – coming ironically at a time when she had inserted the word 'secularism' in the Preamble to the country's constitution – contributed to the institutionalization of communal politics in Kashmir, the potential of which had already been noticed during the first tenure of Sheikh Abdullah's regime. The heightened Hindu-Muslim political tension in Kashmir that we see today was an inevitable outcome of the 1983 electoral politics. Meanwhile, reverberations of the Kashmir issue were felt outside the subcontinent, notably in London. On 3 February 1983, an Indian diplomat, M.H. Mahatre, was kidnapped by a Kashmiri militant group – the Kashmir Liberation Army (KLA). Mahatre's release was made conditional on the release of Maqbool Butt, the Kashmiri extremist who had been imprisoned in India on charges of terrorism. But before a deal could be struck Mahatre was found dead in Birmingham. On 3 February 1984, Maqbool was hanged.

As anticipated in most quarters, Farooq emerged from the 1983 elections with flying colours, the National Conference winning 47 of the 76 Assembly seats. But this election reconfirmed communal overtones in Kashmiri electoral politics when the National Conference won most of its 42 seats from the Muslim-dominated valley, and the Congress secured its 13 seats from the predominantly Hindu-inhabited Jammu. The Government of India, however, refused to accept the popular verdict and sought to project Farooq as a national security risk. Farooq's insistence on the Resettlement Bill, enabling people from across the Line of Control to resettle in Jammu and Kashmir, was characterized by Delhi as 'anti-national'. The Bill proposed resettlements only after careful scrutiny of individual applicants by Indian intelligence agencies. But Mrs Gandhi represented it as a measure to perpetrate Muslim demographic supremacy in Jammu and Kashmir.[107] As Balraj Puri remarked: 'The Congress(I) has chosen to [present the Kashmir issue as a] Jammu versus Kashmir and Kashmir versus Delhi controversy.'[108] On the other hand, Farooq steadily allied himself with the emerging national opposition front against Mrs Gandhi's Congress. Farooq's political realigments coincided with Mrs Gandhi's exercise to impose a uniform polity, making all opposition-led provincial regimes fall victims of the Congress juggernaut.[109] Not unnaturally, the central government used the Jammu and Kashmir Governor Jagmohan's office to engineer dissensions within Farooq's camp and then dissolve the National Front ministry in July 1984.[110] G.M. Shah, the eldest son-in-law of Sheikh Abdullah, formed a new government in Jammu and Kashmir with the help of the Congress and Indian paramilitary forces. Farooq alleged that the entire conspiracy was hatched by Mrs Gandhi herself and executed with the help of the Jammu and Kashmir Governor Jagmohan.[111]

G.M. Shah's regime was unmistakably unpopular in Jammu and

Kashmir.[112] The popular Kashmiri disillusionment with the Indian government's inept intervention in the province was amply demonstrated when during the December 1984 parliamentary elections the National Conference won by considerable margins in all the three constituencies of the Valley. Henceforth, popular alienation of Kashmiri Muslims from New Delhi acquired a new political content. A breach between *Kashmiriyat* and the Indian State appeared to be complete. It seemed as if that there was to be no turning back. An irrational electoral game played by the ruling party in Delhi was now to drive a significant section of Kashmiri Muslims to the path of 'extremism'.

3.3 Economic ingredients of the Kashmir crisis

Political alienation of *Kashmiriyat* – analyzed above – was reinforced by economic factors. Jammu and Kashmir presents a classic congruence of religious and economic boundaries. Although a distinct demographic minority, Hindus of the province had a substantial vested interest in land, business and bureaucracy.[113] On the other hand, the Muslim majority traditionally earned their living either as pastoralists, known as *Gujars* and *Bakerwals*, or as boatmen, known as *Hanjis*.[114] In 1981 while the Hindu majority area in Jammu and Kashmir recorded a 42 per cent literacy rate, the corresponding figure for the Muslim-dominated Valley was only 22 per cent.[115] As late as 1990 George Fernandes, who was then in charge of Kashmir affairs under V.P. Singh's Premiership, admitted that the Kashmiri Pundits, constituting only three per cent of the Valley's population, monopolized 80 per cent of all its professional jobs.[116] Interestingly, during the eight years of Presidents' Rule since January 1990, the Hindu share in central government's Gazetted and Non-Gazetted posts rose to 83.66 per cent and 79.27 per cent respectively. By December 1990, all such pivotal positions as Governor's Advisors, Chief Secretary and Director-General of Police, and ten out of eleven Additional Secretaryships, were held by non-Kashmiri Muslims.[117] According to one estimate, 90 per cent of jobs in the banking, insurance and telecommunication sectors were cornered by the Hindu minority community.[118] In the words of Noorani: '...the Kashmiri Muslims find themselves discriminated [against] even in their home state'.[119] The few Muslims employed by the government suffered from blatant discrimination too. For instance, at the height of the 1990 disturbances when the state was subjected to prolonged curfews and military operations, Muslim employees in the Valley did not receive their salaries, although the Governor reportedly went out of his way to arrange an immediate disbursement of one months's pay to Hindu officers stationed in Jammu.[120] In such circumstances a pre-eminent section amongst Kashmiri Muslims has come to be seized with a belief that their special position within India had 'yielded them precious little economic development'.[121] A new generation of educated Kashmiri youth particularly resent the fact that 'although rich in natural resources, Kashmir continues to be commercially backward'.[122] A pan-Indian bourgeoisie – predominantly Hindu – sees Kashmir as a 'captive market' for its manufactures and not as 'an area of investment'.[123] No major industries are based in Jammu and Kashmir[124], and agriculture remains the mainstay of the economy.[125] Despite its immense hydroelectric potential, acute power shortage, especially in winter, grips the province. Once customs barriers were removed and free trade was imposed on Kashmir following the dissolution of Abdullah's government in 1953,[126] Kashmir's trade with the rest of India developed in the classic manner of internal colonialism – manufactured items being exchanged for Kashmiri raw materials and primary products. Besides, extensive deforestation was carried out in Kashmir to extract timber, mostly for the Indian Railways.[127] The adverse impact of this ecological destruction is described:

> Apart from the widespread ecological impact, a high-value resource was sold at virtually a throwaway price which not only did not bring any substantial monetary benefit in terms of current revenues but also eroded the potential for future income and the State's...self reliance.[128]

Even Sheikh Abdullah's economic reforms did not go too far. The abolition of absentee landlordism was not supplemented by measures to help the tillers to retain their newly-acquired land. Instead, many of the old landed gentry colluded with the new power elites to repossess their holdings and transform them into horticultural lands with government subsidies.[129] Consumer co-operatives established by Sheikh Abdullah also degenerated into hotbeds of corruption.[130] One National Conference member of the Parliament admitted: 'The trouble is that we have failed to deliver on all fronts.'[131]

Present economic hardship in Jammu and Kashmir can also be partly ascribed to New Delhi's dichotomous policy. The Indian Government has apparently adopted a policy of 'economic appeasement' in Kashmir. By the time of the Third Five Year Plan 97 per cent of Kashmir's Plan expenditure was financed by the central government. But in the process Kashmir was caught in a permanent debt trap by New Delhi. This was because the Non-Plan Discretionary Central Assistance to Kashmir came as 70 per cent loan and 30 per cent grant, although for other hill provinces the ratio for such grants was respectively 10 per cent and 90 per cent.[132] The more Jammu and Kashmir received central assistance, the greater was its financial insolvency. A 'discriminatory' fiscal arrangement burdened Jammu and Kashmir with 'greater loan liability…[and] debt servicing ratio'. This left Jammu and Kashmir with no other option but to accept perpetual 'revenue deficits' in its annual budgets.[133] In 1989 Jammu and Kashmir had no developmental funds and was saddled with Rs. 1 billion (US $62.9 million) deficit.[134] In 1991, more than 80 per cent of the budgetary deficit for the state was accounted for by interest payments to the Centre.[135]

Unfortunately, the Indian government was exceptionally slow to rescue Kashmir from its economic predicament. Instead, New Delhi often adopted arbitrary negative postures, as was seen in the abrupt termination of the Rs. 250 *crores* Dhal Rasti Project in November 1981 following differences with the Chief Minister Sheikh Abdullah on the sharing of power to be generated from it.[136] Furthermore, Kashmir did not necessarily enjoy optimum utilization from completed projects. The Salal project can be cited as a case in point. While adequate megawatts of power could not be transmitted from Salal to Srinagar because of the low-quality transmission lines, electricity generated from the same station was transmitted to Delhi through a sophisticated northern grid system. A suspicion was naturally nursed by the Kashmiris that they were being deliberately made to suffer from faulty planning and negligence.[137] All these drove the rapidly rising Kashmiri youth population[138] to a separatist thesis that 'Kashmir, India's only Muslim-majority state, will never be given its rightful place among the states of Hindu-dominated India.'[139] In the words of the noted Indian journalist Rajinder

Sarin: 'The rise of fanaticism in the valley highlights the failure of our development strategy, educational system and so on.'[140]

It would be, however, inaccurate to argue that no one within Kashmiri society benefited from the post-1947 developments. Recent studies draw our attention to a nexus of businessman-politician-bureaucrats, cutting across religious lines, which has prospered by misappropriating funds earmarked for schemes of public welfare. One analysis reckons that by 1974 more than 3,000 families in Jammu and Kashmir had amassed 'amazing' fortunes from an underground narcotic trade in *charas*.[141] But an entire spectrum of the primarily Muslim population was deprived of the fruits of economic development. In 1989 one-third of the state's population was unemployed. The figure for educated unemployment surged from 100,000 in 1986–7 to 300,000 in 1991.[142] Schools, hospitals, bridges and roads lay badly damaged; much of the Valley remained without electricity at nights.[143] It is this section of the Kashmiri population which provides the backbone for the current unrest. Sheikh Abdullah was perhaps anticipating the present crisis when he exclaimed in utter frustration:

> I had told my people that their interests are safe in India. But educated unemployed Muslims look towards Pakistan because while their Hindu compatriots find avenues in India open for them they [Muslims] are debarred from getting Government services. When I point out these difficulties, I am dubbed as a communalist.[144]

Some Indian analysts argue that economic frustration of the rank and file in Kashmir is not qualitatively different from their compatriots in other parts of India.[145] But the economic resentment of Kashmiri Muslims acquires a particular dimension when viewed in the context of a 'feeling of being deprived of their right to establish and institutionalize their separate identity *vis-à-vis* the Indian state'.[146] This distemper was expressed when a Kashmiri Muslim government employee recalled to a group of investigative Indian journalists that he was not an Indian by accident of birth, but when Kashmir chose to accede to India he became an Indian by conviction. After all these years, he exclaimed, 'where is my conviction now?'[147] The following quote from a moderate Kashmiri politician also reveals the helplessness of a large segment of Kashmiris:

We are branded Pakistanis. We have always been objects of suspicion. Even if we pick up the Indian flag, and start shouting *Jai Bharat ma*, the suspicion will remain. They do not trust us. Our elders fought against the Pakistanis in 1947, we fought against them in 1965 and 1971, but I do not know why we are still not trusted.[148]

A separatist militant would extend this disillusionment to assert: 'We will win independence one day. The question is whether India wants to leave Kashmir gracefully or after a massacre?'[149] As early as 1968 Sheikh Abdullah had anticipated such a fear and his remark is worth quoting:

...we felt that our ambitions, and our hopes, for which we had made huge sacrifices since 1931, would be fulfilled by allying ourselves with [India] which believed in democracy, in the rule of law [and]...equality of man. We believe in the high ideals which Mahatma Gandhi preached. Now look at the treatment Kashmir has received. That is an open book... Let every Indian search his own heart.[150]

4. THE ISLAMIZATION OF KASHMIRIYAT

The assertion of Kashmiri ethnicity along Islamic lines effectively coincided with Farooq's National Conference abandoning its anti-Delhi stance and alliance with Rajiv Gandhi who had assumed the mantle of both the Congress party and the Indian government after Mrs Gandhi's tragic assassination in September 1984. In 1986 Farooq signed an accord with Rajiv, justifying it as a 'hard reality'.[151] But this alliance was widely interpreted by Kashmiri Muslims as a betrayal of the Kashmir cause. What followed was a tragedy of circumstances. Farooq, who had risen on the crest of Kashmiri identity, was now condemned for having abandoned it. At this juncture *Kashmiriyat* was appropriated by Islamic fundamentalism under the banner of the Muslim United Front. This Islamization of Kashmiri ethnic assertion was accelerated when the National Conference-Congress combine, alarmed at the upswing of the Muslim United Front's popularity, allegedly rigged the provincial legislative elections of 1987 and perpetrated violence on the Muslim United Front activists. It was these disgruntled sections within the Muslim United Front who later provided much of the leadership to insurgency politics in Jammu and Kashmir.[152] Farooq did form a ministry in Jammu and Kashmir with Congress support. But he could not stem the tide of popular anger – mostly asserted along violent lines – at his blatant surrender to Delhi's authority. By 1989 matters were out of Farooq's hands. On 18 January 1990 he resigned in protest against Delhi's undue interference when, despite his reservations, the non-Congress Government of V.P. Singh appointed Jagmohan as Governor of the province. Jammu and Kashmir was then brought under President's rule. The review of all Parliamentary legislation extended to Kashmir promised under the 1975 February Indira Gandhi-Sheikh Abdullah Accord was put in cold storage. Instead, the government of India empowered itself to legislate in Kashmir on any subject within the State List.[153]

Once secular politics failed to be a viable vehicle for the expression of *Kashmiriyat* and existing political institutions failed to mitigate the sufferings of Kashmiris, the mosque emerged as the central rallying point for disgruntled Kashmiris.[154] The rapid growth of *madrasas* (Muslim schools) financed by Gulf oil money facilitated a further injection of fundamentalism into Kashmiri society.[155] All these provided an ideological backdrop for Kashmiri ethnicity to develop an external dimension, looking to the neighbouring Muslim state of Pakistan for sustenance. Kashmir degenerated into a battleground between Indian security forces and a Kashmiri self-assertion movement, tinged with Islamic fundamentalism, and driven by the idea of secession from the Indian union.

5. KASHMIRI SEPARATIST POLITICAL ACTORS AND THE OBFUSCATION OF BOUNDARIES BETWEEN DOMESTIC AND FOREIGN AFFAIRS

The insurrection in Kashmir has been described in many circles as an 'intifada', having a Pan-Islamic flavour of the Palestinian variety. Whether or not this characterization is correct, the fact remains that Kashmiri rebels seeking the secession of Jammu and Kashmir from the Indian Union draw sustenance from Pakistan. An index of this transfer of loyalty from India to Pakistan is the manner in which political events in Pakistan tend to have an emotive impact on the rebel mind. Such incidents as the fall of Dhaka in 1971 or the Ojhri ammunition camp blast in April 1988 made Srinagar restive, gripped as it was by a feeling that India's invisible hand was trying to jeopardize Pakistan's national integrity.[156] The Valley experienced *bandhs* (strikes) when the Bhawalpur plane crash ended the life of the Pak President Zia-ul-Haq.[157] Hoisting the Pakistan flag on 14 August (Pakistan Independence Day) and a black flag on 15 August (Indian Independence Day), and celebrating Pakistan's victory against India in a hockey or cricket match are not uncommon.[158] A Pakistani analyst proudly recalled how 'Indian-held Kashmir observed *hartal* (general strike)' at the call of Zulfikar Ali Bhutto.[159] Subsequently, when in February 1995 Zulfikar's daughter, the then Pakistani Premier Benazir Bhutto, called for a general strike to 'express solidarity with the people of Kashmir', it incited a response in Jammu and Kashmir. Assumption of office by a new President or Premier in Islamabad also occasions thanksgiving prayers in Kashmir.[160] Even disgruntled political leaders in Jammu and Kashmir would not hesitate to express their dissatisfaction by demonstrating solidarity with Pakistan. Thus G.M. Shah, who lost his office of Chief Ministership in 1986 due to New Delhi's pressure, held a demonstration in Srinagar's Iqbal Park, unfurled a Pakistani flag and publicly admitted his folly for 'falling in the trap' of the Indian government.[161] Pro-Pak sentiments in Kashmir are also expressed to vent popular Muslim Kashmiri resentment against 'an inefficient and unresponsive Indian administration'.[162] Thus demonstrations in Jammu and Kashmir on such domestic issues as increase in electricity charges had spill-over effects in Pak-occupied Kashmir.[163] To quote a US study:

> …the rise of Islamist ideology to predominance throughout Indian Kashmir facilitated the emergence of a tight link between Indian Kashmiri insurgents, their supporters and Islamabad. Thus it was with the widespread adoption of Islamist ideologies that Kashmiri Muslims could 'now seek ideological sustenance from a transnational Islam, while simultaneously basking in the guaranteed patronage from across the border'. Concurrently, for the Pakistan defense establishment, the Kashmir cause constituted a combination of regional interest and commitment to the global

Islamist cause. Muslim fundamentalists in Pakistan...see the Islamic surge in Kashmir as the long-awaited hour for jihad against Indian infidels, a holy war for which Pakistan must funnel material and moral backing.[164]

Secessionist politics in Jammu and Kashmir is not, however, played under one umbrella. Instead, a number of militant organizations are involved, estimates of their numerical strength varying from 30-plus[165] to 158.[166] However, two broad strands are usually discerned. On the one hand, we have pro-Pakistani Islamic fundamentalists like Jamaat-e-Islami, Hizbul Islami, Hizbul Mujahideen, Al-Barq, Ikhwanul Muslimeen, Muslim Student Federation, Allah Tigers, Islami Student League, Al Umar, Mutahid Jehad Council, Tehrik-e-Kashmir, Al Jehad, Tehrik-e-Amal, People's League and Laskar-e-Taiba whose general contention would be: 'Kashmir is a Muslim majority region and nobody can deny us the right to bring about Islamic revolution to get rid of Indian domination.'[167] In Rajouri, Kalakote, Poonch, Kupwara and Baramullah handwritten posters were circulated urging 'all possible co-operation and assistance to our friends who have crossed into the state [i.e. sympathizers from Pakistan] to do away with Indian domination'. During the heyday of the 1990 insurgency in Rajouri and other places there was an increase in circulation of Pakistani currency notes inscribed with the following message: 'Time is not far off, when Pakistani currency alone will be in circulation in this region too.'[168] The Indian press still regularly reports security personnel apprehending followers of these fundamentalist groups who have received military training in Pakistan. Such militant leaders as Ghulam Mohd, Mir Shamshul Haq, Bilal Ahmed Siddiqui, Hamid Gul, Nayeem-ul-Haq, Ali Mohd Dar and Ashan Dar are alleged to have made Pakistan their bases of operation.[169] Amongst the Islamic militants the Hizbul Mujahideen, whose chief commander Ahsen Dar claims to command a cadre of 11,000 armed young men, emerged by 1990 as the most 'credible force' in Kashmir's centrifugal politics. The group insists on the observance of Islamic moral code, and advocates prohibition and closure of bars, cinema halls and beauty parlours in areas under its control.[170] This section of Kashmiri militants also vent their wrath on Hindu Pundits who are identified as representatives of a 'Hinduized state polity' which caused large-scale migration of Kashmiri

Hindus from the Valley to Jammu. Massacres carried out in the Hindu hamlets of Udhampur, Poonch and Rajouri are common, one of which provoked Omar Abdullah, the son of the state Chief Minister, who won a seat in the parliamentary election of 1998, to remark in anguish: 'This mindless act of violence has once again shown the desperation of the militants.'[171] According to one estimate 100,000 Pundit inhabitants of the Valley left their homes by January 1990. Others push the figure of Hindu refugees to 200,000.[172] Recent studies, however, dismiss the RSS and Hindu sectarian claims of violence against Pundits as 'a pot-pourri of fabrication and exaggeration'.[173] Kashmiri militants have also resorted to kidnapping of civilians to force the Indian authorities to release their colleagues from jails. The Indian government alleges direct patronization of Hizbul Mujahideen by Pakistan's Inter-Service Intelligence (ISI). Separatist leaders like Mast Gul are frequently found addressing Jammat-e-Islami workers in Rawalpindi and other areas to unite all Pakistanis in the jihad for liberating Kashmir.[174] The Hizbul is even believed to have links with Afghan mujahedin.[175]

At the other end of the spectrum lies the Jammu and Kashmir Liberation Front (JKLF) and groups affiliated to it. Founded by Maqbool Butt and Aminullah Khan, the party wields considerable support in the urban sector. It has organized a number of terrorist plots, including the hijacking of an Indian Airlines aircraft and kidnapping the daughter of India's former Home Minister, Mufti Muhammad Sayeed. The organization apparently distances itself from pro-Pak Islamic fundamentalists and theoretically advocates a secular independent Kashmir. But in reality this 'distancing' has proved more to be a myth. In the case of the JKLF, too, the obfuscation of internal/external boundaries is apparent. Its major support base remains in Pakistan.[176] One of its prominent leaders Noor Khan candidly stated: 'The ultimate goal of our organization is the establishment of Nizam-e-Mustafa (regime of the Prophet) in Kashmir.'[177]

A 1990 press report estimated that 10,000 armed JKLF Members were trained in Pakistan[178] to organize 'sabotage, kidnappings and executions' in Jammu and Kashmir.[179] On 17 December 1989, the JKLF supremo Amanullah Khan advised his followers from his Pakistani base in Rawalpindi: 'Don't touch our people, but hit Indian property, including airlines, post offices and public buildings.'[180] On 14 August 1989, the JKLF held a gathering of 5,000 at the Ghani Stadium in Srinagar to observe Pakistan's Independence Day. Its underground leader Shabir Shah took the salute and 21 guns were fired on the occasion. On the next day – India's Independence Day – the JKLF volunteers burned the tri-colour and observed a blackout in Srinagar.[181] In September 1990, the JKLF even joined United Jihad Council, an apex body of such top pro-Pak militant Kashmiri outfits like Hizbul Mujahideen, Muslim Janbaaz Force, Tehrik-i-Jehad-i-Islami, Al Umar Mujahideen, Hizbullah and Operation Balakot to evolve a 'common programme of action'.[182] The Indian government has mentioned the names of JKLF leaders like Ghulam Nabi Butt, Sher Mohd and Abdul Rashid Jalal who work closely with Pakistani Intelligence agencies.[183] The Party even reportedly established contacts with Khalistanis.[184] The JKLF also had planned to undertake in March 1992 a 'long march' from 'Azad Kashmir' across the 1949 cease-fire line into Jammu and Kashmir. Thanks to the Pakistan army's good sense, the 'march' did not materialize and an Indo-Pak crisis was averted. It is, however, doubtful if Pakistan's action was prompted by an understanding that the JKLF's march was 'philosophically wrong' or by a realization that it would be strategically unsound to place the 'innocent people before the Indian firing squads.'[185] An Indian news-paper was not wide of the mark in commenting:

> ...nor should the reported action to prevent them [JKLF volun-teers] from [crossing the Line of Control] lead anyone to believe that it was an aberration in which Pakistan had no hand. The whole drama is part of a calculated Pakistani design to capture Kashmir – a blueprint of direct and indirect action.[186]

Even when the entire world hailed the February 1999 Lahore summit between the Indian Premier Atal Behari Vajpayee and his Pakistani counterpart Nawaz Sharif, the JKLF leader Amanullah Khan directed his supporters to organize protests against Vajpayee's visit. He lost no opportunity to voice his anti-India feelings: 'We believe that unless we shed blood – our own and that of the enemy – we won't get freedom.'[187]

Interestingly, the late 1980s witnessed the establishment of women's organizations like the Dukhtaran-e-Millat (Daughters of Faith) and Muslim Khawateen Markaz (Muslim Women's Centre) with the explicit purpose of defending male militants from the aggressions of Indian security forces.[188] By May 1990 the Dukhataran-e-Millat was believed to have enrolled 70,000 volunteers.[189] Three years later, Indian security forces rounded up the main organizer of this group, Asiaya Andrabi.[190]

Transfer of loyalty from the Indian state on the part of the Kashmiri militants has gained encouragement from the triumph of Islamic fundamentalism in Iran and Afghanistan. In the words of one of the analysts supportive of this trend: 'The temptation to look around for international linkage of self-determination movements is fairly common.'[191] With the improvement of Iran-Pak relations since 1986, the Iranian factor in Kashmir politics became pronounced. The first public indication of an Iranian interest for the 'struggling Kashmiris' came when the Iranian President during his 1986 meeting with the Pakistan Prime Minister Junejo went out of his way to describe himself as a student of the freedom movement of South Asian Muslims and a devotee of Allama Iqbal, whose ancestors were Kashmiris.[192] The Iranian President's hidden agenda was clarified by his Ambassador in Pakistan: 'Ever since our [Iranian] revolution we have supported the freedom fighters and waged struggle against aggressors and despots as we are fighting for true independence and rule of the people.'[193] Within two years of this declaration an Iranian diplomat was invited to Jammu and Kashmir by pro-militant forces to attend the foundation stone-laying ceremony of a college in Srinagar. The diplomat's visit could not, however, take place because the government denied his entry into the province.[194]

By 1990 Iranian support for the Kashmiri Muslims' struggle had become overt. In January Tehran unceremoniously called off the visit by the Indian Foreign Minister in protest against India's treatment of the people of Jammu and Kashmir.[195] In April Morteza Sarmadi, a Foreign Ministry spokesman of Iran, warned that 'Indian rule [in Kashmir] injured the religious sentiments of Muslims throughout the world.'[196] Not surprisingly, the Ayatollah's pictures began featuring prominently in processions of Kashmiri militants. A team of Indian observers wrote: 'Judging by the display of pictures of Khomeini in the streets of Srinagar, we felt that the impact of the Iranian-type militant Islamic fundamentalism also could not be ruled out.'[197]

The growing Pan-Islamic edge to Kashmiri insurgency is also evident from the participation of Afghan mujahedin and 'other fighters' from Sudan, Algeria, Yemen and Libya in what has come to be termed 'the

Kashmir jihad'.[198] Speaking of the Afghan connection, a Western commentator quoted a Kashmiri militant: 'If the Afghans can do it, then why not us?'[199] Pro-Pakistani Kashmiri activists were also involved in organizing cross-border militant conclaves in the Middle East.[200] The Hizbul Mujahideen, Al Umar, Harkat-ul-Ansar and Laskar-e-Toiba have been particularly active in employing foreign mercenaries to attain their objectives.[201] Many commentators believe that the current phase of militancy in Jammu and Kashmir is the handiwork of foreign mercenaries employed by the ISI rather than of local militants.[202] Particular mention has been made of Afghan-Taliban mercenaries who, by the beginning of 2001, succeeded in expanding their activities from mountainous terrain to the interior of Udhampur district by using sophisticated weapons such as the Strella SA-7 Grail Missile, which is capable of bringing down aircraft flying in the range of 3,500 to 4,500 metres. In an interview with *The Times*, the spokesman of Laskar-e-Taiba noted with pride how fighters from all Muslim nations, particularly Pakistan and Afghanistan, were swelling the ranks of insurgents in Jammu and Kashmir.[203] It is also believed that the Saudi militant leader Osama Bin Laden, now settled in Afghanistan, himself once planned a major 'Islamic offensive' in Jammu and Kashmir.

Nevertheless, the presence of foreign mercenaries need not be overstressed. Although Indian officials are increasingly speaking of proxy war in Jammu and Kashmir at the behest of Pakistan and 'international terrorism', the actual figure of foreign mercenaries in the province seems to be declining. It becomes evident from an official report which estimates that between January 1997 and August 1999 amongst the total number of militants killed 1,334 were locals and only 328 foreigners.[204] Many commentators thus stress the growing importance of local components in Kashmir's insurgency politics.[205]

6. THE PAKISTANI RESPONSE TO INSURGENCY IN KASHMIR

There are strong indications to demonstrate Pakistan's positive response to any instance of threatened Kashmiriyat's transfer of loyalty from India. In a sense this is natural. For, as Urmila Phadnis contended:

The imperatives of *realpolitik* coupled with that of cross-boundary ethnic links have at times created situations in which the externality of such movements induces a sort of pressure leading to an interventionist role of the neighbour through mediation or confrontation.[206]

Yet analysts like Ayesha Jalal do not consider Pakistan's expressions 'of concern and moral support' for Kashmiri Muslims in India as

evidence of a subversive foreign hand… In Islamabad there seems to be a sense of the limits of power; circumspect state officials are not prepared to risk the future of Pakistan for a military adventure to regain a lost letter.[207]

In reality, the ruling elites in Pakistan can hardly reconcile themselves with the loss of Kashmir, just as their counterparts in India would not like to preside over the secession of Kashmir. For Islamabad the acquisition of Jammu and Kashmir remains an 'unfinished agenda of Pakistan'. As early as 30 October 1947 a Pakistan government communiqué had emphasized: 'The Government of Pakistan cannot accept the version of the circumstances in which Kashmir acceded to the Indian Dominion.'[208]

Accordingly, it came to view the 'struggle for Kashmir' as a part of the unaccomplished task of establishing a consolidated Muslim home-land in the subcontinent.[209] Kashmir was presented as 'an article of faith' and the Pakistanis were urged to fight: 'for Kashmir on the same principle as that on which we fought for Pakistan..[to] secure for all areas of the subcontinent where Muslims were in the majority, the fundamental right of self-determination.'[210]

Muhammad Ali Jinnah, the father of Pakistan, himself reiterated the duty of Kashmiri Muslims to unite with their subcontinental coreligionists to make the 'Muslim nation' a reality.[211] The Pakistan government's White Paper on Kashmir admitted the 'natural instinct of the Qaid-i-Azam (Jinnah)…[was to] go effectively to the aid of…beleaguered brethren in Jammu and Kashmir'.[212] M.A. Gurmani, the Pakistan Minister for Kashmir Affairs till November 1951, noted:

Kashmir is an article of faith with Pakistan and not merely a piece of land or a source of rivers… We are fighting for Kashmir on the same principle as that on which we fought for Pakistan. We took a solemn vow that we would secure for all areas of the subcontinent where Muslims were in the majority, the fundamental right of self-determination.[213]

The Pakistani ruling elite – like its Indian counterpart – had been thus driven by the notion of Kashmir's strategic importance for national security. As early as December 1947 the Prime Minister of Pakistan wrote to Jawaharlal Nehru: 'The security of Pakistan is bound up with that of Kashmir, and ties of religion, cultural affinity and economic interdependence bind the two together still closer.'[214] Likewise, the Founder-President of Azad Kashmir elucidated the 'geopolitical link' between Pakistan and Kashmir:

The Hindu-Kush ranges in the North, the hilly tracts of land in the North-West, common between the adjoining districts of West Pakistan on the one side, and the Jammu and Kashmir State on the other, prove…geographically, Kashmir and Pakistan are one. No natural barriers separate Kashmir from Pakistan, as is the case with respect of India. It is only a man-made and artificial line which separates Pakistan from Kashmir.[215]

The two metalled roads – the Banihal Cart Road and the Jhelum Valley Road – connecting Kashmir to the outside world pass through Pakistan; the two main road and railway systems of West Pakistan run parallel to Kashmir. The Pakistan Foreign Minister thus submitted before the United Nations Security Council on 8 February 1950:

The whole of the defence of that area…is based upon the fact that this line would not be threatened from the flank. If Kashmir acceded to India, the whole of that flank would be threatened…and broken… India would obtain direct access to the tribal areas and through [them], on to Afghanistan.[216]

During his interview with David Lilienthal, the Pakistan Prime Minister Liaquat Ali Khan remarked in metaphorical terms: 'Kashmir, as you will see from this map, is like a cap on the head of Pakistan. If I allow India to have this cap on our head, then I am always at the mercy of India.'[217] Besides, Kashmir was viewed by the Pakistani government as an 'economic life-line'. For instance, the 'headwaters' of Pakistan's major rivers and canal systems lie in Kashmir. One Pakistani commentator aptly underlined how his country's

> agricultural economy was dependent partly on the rivers coming out of Kashmir. The Mangla Headwaters were actually in Kashmir and the Marala Headwaters are within a mile or so of the border. What then would be our position if Kashmir was to be in Indian hands?[218]

Pakistan has been also interested in Kashmir's timber, fruit and vegetables, woollen products, mineral deposits and hydroelectric potential.[219] Zafrullah Khan, Pakistan's former Foreign Minister, summed up Kashmir's importance to Pakistan thus: 'If Kashmir should accede to India, Pakistan might as well, from both the economic and the strategic points of view, become a feudatory of India.'[220]

In the context of national pressure to launch a Kashmir recovery mission it was not unnatural for the Pakistani government to organize an infiltration of tribes into Kashmir on 23 October 1947 to secure the region's accession to Pakistan. Although Pakistan officially denied its involvement in the episode, the following quote from a recent memoir of the then Pakistan cabinet member Sirdar Shaukat Hyat Khan speaks otherwise:

> Seeing the Maharaja's and India's bad faith, we decided to walk into Kashmir. I was put in charge of the operations. I asked for the services of Brigadier Sher Khan and Brigadier Akbar, both of 6/13th Frontier Force (Piffers) and requested that we should be allowed some arms which we could retrieve from…Lahore fort… We lost Kashmir through our own blunders. The people there were jubilant over Pakistan's actions and wanted to join it, but the tribes fell back pell-mell.[221]

At the same time in 1948 some Kashmiri political actors had transferred their loyalty to Pakistan.[222] Sardar Ibrahim, the leader of the pro-Pak Muslim Conference, crossed into Pakistan in search of military assistance to forestall the Maharaja's accession to India and make Kashmir a part of Pakistan.[223] Ibrahim's moves were promptly reciprocated by Pakistan's ruling party, the Muslim League. Akbar Khan, then Director of Weapons and Equipment in Pakistan, himself recorded how 4,000 military rifles destined for the Punjab police were diverted to the hands of the pro-Pakistani Kashmiri political groups.[224] Pakistani commentators wrote about 'full sympathies of the people of Pakistan'[225] for the tribal warriors in Kashmir. An 'unanimity of tribal feeling' was reported, the like of which had hardly been seen in such tribal areas'.[226] But this popular hysteria in Pakistan could not have been generated unless the people had been fed with stories of Hindu atrocities in Kashmir through inflammatory pamphlets and provocative speeches of *maliks*, *mullahs* and *pirs* at religious congregations.[227] Meanwhile, the pro-Pakistani Kashmiri migrants to Pakistan established at Muzaffarabad on 4 October 1947 the provincial government of Free Kashmir (the Azad Kashmir government) with Sardar Mohammad Ibrahim Khan as its President. The incident prepared the ground for the future trend of obfuscation of internal and external differences in Kashmiri ethnic politics.[228]

All future Pakistani heads of state subscribed to the Kashmir policy enunciated in the immediate aftermath of the decolonization of the subcontinent. In the words of an Indian commentator: 'Pakistan's oligarchical inheritors of the two nation theory need the Kashmir conflict to keep themselves in power.'[29] President Ayub Khan considered Kashmir as 'the test case' for Pakistan's national strength.[230] Zulfiqar Ali Bhutto openly spoke of dismantling the 'barrier' between the people of Jammu and Kashmir and 'their kith and kin in Azad Kashmir and Pakistan'.[231] He had even once advocated the use of force to resolve the 'fight between Indian imperialism and Kashmiri democracy'.[232] Not surprisingly, shortly after signing the 1972 Shimla Accord, Bhutto took the first opportunity of assert: 'On the vital question of Kashmir, we have made no compromise.'[223] Five years after the Shimla Pact he candidly declared in Beijing: '…normalization of relations [with India] does not mean that Pakistan should abandon its traditional support for the rights of the Kashmiris.'[234] General Zia-ul-Haq, who subjected Pakistan to an era of unprecedented 'militarization of economy and polity',[235] also reiterated in no uncertain terms: 'Our Muslim Kashmiri brothers cannot be allowed to stay with India for any length of time now.'[236] President Qayum of Azad Kashmir himself paid tribute to President Zia-ul-Haq for his important role in helping Kashmiri separatists.[237] In February 1993 the Pakistan Minister of State for Foreign Affairs went a step further to compare the 'epic Kashmiri struggle' to 'the struggle of the Afghan people against Soviet intervention'.[238]

In fact, no government in Pakistan can afford a 'soft line' on Kashmir.[239] This fact was revealed in no better way than the manner in which Benazir Bhutto as the Prime Minister changed tack after her initial euphoria for Indo-Pak normalization. Faced with the critique of being 'an appeaser' of India in Kashmir, she declared in her address to the National Defence College on 22 March 1990: 'What is happening in Kashmir cannot remain a permanent fact of life. A people cannot be kept in permanent bondage.'[240] Bhutto described the Kashmir valley as awash 'in blood and tears' and 'crying for freedom'.[241] On one occasion she promised 'a thousand years of war' to help the Kashmiris and pledged $5 million to this 'Muslim cause'.[242] In May 1990 Bhutto undertook a tour of Muslim countries, 'seeking support for the Kashmiris' right to self-determination'.[243] She charged India with perpetrating 'genocide' in Kashmir and insisted that Kashmir's freedom was 'the freedom to join Pakistan'.[244] As late as December 1998, on the occasion of the 50th anniversary of the UN Declaration of Human Rights, the Pakistan Information Minister Mushahid Hussain declared his country's resolve to provide 'moral and material support to Kashmiris in their struggle for the right to self-determination'.[245]

Other national politicians in Pakistan have been equally enthusiastic in responding to developments in the Indian part of Kashmir. Haji Moula Baksh Soomru of the Republican Party summed up the mood of the Pakistan National Assembly in 1957: 'Our country is incomplete without Kashmir. We cannot go without Kashmir.'[246] Air Marshal Asghar Khan, the leader of the People's Democratic Party, called for a 'Vietnam-style war' in Kashmir.[247] The Jamaat-e-Islami and the Tehrike Takmeel-e-Pakistan have been consistent in organizing nationwide campaigns for the 'Kashmiri Freedom Movement.[248] Indian Republic Day is still commemorated as a Black Day throughout Pakistani Kashmir. To quote Cohen: 'For Pakistan leaders, both civil and military, Kashmir was a useful rallying cry and a diversion from the daunting task of building a nation out of disparate parts.'[249]

The Pakistan government has been systematically utilizing the mass media to incite national passions 'for the liberation war in Kashmir'.[250] Any 'adverse' event in Jammu and Kashmir is exploited to provoke anti-Indian protests in Pakistan. When Sheikh Abdullah's government was dismissed for the first time, none other than Fatima Jinnah, the sister of Muhammad Ali Jinnah, led demonstrations in Karachi, imploring the 'Pakistanis to volunteer their services and join their Kashmiri brethren in their righteous cause and fight for freedom'.[251] National occasions in Pakistan like Jinnah's birthday are used to remind the people about their responsibility for the people of Kashmir. Every 5 February Pakistanis join their government in observing a 'Solidarity Day, in support of the Kashmiri freedom fighters against Indian occupation'. The mammoth Lahore rally of 20 March 1990 to solemnize the Golden Jubilee of the Pakistan Resolution[252] recalled Pakistan's full 'support [for] the movement in Kashmir for secession from India'.[253] When in the early 1990s the Kashmiri insurrection turned open and violent, Islamabad sponsored solidarity 'rallies and days' throughout Pakistan.[254] 'Jehad Conferences' were held in the Pakistani Punjab, which occasioned the burning of effigies of the then Indian Premier V.P. Singh.[255] During this period, one of the largest processions in Islamabad was led by Ijazul Haq, son of Pakistan's late President Zia-ul-Haq. The US-based *Asia Watch* even cited evidence of the 'perfidious role' of Brigadier Imtiaz of the Inter-Services Intelligence (ISI) in pressurizing Kashmiri militants to execute the Vice-Chancellor of Kashmir University Mushirol Haq in April 1990. In October 1992 the Pakistan National Assembly unanimously resolved to express 'total and unflinching solidarity with the people of Kashmir for their valiant struggle to realize their right to self-determination'.[256] At an all-party conference in Islamabad in February 1993 the Pakistan government's Minister for Religious Affairs, Maulana Abdus Sattar Niazi, declared that 'Jehad for the liberation of Kashmir was obligatory for Pakistan' and specially urged 'able-bodied youth of age 15 to 35' to sacrifice their lives for this cause.[257] Leading Pak newspapers like *The Muslim* (7 April 1993) carried such exhortations as:

HELP THE KASHMIRIS
KASHMIR IS BURNING
Please Rush Your Contributions to
Kashmir Freedom Council, A/C 2629–69 H.B.L. City,
Saddar Road, Rawalpindi.

HELP YOUR BROTHERS
ALLAH WILL HELP YOU
Kashmir Freedom Council, PO Box-393, Rawalpindi, Pakistan.
Ph: 9251–587062; Fax: 9251–5851

On 5 February 1994 Prime Minister Bhutto herself called for a general strike in Pakistan to demand the implementation of the UN Resolution of Plebiscite in Kashmir. This occasioned anti-India demonstrations all over the country during which an irate crowd even tried to storm the Indian Consulate in Karachi.[258] There are also reports of Islamabad keeping a number of key Jammu and Kashmir government officials on its payroll.[259]

Having, however, failed thrice[260] to take Kashmir by storm, Pakistan now prefers to respond to Kashmir's ethnic assertion by sending 'saboteurs' into Jammu and Kashmir or training pro-Pakistani political groups in subversive activities.[261] President Zia was perhaps hinting at this strategy in his July 1989 address to his military: '...we must adopt those methods of combat which the Kashmiri mind can grasp and cope with – in other words, a co-ordinated use of moral and physical means, other than [pure] military operations.'[262]

Although Islamabad officially denied its involvement in Jammu and Kashmir,[263] what followed was Pakistan's proxy war there to erode India's economic and human resources in the region. Two phases of Pakistan's low intensity conflict in Jammu and Kashmir have been identified: the first between 1987 and 1989, when the local Kashmiri population was mobilized for the Islamic militant cause, and the second from 1990 to 1991, which was characterized by 'the escalation and professionalization of the insurgency'.[264] Indian newspapers are replete with accounts of the 'smashing of Pakistani spy ring' or 'capturing of Pakistani armed intruders'.[265] We also learn from the pro-Islamabad Urdu daily *Imroze* (Lahore) how a plan was afoot under the auspices of Al-Mujahid to sponsor an Al-Fateh-type guerrilla movement in Kashmir with the help of a group of educated youth from Srinagar who had been trained in the use of arms and subversive strategies.[266] Indian sources allege the setting up of 46 training camps in Muzaffarabad, Loha, Bult, Aliapur, Ojehra, Aliabad, Kachigarhu, Peshwar and Faisalabad to provide training for Kashmiri militants by the Field Intelligence Unit of Pakistan Army and ISI personnel.[267] Reports indicate the high level of organized training imparted to the trainees. To quote one such description: 'They [trainees] crawl on their bellies, plant land mines and practice marksmanship. Their enemies are the Indian soldiers trying to crush a decade-old-insurgency in the Indian-controlled portion of Kashmir.'[268] Some of these camps train 600 to 700 militants every summer. Even Islamabad's Foreign Minister Sartaj Aziz could not deny that Kashmiri militants were attending religious schools in Pakistan.[269] Organizations like Markaz-Ud-Dawa-Wal-Irshad reportedly run 2,200 religious schools across Pakistan whose students 'learn Islam and prepare for jihad' in Jammu and Kashmir.[270] Another press report identified 4,500 *madrasas* in Pakistan which are funded, and often manned, by well-known terrorist groups to motivate volunteers 'who believe that their mission in life is to free Kashmir from the hands of Indian infidels'.[271] While all students are given Islamic indoctrination and provided with training in guerrilla warfare, the brighter ones are given a six-month course in intelligence operations.[272] The trainees do not cut their hair, grow a beard and wear *salwars* above the ankles. The Nawaz Sharif regime even reportedly earmarked a plot of land to establish a university for the youngsters who after religious and military training were to be sent for terrorist acts across the border.[273] If anyone dies in such actions the following is the standard letter in the name of the 'martyr' by the concerned militant outfit to his family:

My dear father, mother, brothers and sisters

If you really love me, you should bear the news of my martyrdom with courage and be thankful to God. I request my mothers and sisters to observe purdah, shun sin, say their prayers and pray to God to accept my martyrdom. I request my father to send my brothers for training and also to educate others about jihad. It is an excellent path, which leads straight to paradise. I request you to break your television set soon after reading my will so that our house is free from the influence of Satan and God is pleased with us all.[274]

In a press interview Zakirur Rahman Lakhvi, the chief of Lashkar-e-Toiba, claimed no dearth of recruits but regretted that many of them had to be turned back for lack of adequate training facilities.[275] In early 1990 the then Pak army Chief of Staff General Mirza Aslam Beg proudly recalled:

In the last six months our boys [militants trained in Pakistan] have knocked off about two dozen [Indian] posts completely, killing several Indian soldiers. The summer of 1992 will be decisive... we are in full control of the situation in the valley.[276]

The ISI has reportedly raised a highly professional group called Janbaz Mujahideen – comprising Kashmiris and Afghans – for subversive operations in Jammu and Kashmir.[277] There are references to such ISI officers as Brigadier Mohammad Salim having developed a particular expertise in promoting insurgency operations in Jammu and Kashmir.[278] The noted Pakistani writer Muneer Ahmed has himself testified to the political role of the ISI in Jammu and Kashmir.[279] We have depositions from arrested militants of 'Pakistani boys' fighting in Kashmir.[280] Since the latter half of 1990 Pakistan has used heavy artillery and mortar fire to help infiltrate trained guerrillas into Indian territory. Leading Pakistani politicians like Maulana Fazlur Rahman – the chief of the fundamentalist Jamiat-i-Ulema and former Chairman of the Foreign Relations Committee of the Pakistan National Assembly – maintain close connections with Kashmiri militant organizations like Al Faran.[281] Senator Naam Singh allegedly openly supported terrorist and subversive activities inside India.[282] Indian sources even claim to have uncovered Pakistan's 'grandiose K-2 project' of uniting the Kashmiri and Sikh 'terrorists' and using the international border across Rajasthan and Gujrat as an 'operating base'.[283] The Indian security forces unearthed in July 1993 the Harquat-ul-Jehad-Ishami (HUJI) plan of the ISI to undertake subversive activities all over the country. In November 1993 the Indian government alleged Pak involvement in a project of Kashmiri militants to occupy and then blow up the Hazratbal shrine – believed to be a repository of the Prophet's hair – in an effort to incite religious strife in Jammu and Kashmir.[284] Not surprisingly, the militant Mast Gul – reportedly the brain behind the desecration of Char-e-Sharif – was accorded a hero's welcome in Pakistan.[285] By October 1995 India's Border Security Force estimated the presence of about 3,000 foreign mercenaries in Kashmir.[286] *The Pioneer* reported on 12 May 1997 that Islamabad itself admitted having organized 38 terrorist camps for 'freedom fighters' in Jammu and Kashmir. New Delhi also claims that Pakistani military intelligence uses the profit from trade in narcotics to fund separatism in India.[287] During the November 1998 Indo-Pak talks on terrorism and narcotics the New Delhi representatives noted that while 243 Pakistani and 48 residents of Pakistan-occupied Kashmir belonging to various fundamentalist organizations were killed by Indian security forces, 91 Pakistanis and 34 Azad Kashmir inhabitants had been put behind Indian bars on charges of Pak-sponsored terrorism in Jammu and Kashmir. In November 1998 Indian security forces recovered 47,000 firearms and 30,000kg of explosives from the Pak-trained Kashmiri militants and seized from the forests of Rajouri two micro-light aircrafts that were reportedly used for 'cross-border terrorism'. The fact that foreign mercenaries losing their lives in Jammu and Kashmir are celebrated as martyrs by such Pakistani organizations as Lashkar-e-Taiba and Al-Badar also testify to their connections with Islamabad. India alleges that Pakistan has also established a clandestine radio station across the Line of Control in Kashmir and is using cyber connections for propaganda warfare.[288] For the Indian government the Pakistani response in Kashmir is thus nothing short of 'a proxy war, a well-calculated sinister move to send arms and ammunition and trained militants across the border'.[289] Prem Bhatia clearly stated the Indian position on the issue: 'If Pakistan [seeks] to see the glorification of its flag on the soil of Kashmir…the reaction in India is equal and opposite'.[290] Interestingly, some see the Kashmir 'turbulence' as a 'rerun of the Bengalee belligerence in the then East Pakistan in the early 1970s…with the role of India and Pakistan being reversed this time'.[291]

Indian analysts have often been criticized for overemphasising the Pak involvement in Kashmir. For instance, K. Subramanyam once spoke of General Zia-ul-Haq's *Operation Topac* to start a Kashmiri uprising, only to later acknowledge it to have been a mistake.[292] Nevertheless, the fact of Pakistani complicity in Kashmiri insurgency is explicitly corroborated by Western sources. American and European observers have lent credence to Indian allegations of Kashmiri guerrillas being provided by Pakistan with 'spanking new uniforms and…modern weapons'.[293] According to an official US estimate, by 1990 about 5,000 Kashmiris had been trained in Pakistan and about 20,000 AK-47s were in use in Jammu and Kashmir.[294] *The US News & World Report* (11 June 1990, p. 42) cited an American official confirmation 'that Pakistanis are providing aid and sanctuary to Kashmiri insurgents'. The *Washington Post* (16 May 1994) reported how the ISI operated within India through private organizations like Jamaat-i-Islami.[295] The US Deputy Assistant Secretary of State John Mallot admitted in 1993 that the ISI was behind terrorist acts in Kashmir and the Punjab.[296] A 1993 US House Republican Research Committee Report on 'Terrorism and Conventional Warfare' confirmed Pakistan's direct sponsorship of 'transborder Islamic terrorism' in India and affirmed:

> The ISI…was completing a vast training infrastructure for the Afghan resistance movement that could just as well be used for the training and support of other regional groups. Therefore, it was not long before Afghan terrorists trained by…CIA instructors had been smuggled into India with the purpose of organizing acts of terrorism against…members of the Indian government and foreign diplomatic representatives.[297]

The 1994 US House of Representatives Report estimated that 20,000 young Kashmiris had been trained and armed by Pakistan.[298] Human Rights organizations have documented the use of Pakistani weapons by Kashmiri militants. To quote from one such report:

> As anyone who has travelled [in] northwest Pakistan knows, weaponry siphoned off from supplies provided by the United States during the Afghan war is readily available in the arms bazaars of the North-West Frontier Province.[299]

The US State Department has specifically branded groups like the Harkat-ul-Ansari as terrorist outfits fighting in Kashmir 'with passion for Jehad'.[300]

Kashmir and Sindh

In the beginning of May 1999, the Indian army and air force was involved in a number of clashes with Pak-sponsored infiltrators in the high-altitude barren terrain of the Drass-Kargail-Batalik sector of Jammu and Kashmir. Direct involvement of Pakistan with this infiltration was proved beyond doubt by the recovery of Pak Army identity cards from one of the captured intruders.[301] Interestingly enough, *Jasarat*, a Jamaat-i-Islami newspaper, itself exposed the Pak intervention in Kargil. It carried an article by the Jammat activist Abdul Karim Abid condemning the Pak government for its hypocritical attitude towards the militants and the Kargil situation:

> We must come out in the open as men [to fight the Kashmir war]. The hypocritical attitude of first preparing the militants for the fight and then denying the same in the international forums will not do... This lie did not help Pakistan earlier nor will it do in future. Jihad cannot be conducted on lies. Pakistani policy makers must make it very clear (to the world) that the fight the Mujahideen are fighting is our fight. Our army is backing them, and [will] provide all kinds of help, and if needed it will participate in the war activities.[302]

Islamabad also has reportedly supported the formation of a United Jihad Council to bring together at least 14 militant organizations to join the recent operations in the Kargil sector of the Indo-Pak border in Jammu and Kashmir.[303] A May 1999 press report referred to members of the Pakistan parliament such as Mian Ghulam Rasool being closely involved with the training programme of Kashmiri extremists on Indian soil.[304] Islamabad's Foreign Minister Sartaz Aziz was himself forced to admit the intrusion of Islamic militants in the Kargil region, although he denied his country's responsibility for this.[305] According to a report in *The Times* many British Pakistanis have even landed in Kargil to fight the Indian security forces.[306] Western correspondents have generally supported the Indian claim of a Pak hand behind the Kargil episode. To quote one such observer:

> Our view is that the Indian account of events is correct. This is simply too large an incursion, too well-equipped and extensively

planned, to have happened without the sanction of the highest powers in Pakistan.[307]

Foreign observers also testify to the militants' use of US-made Stinger missiles – made available by Pakistan – to ground Indian helicopters.[308]

The Kargil event should not, however, blind us to dissenting voices within the Pakistani part of Kashmir which makes one suspect whether the notion of Azad (Free) Kashmir is becoming a misnomer. Pakistan-controlled Kashmir comprises two distinct geographical regions: (1) the five districts of Muzaffarabad, Bagh, Rawalakot, Kotli and Mirupur constituting 'Azad Kashmir' proper; and (2) Gilgit, Baltistan and the contiguous upper Himalayas known as the Northern Areas. While since 1947 the latter has been directly ruled by Pakistan's Ministry of Kashmir Affairs without any genuine election and proper judicial system, the government in 'Azad Kashmir', although theoretically empowered to administer local subjects, is also actually controlled by Islamabad. The inhabitants in Pak-controlled Kashmir are deprived of political rights granted to other parts of Pakistan. On 25 April 1994, Islamabad proclaimed a package of constitutional reforms for this part of Pakistan. But they fell far short of popular demands and were rejected by all local parties, which made the 12-party alliance charge the federal government with denying the region those customary rights even recognized by the erstwhile Hindu Maharaja. All key officials, in 'Azad Kashmir' like the Chief Secretary and Inspector-General of Police, are thus appointees of the Federal Government. The Constitutional Acts of 1960, 1964 and 1974 were ostensibly designed to make the 'Azad' government 'more democratic'. But each of these Acts maintained the preeminence of the 'Azad' Council functioning under the chairmanship of the Pakistan Prime Minister.[309] Urdu has been imposed on 'Azad Kashmir' as the official language; the province remains economically backward, which makes it completely dependent on Islamabad's financial assistance; the armed forces in 'Azad Kashmir' function under Federal command.[310] Although Islamabad proclaims the insurgency in Jammu and Kashmir as a fight for the right of self-determination, the same principle of self-determination under the election laws of POK (Pakistan Occupied Kashmir) means the right to determine only in favour of Pakistan.[311] A Kashmiri in 'Azad Kashmir' is debarred from participation in election process if:

He [or she!] is propagating any opinion or action in any manner prejudicial to the ideology of Pakistan…or the sovereignty or integrity of Pakistan or security of Azad Jammu and Kashmir or morality or the maintenance of public order or the integrity or independence of the judiciary of Azad Jammu and Kashmir or Pakistan or who defames or brings into ridicule the judiciary of Azad Jammu and Kashmir or Pakistan or the Armed Forces of Pakistan.[312]

No person or political party in 'Azad Kashmir' is permitted to propagate against or take part in activities prejudicial or detrimental to the ideology of the State's accession to Pakistan.[313] Such constitutional clauses were reiterated by the 'Azad Kashmir' High Court in August 1991 when it characterized it as an 'electoral offence' for any citizen

(a) to criticize the territory's incorporation in Pakistan;
(b) to advocate the reunification of Pakistan Occupied Kashmir, Gilgit and Baltistan with Jammu and Kashmir in order to restore the 1947 position;
(c) to advocate independence for Jammu and Kashmir;
(d) to criticize the Partition of India;
(e) to criticize the Pakistan armed forces for their continued presence in Pakistan Occupied Kashmir, Gilgit and Baltistan or their violation of Human Rights of the state subjects of the Pakistan Occupied Kashmir and the Northern Areas.[314]

If politicans of 'Azad Kashmir', hailing mostly from the local *biradaris* (landed elites), fail 'to bow to whoever happens to be in power in Islamabad'[315] they lose their offices. This was aptly demonstrated in July 1991 when 'Azad Kashmir's' elected Premier Mumtaz Rathore not only had his cabinet dismissed, but found himself behind bars for being at odds with Islamabad.[316] As Rose aptly comments, '…Muzaffarabad (capital city of Azad Kashmir) may be no more 'azad' (independent) of interference from Islamabad now than Srinagar is from New Delhi.'[317] A continuation of this trend could in the long run result in a clash between the 'Azad Kashmiris' and the Pakistan state.[318] Areas like Mirpur are particularly reacting to the federal government's policy of economic discrimination. For instance, while the Mangla dam supplies power to Karachi and acts as a reservoir for Pubjab's canal system, it has subjected Mirpur to extensive flooding and considerable environmental imbalance. Mirpuris also suffer from an acute shortage of electricity. In 1998 anti-Islamabad feelings were noticed in 'Azad Kashmir' following the alleged abduction of some leading 'Azad' Kashmiri politicians by the ISI. Demands were even raised for international intervention in the matter.[319] 'Azad' Kashmiri groups like the Kashmir Democratic Front are increasingly asserting their autonomy from Islamabad, rejecting the Two Nation Theory and calling for a negotiated resolution of the Kashmir issue. One may recall here the experience of Aftab Hussain of Poonch district in Azad Kashmir. While filing his nomination as an independent candidate in the 1991 Provincial Assembly election, Aftab deleted the words 'the ideology of Pakistan, the ideology of the State's accession to Pakistan and the integrity and sovereignty of Pakistan' and replaced them by 'Freedom of Jammu and Kashmir State'. But he had his nomination paper rejected.[320] Such incidents confirm a growing 'pro-independence sentiment in "Azad Kashmir" in the last few years'.[321] There are tensions even amongst 'Azad' Kashmir's inhabitants, which often find expression in open clashes. For example, on 27 April 1998 'unknown gunmen' slaughtered 22 people in a village, 275km away from Muzaffarbad,[322] although Islamabad alleged an Indian hand behind the incident.[323] It would be, however, overstressing the point to argue that 'Azad Kashmir' 'at the hands of military-bureaucratic Pakistan bears a remarkable similarity to what Kashmiris in the Valley have suffered in democratic India'.[324] At least in Jammu and Kashmir the instruments of political democracy exist, although at times their workings are distorted. Elections in Jammu and Kashmir might not always have been fair. But both international and national observers single out the 1977 legislative elections as a fair poll by all standards. Is it possible to identify any such election in 'Azad Kashmir'? There have not been reports of major irregularities in Jammu Kashmir in the last national and provicial elections. Voter turnouts in these elections, too, were fair. Further, antagonism against the Indian state can be voiced in Jammu and Kashmir both inside and outside institutional politics, which is hardly feasible in 'Azad Kashmir'.

7. THE INDIAN STATE AND THE PRESENT KASHMIR IMBROGLIO

The Indian state's basic response to the Islamization of Kashmiriyat and its threatened transfer of loyalty across the border has been attempts to impose 'state-sponsored Pan-Indianness' which by 1990 had become, in the words of a commentator of *Economic and Political Weekly*, 'the hegemony of Hind-Hindu nationalism'.[325] This provoked a feeling of cultural marginalization amongst the Kashmiri Muslims. The process of pan-Indianism was often pushed to such absurdities as introducing linguistic uniformity in official releases. For instance, a circular of 12 January 1990 from the News Service Division of All India Radio reminded:

> the newsreaders-translators in the respective languages includ-ing Hindi, Urdu and Kashmiri, that 'rastrapati' will be used for President, 'up-rastrapati' for Vice-President and 'pradhan mantri' for the Prime Minister. For India the language version will be Bharat.[326]

At the same time the Indian state resorted to stringent repressive measures to maintain law and order in Jammu and Kashmir. By the middle of 1993 New Delhi had deployed an estimated 175,000 soldiers and 30,000 paramilitary personnel in the province.[327] Almost 60 per cent of Jammu and Kashmir's annual expenditure is concerned with 'security-related activities'.[328] People in the province have come to live with house-searches, arrests by security forces and 'endless Curfew Raj'.[329] Atrocities were committed during house-searches. As one victim recounted: 'They [security forces] would mix oil in my rice, chilli powder in my Kahwa [Kashmir tea] and [leave] the entire house in total chaos.'[330]

Recalling the highhandedness of security personnel two Indian journalists noted:

> *Oye chathloo* (Kashmiri profanity) *ye bakwas bandh Karo* ('You scoundrels, stop this nonsense'), snarled the gun-toting BSF jawan as he emerged from his bunker and gingerly walked towards a group of ragpickers huddled on the pavement. That single, deflating remark was enough to smother the loud chatter.[331]

70

Incidents like the *jawans* mistaking a gas cylinder's explosion or a tyre-burst as firing from militants and adopting retaliatory measures leave deep adverse imprints on the Kashmiri Muslim psyche.[332] While impressions of the anti-Muslim bias of paramilitary forces[333] strengthen the militants' loyalty to Pakistan, the assassination of such respected Kashmiri personalities as the cleric Maulavi Mohammed Farroq and the physician Dr Farooq Haider – widely believed to be perpetrated at the behest of Indian law-enforcing agencies – or the gunning down of about 50 mourners during the Maulavi's funeral have eroded the confidence of a large section of Kashmiris in the Indian state.[334]

Investigative reports have cited numerous instances of how inept handling by security forces turned 'innocents into militants'.[335] The Armed Force (Jammu and Kashmir) Special Powers Ordinance of 1990 offers 'enormous latitude' to security forces and 'absolves' them of popular accountability in many matters.[336] 'Operation Tiger' and 'Operation Shiva' were particularly severe 'crackdowns' by the Indian army.[337] At one point India reportedly toyed with a plan to secure Israeli help to fight the Pak-sponsored terrorism.[338] While officials estimate that till 1993 the insurgency caused a loss of at least 7,000 lives, the militants push the figure to 25,000.[339] According to another study the Kashmir violence between 1990 and 1995 claimed at least 12,000 civilian lives.[340] Between January and August of 1995 2,170 cases of firing by Indian security forces were recorded. During the same period 650 civilians and 160 army personnel lost their lives, 80 militants having been killed on the Line of Control alone while attempting to infiltrate into India.[341] Most human rights organizations also charge the Indian government with a lack of transparency on Kashmir. About 30,000 Kashmiri insurgents are still reportedly languishing in Indian jails and human rights groups continue to allege India's violation of fundamental civil rights in Kashmir.[342] Detainees in Indian camps are allegedly tortured, refused access to law-courts and very often listed as having 'disappeared'.[343] Cases filed against Indian security forces are obstructed. Even such leading Kashmiri lawyers as Jalili Andralei have not been spared. In 1996 uniformed Indian soldiers pulled him out from his car, and then tortured and shot him.[344] On a number of occasions the Indian government faced indictment from the Srinagar High Court itself for the disappearance of young boys taken to custody.[345] A panel report of the Press Council of

India explained the national implications of the violation of human rights in Jammu and Kashmir:

> Human rights cannot be safe in [the rest of] India if they are trampled upon…in Kashmir. Such violations are brutalising and threaten the democratic edifice of the country. More precisely, far from subduing aggrieved communities, Kashmiris in this case, they can only alienate them further, especially if their women are dishonoured and their collective psyche hurt.[346]

Jagmohan's Governorship in Jammu and Kashmir has been singled out by many commentators as 'most repressive', converting 'minor insurgency into a full-blown popular revolt'. In the words of a senior Indian Administrative Service officer Ashok Jaitley: 'What Jagmohan did in five months they [the militants] could not have achieved in five years.'[347] The noted Indian journalist M.J. Akbar alleged that Governor Jagmohan even imparted – perhaps under instructions from the RAW[348] – a communal edge to the Kashmir crisis by encouraging the exodus of Kashmiri Hindus from the Valley.[349] Many analysts assert that women have been the worst to suffer – often in silence – in the 'war' over Kashmir. 'They have been killed in crossfire, shot in public demonstrations, blown up in grenade explosions or shellings along the Line of Control and have been raped by the security forces, by anti-government militants and by pro-government militants.'[350] Reports are not uncommon of 'command marriages' which occasion sexual exploitation of local women by militants.[351] It needs, however, to be emphasized that human rights violation by security personnel should not blind us to organized unprovoked attacks by militants on security forces themselves. Similarly, the imposition of their politics upon the civilian population by the militants also amounts to an infringement of the civil liberties of the general populace. Unfortunately, the mainstream Indian press has failed objectively to represent the gross violation of human rights in Kashmir, whether by security forces or militants, tending to fall back on a state-centric approach.[352]

The Indian state's strategy in Jammu and Kashmir has produced the contradictory effect of strengthening secessionism in Kashmir. Clashes between Indian security personnel and Kashmiri militants, ransacking of police stations resulting in loss of weapons and ammunitions, attacks on government property and general strikes (*hartals*) are regular occurrences. In some instances protest marches against the 'Indian administration' have mobilized as many as 30,000 people. While hundreds of Kashmiris regularly cross the barriers of deep snow, difficult mountain terrain and eyes of the Indian *jawans* to escape to POK, thousands raising anti-Indian slogans try to enter Jammu and Kashmir from Pakistan causing exchange of fire between Indian and Pakistani troops.[353] *India Today* (15 May 1990) records how families in Jammu and Kashmir sent their 15-year-old sons to Pakistan for training after a 'special Mehndi ceremony'. The following report – perhaps with little exaggeration – typifies the situation:

Syed Anwar Shah, a Kashmiri village chief, explained that Indian troops turned his village into an armed camp, taking over the school, closing the mosques and banning Friday prayers. 'I told everyone I was leaving, and it was time for them to save their own skins,' he said. Now he and 150 other villagers live across the cease-fire line in Muzaffarabad.[354]

A Pakistani commentator might not have been far from truth when he reported:

In the summer of 1990 the present writer happened to meet two freedom fighters in Rawalpindi, one seventeen, the other eighteen. In reply to my question as to why he had come to Pakistan, the first one said he had two elder brothers: the eldest was killed by the Indian forces and the other was picked-up whose whereabouts are still unknown... His college was also closed. So he asked for the permission of his parents to go across for some training and weapons so that if he could return, he could die fighting like a hero, not get killed like a rat. The second teenager said his father had died by a stray bullet of the Indian military... It was his widowed mother who told him: 'Son! Why wait for being killed or caught? ... Go across to Pakistan and if you can come back, trained and equipped, kill these cruel Indians before you become a martyr.'[355]

According to Rahatullah Khan, the Chief Secretary of 'Azad Kashmir', about 5,000 refugees from Indian Kashmir arrived in May 1990 alone.[356] The majority of them were young men aged between 18 and 30 and included bank managers, students and talented artists.[357]

New Delhi's diabolical Kashmir policy has thus created 'a situation where the hitherto non-committed masses are being pushed...to feel that independence from New Delhi is the only way of escape from state repression'. This feeling was eloquently summed up by a Kashmiri government officer: 'Till January 1990 I was against militants. Today I am for them.'[358] The Kashmiri loss of confidence in the Indian state was restated in the Kashmiri leader Maulana Ansari's retort to the former Indian Prime Minister Narasimha Rao's call to create conditions for holding elections in the province: 'It's absurd to talk of reviving the political process when every house is involved. Even those who had a vested interest in maintaining links with Hindustan have been victimized.'[359] In the same tone Abdul Ghani, leader of the pro-Pak Moslem Conference Party, discounted the possibility of fair elections in Jammu and Kashmir: 'India has burnt all its bridges in Kashmir, now they want to build bridges where no river exists.'[360] The Hindu communal backlash following the demolition of the Babri Masjid on 6 December 1992,[361] and assertions of the Shiv Sena leader Bal Thackeray such as that those not loyal to India should vacate Kashmir, have reinforced the fear psyche amongst the Kashmiri Muslims about Hindu tyranny. To quote a report from the *New York Times* (15 January 1990): 'Visitors to the Indian...Kashmir find a common theme in most conversations: admiration for the militants, anger towards the government and a wish for separation from India. The same sentiment runs equally among women.' *Newsweek* for the period ending 5 February 1990 reported too: 'On every available inch or wall is scribbled the same unambiguous message: "Indian Pigs Go Home." The Kashmiris have risen...in a movement that bears close comparison with the Palestinian intifada'. As often happens with foreign journalists, they were perhaps overreacting. But even Mufti Mohammad Sayeed, a former Home Minister of the Government of India, acknowledged: 'The people, seeing no alternative to the present situation, are looking forward to militants. There is a total collapse of administrative machinery and other institutions in Kashmir.'[362]

Some scholars do not find any 'reactionary' element in the Islamization of the Kashmiriyat.[363] But it is hard to ignore the conservative social values imposed by the Islamic fundamentalists in the Valley. The militants espouse a philosophy bearing similarities to the Taliban ideology. They impart 'a restrictive and austere interpretation of Islam' which prohibits any form of light entertainment, including music and television. Western clothes are forbidden by them. The militants have untrimmed beards, wear traditional baggy pants and long shirts and do not like having their photographs taken.[364] Christopher Thomas, a journalist of *The Times*, aptly described the grip of Islamic fundamentalism imposed by extremist organizations in the Valley:

> Nearly every woman was shrouded in a burqa. Video shops sold only Pakistani films. Shoppers hurriedly erected new Urdu-script signs above their stores. Cinemas, condemned as decadent, were shuttered. Barkeepers, branded as un-Islamic, served tea instead.[365]

Since the early 1990s the militants have tended to boycott anything perceived as Indian.[366] The Indian Republic Day, the Indian Independence Day and Nehru's birthday are commemorated as 'Black Days'. Sheikh Abdullah's death anniversary on 8 September is called 'Day of Deliverance'. On the other hand, Pakistani and JKLF flags are hoisted at every opportunity. At one point Kashmiri militants insisted on the changing of clocks to Pakistan Standard Time.[367] They seem to rely on the BBC and Pak TV, rather than the Indian *Doordarshan*.[368] *India Today* (31 May 1993) reported the establishment of 'liberated zones' by the insurgents in pockets of Baramulla, Srinagar and Anantnag districts, which resembled 'fortified garrisons that even the Indian armed forces cannot enter'. Some areas in Anantnag came to be called 'Chhota Pakistan' (small Pakistan). During the tumultuous days of the early 1990s Kashmiri militants freely carried sophisticated weapons and openly met journalists, and their erstwhile leaders addressed Friday congregations in mosques.[369] A section of Kashmiri Muslim lawyers and government officials also supposedly openly helped the militants.[370] On 22 April 1993 even Kashmiri policemen went on strike to protest against the death of their colleague in the custody of paramilitary forces. The Indian army could not disarm and arrest the mutinous policemen until six days later. The Chaar-e-Sharief episode of March 1995[371] and the subsequent failure of the government to secure the release of foreigners held captive by the Al-Faran extremists are other apt commentaries on the state of administration in Jammu and Kashmir.[372] The fact that between 1993 and 1995 four of Governor K.V. Krishna Rao's advisors were made to quit, and two Chief Secretaries had to be shifted, indicated the level of administrative instability in Kashmir.[373] All these demonstrated a dual truth: the failure of the Indian state to adequately tackle the insurgency, and an open blurring of the distinction between home and foreign affairs on the part of Kashmiri militants. At the dawn of 1990 Kashmir appeared a divided house: the Muslim-dominated Valley asserting its identity by very often transferring its loyalty away from India, and the Hindu-concentrated Jammu looking more towards Delhi for survival.[374]

CONCLUSION

The present submission has hopefully demonstrated that the crux of the current ethnic insurrection in Jammu and Kashmir lies in the lack of a reconciliation between Indian nationalism and Kashmiri ethnonationalism, or what Sumit Ganguly calls Kashmiri 'ethnolinguistic assertion'.[375] It is the outcome of a failure to harmonize the twin processes of nation-building and democratization.[376] Immediately after Kashmir's accession to India Jawaharlal correctly assessed the special strength of Kashmiri ethnic identity, evident from his joint statement with Sheikh Abdullah issued on 24 July 1952.[377] But he failed to reconcile this feeling with his nation-building strategy that emphasized unity rather than diversity in our national politico-cultural life.[378] For the Indian ruling elites Kashmir became a prized possession to vindicate their secular concerns and satisfy their 'security psyche'. Jai Prakash Narain recognized the fallacy of such an approach many years before when he warned: 'But suppose we had to keep the Muslims of Kashmir within India by force: would that also be an example of our secularism? The very question exposes its absurdity.'[379] What was required was the Indian state's respect for the *Kashmiriyat*. But New Delhi preferred to treat any Kashmiri dissent as a law and order issue. To quote a celebrated Indian columnist:

> The only tangible evidence of New Delhi's concern and interest in Kashmir was the despatch of forces in greater number…

India's democracy can never sustain itself by stamping the jack-boot on the people in any part of our far-flung republic. Kashmir summons us to heed the voice of our conscience.[380]

The dominant Kashmiri concern for a considerable period of time was 'not about secession but...the quantum of autonomy [from Delhi]'.[381] Unfortunately, the Indian state failed to appreciate this spirit. Instead, it provided the Kashmiris with 'misrule, rising unemployment and rampant corruption in the administration'.[382] Consequently, a Kashmiri, as M.J. Akbar succinctly remarked,

asks a good question these days. He does not deny that he joined India in 1947. All he wants to know is if this is the same India that he joined in 1947. He wants to know whether the values of Mahatma Gandhi – who was cheered by the Muslims of Srinagar less than a fortnight before Pakistan was born – still mean anything to the men and women who exercise power in Delhi... The Kashmiri could be expected to fight the fundamentalist raider from Pakistan in defence of such a promise, but not to exchange the raider for a Delhi in which the secular (and democratic) faith had died.[383]

In a conjuncture of historical circumstances, as delineated above, the politics of Kashmiri ethnicity was transmuted into ethnonationalism, associated with a distinct Islamic tinge and a transfer from Indian to Pakistani loyalty. The ruling elite of Pakistan, unreconciled with the idea of the 'loss of Kashmir', readily responded to this historic opportunity. Kashmir became one of the worst tragedies of international politics, degenerating into a pawn in Indo-Pakistani rivalry. The unfortunate victim of this process has been the people of Kashmir.

What is the way out of the present impasse in Kashmir? An Indo-Pak war is certainly not a solution for the Kashmir issue. Both New Delhi and Islamabad realize the prohibitive cost such an encounter will involve.[384] Many commentators argue that the exercise of nuclear options by both India and Pakistan would have a further deterring effect on a military conflict between the two neighbours. Similarly, it would be unrealistic to question the legality of Kashmir's accession to India at this late hour.[385] Instead, there is an increasing body of public opinion in both countries which recognizes the need to acknowledge the current Line of Control in Kashmir as the international border between India and Pakistan. During the Tashkent treaty of January 1966 the Indian Premier Lal Bahadur Shastri was believed to have consented to his Soviet counterpart Kosygin's proposal of converting the Line of Control into a permanent Indo-Pak border, although the Pak President Ayub Khan preferred to reject the suggestion. But during the Shimla talks of 1972 the Pak Premier Zulfiqar Ali Bhutto reportedly toyed with the same idea of conversion. Inside India Farooq Abdullah, the present Chief Minister of Jammu and Kashmir, is a strong proponent of this idea. New Delhi is yet to buy the idea. But Indian diplomats like the former Foreign Secretary J.N. Dixit consider this proposal as one 'which makes ground realities and which safeguards the territorial integrity of both India and Pakistan'.[386] Prakash Singh, former Director-General of India's Border Security Force, also feels: 'The one and only option which should have the best chance of success would be to freeze the line of actual control and declare it as an international border.'[387]

The acceptance of the Line of Control as the international border could pave the way for stabilization of Indo-Pak relations, thereby creating opportunities of interactions between Kashmiris on both sides of the frontier. Once border tensions are subdued, Kashmiri ethnic aspirations can be addressed by ensuring greater autonomy for the two provinces within their respective national political structures so that the national identities in India and Pakistan alike could become harmonized with respective Kashmiri subnational feelings.[388] In this context a leading Indian commentator remarks:

> ...it does not lie in the enlightened national interest of India to push dissidence in Kashmir towards extremism. For a humiliated Kashmir is no asset for the nation. Other than economic incentives and constitutional guarantees new ways for restoring a sense of Kashmiri pride and honour need to be thought out. Violence and repression is as self-defeating for the government as it is for the Azadi leaders. Both sides must realize that violence is enormously counter-productive.[389]

Instead of seeking to stifle ethnic dissent through such draconian measures as the TADA (Terrorism and Disruptive Activities Prevention Act) and Jammu and Kashmir Public Safety Act or bolstering up groups of anti-terrorist militias like Jammu and Kashmir Ikhwan factions, New Delhi needs to realize that in a multi-ethnic society it is 'possible to manage or reduce ethnic tensions…[but] not…to obliterate those tensions'.[390] Nor would such provocative Hindu nationalist stances as the BJP's commemoration of the death anniversary of Shyama Prasad Mukherjee with a *Jana Jagaran* (public awareness) campaign against Article 370 of the country's constitution[391] or the BJP President Kushabahu Thakre's threat to recapture Pakistan-occupied Kashmir[392] would contribute to a resolution of the Kashmir problem. Since ethnic conflict in the modern age has a 'highly focused relation to the state'[393] – and the Kashmir case is no exception – the two possible approaches towards 'interethnic accommodation' are 'negotiation or reciprocity, on the one hand, and legislation or public policy-making, on the other'.[394] A proper assessment of the Kashmir issue calls for an understanding of the 'human factor' in Kashmiri ethnic conflict and not its treatment as a mere law and order problem.[395] In the words of Ayesha Jalal: 'The challenge…is to reconcile the principle of self-determination with the realities of regional power.'[396] Such an accommodation of Kashmiri sensibilities, as Cohen rightly points out, 'should not be a prelude to the break-up of either state [India or Pakistan]'.[397]

Restoration of Article 370 to its original strength, enquiries into alleged excesses of security forces, making local administration accountable to popular will, revival of electoral process, the introduction of new packages of economic development and initiation of political dialogues with militants – all these can make the Kashmiris feel that the Indian political system is not necessarily hostile to their democratic aspirations.[398] New expectations for order and progress were generated when the current National Conference government was elected to power. These should not be belied. For, as has been aptly remarked:

> The people [of Kashmir], regardless of propaganda in Delhi, are peace-loving and detest discord and strife. They reached out to embrace the democratic option but were left alone facing the gun. It is the people who have paid for the deliberate mistakes of

the political class. It is the people who have been caught in the crossfire between the Pakistan-backed militants and the security forces. It is the people who go to sleep hungry, without jobs. The people of Jammu and Kashmir are not the enemy. They are the victims who are being hurt, and are hurting.[339]

The hardliners in Delhi's South Block also need to realize that a basic distinction between Kashmir's demand for autonomy and similar demands voiced in other parts of the country lies in the fact that Kashmiris are seeking not the grant of special privileges, but a restoration of powers of which they have been deprived. Notwithanding the contentions of some political parties, the Supreme Court in its 1984 judgement in Khazan Chand versus the State of Jammu and Kashmir had clearly upheld the special status of Jammu and Kashmir within the Indian constitutional format.[400] The judgement recalled that in some matters special dispensations are also provided to the states of Maharashtra, Gujrat, Nagaland, Assam, Manipur, Andhra Pradesh, Sikkim, Mizoram, Arunachal Pradesh and Goa. Leftist political parties in India, notably the CPI(M), have thus consistently advocated the grant of autonomy to Jammu and Kashmir within the Indian federal polity.[401] The former Union Home Minister Mufti Mohammad Sayeed, too, underlined the 'crux' of the Kashmir problem when he remarked: '…all Kashmiris are not for Pakistan. They want to remain part of India. We have to identify those people, involve them in administration to strengthen the State's irrevocable links with India.'[402] In this connection the 'Autonomy Resolution' passed by the Jammu and Kashmir Assembly at the behest of the Farooq Abdullah government deserves serious consideration.[403] Such constitutional reforms are considered by their advocates as the only way 'to ensure that the state's (Jammu and Kashmir's) diversity becomes a strength, not a weakness and source of tension'.[404]

Fortunately, we are noticing some healthy signs in Kashmir politics. For instance, the killing of a foreign hostage in August 1995 by Al-Faran prompted a strong condemnation from the All Party Hurriyat Conference, which described the incident as 'killing of humanity, human values and human liberty'. A general strike was also organized in Kashmir valley on 16 August 1995 to protest about the brutality. Many political leaders aligned with militant groups now admit that kidnapping and other forms of violence committed against ordinary civilians have undermined popular support for the militant cause in Jammu and Kashmir.[405] On 20 June 1994 50,000 demonstrators voiced anti-Pak and anti-Hizb slogans while protesting the killing of Qazi Nisar Ahmed, the Mirwaiz of South Kashmir, by the Anantnag militants. Desecration of the holy shrine Charar-e-Sharief in the spring of 1995 also received widespread public condemnation in Jammu and Kashmir. Recently the Hizbul Mujahideen itself has criticized the 'gun-wielding youth…harassing the innocent people, kidnapping local officers and threatening intellectuals, besides interfering in the working of government offices'.[406] The JKLF itself is today a divided house, the Pak-based Amanullah Khan and the India-based Yaseen Malik leading the two factions.[407] The fact that the people in Kashmir turned out in large numbers to vote in the May 1996 and 1998 parliamentary elections, despite calls of boycott by the Hurriat Conference, demonstrates that the Kashmiris are today eager to restore the normal functioning of the State. By the end of 1995 considerable Hindu-Muslim amity was noticeable even in areas like Baramulla, which had once been a witness to the worst forms of sectarian violence.[408] The sentiment in the Valley today is 'not as much pro-Pakistani as…anti-establishment'.[409] In April 1999 the pro-Pak hardliner of All Party Hurriyat Conference, Abdul Gani, broke his earlier stance and called for a dialogue with mainstream political organizations in Jammu and Kashmir for a 'lasting resolution to the dispute in accordance with the aims and aspirations of the people'.[410] Even the Jamaat-e-Islami is moving away from its earlier commitment to join Pakistan to the notion of an independent Kashmir.[411] It is also important to note that Pakistan has so far failed to evoke support from Islamic countries for its stand on the Kashmir question. After its recent visit to Jammu and Kashmir even a US-based team recommended the maintenance of the status quo. It disapproved of the idea of a referendum and advocated greater autonomy of the state of Jammu and Kashmir within the Indian Union. The group suggested: 'Over the longer term the complexities of the Kashmir conflict may require…innovative, even what may now seem radical experiments… Among such experiments…schemes for devolving maximum political authority to a state or sub-state regimes should certainly be closely examined…'[412]

Besides, Kashmir as an issue is increasingly losing its 'homogeneity both in India and Pakistan'. Cohen rightly contended:

The further one travels from Delhi and Islamabad the less passion there is about Kashmir. In Madras, Calcutta, Hyderabad (Deccan) and Bombay Kashmir is seen as New Delhi's obsession; in Karachi, Quetta, Peshwar and Hyderabad (Sindh), it is seen as a secondary issue; relations with Islamabad and the Punjab come first.[413]

No less a person than Pakistan's former Air Force Chief Asghar Khan expressed scepticism about his country's 'proxy war policy' in Kashmir. He told a group of non-resident Pakistanis: '…their country cannot afford to wage a war over Kashmir. We are in a no-win situation in taking up the Kashmir jehad; Pakistan cannot attain Kashmir by jehad; people in Kashmir who talk of jehad are either naive or outright stupid or hypocrites. Pakistani politicians are using Kashmir to whip up sentiments for their selfish ends…under such circumstances, no Kashmiri would like to join Pakistan and it is my clear belief that Pakistan should stop meddling there and leave the issue to be settled by the people of the state.'[414] In a similar vein the Tehriki-Istaql chief had warned that, 'unless the present Nawaz Sharif government takes drastic and far-reaching measures and desists from continued meddling in Afghanistan and Kashmir, Pakistan is headed for a disastrous course.'[415] Yet another former Pakistani Air Force Chief, Noor Khan, urged Islamabad to 'stop considering Kashmir as its jugular vein and allow Kashmiris to settle the contentious issue themselves'.[416] It is not without significance that during the last Parliamentary election in Pakistan the question of Kashmir was not raised as a major issue in political discourse. A recent study also demonstrated that while Punjabis, Pakhtuns and a majority amongst the Muhajirs would support Islamabad's stand on Kashmir, Sindhi and Baluchi intellectuals would opt for an 'independent, secular, demilitarized and neutralized' Kashmir.[417] Young Pakistani scholars – although propounding a moral indictment on India's role in Kashmir – are also appreciating the need for 'demilitarization to allocate resources to socio-economic welfare'.[418] Likewise, in May 1990 a group of academics met at the Indian Institute of Technology in Delhi to protest against the war psychosis being generated by both Indian and Pakistani governments.[419] Despite recent nuclear tensions, dialogues between Indian and Pakistani scholars – though limited – are continuing, and this can contribute to the breaking of 'conventional barriers' between the two countries. If dissenting voices can be raised in both India and Pakistan against the nuclear race there should not be any reason why we should lose hope for a negotiated settlement on Kashmir. Significantly enough, the Lahore Declaration of 21 February 1999 following the Indian Premier Vajpayee's historic bus trip from Delhi to Lahore have bound both countries to an under-taking to resolve all bilateral issues, including Kashmir, through peaceful means.[420] The former Pak Prime Minister Benazir Bhutto, too, admitted in Washington in May 1999 her mistake in holding relations with India 'hostage' to the Kashmir issue. She acknowledged that her hardline anti-India stance was adopted to 'pander' to the 'Punjabi constituency and hawkish elements within the military'. Mrs Bhutto regretted her decision to shun liberal advice to promote co-operation with India on trade, commerce and other economic matters of mutual interest.[421] Mrs Bhutto has recently gone to the extent of suggesting the following confidence-building measures, which could be a prelude to a Camp David-type settlement on Kashmir:

(a) The two sections of Kashmir should be open and porous;
(b) Both sections are to be demilitarized and patrolled by either an international or a joint Indian-Pakistani Peacekeeping Force;
(c) Legislative Councils in both parts of Kashmir are to meet separately and on occasions jointly;
(d) People on both sides of Kashmir are to meet and interact freely and informally;
(e) Tariffs and quotas are to be eliminated; educational and techno-logical exchanges and expansion of the South Asia Free Market Zone are to be modelled along the lines of the European Community and NAFTA.[422]

Even at the height of tensions in the Kargil sector which brought the two countries to a war-like situation, noted personalities of India and Pakistan through organizations like the Association of Peoples of Asia and Pakistan-India Forum For Peace and Democracy pleaded restraint on the part of New Delhi and Islamabad in the interest of people on both sides of the border. They have also proposed a demilitarized zone along the Line of Control.[423] The distinguished Pakistani columnist

Afrashiyar Khattak regretted in *The Frontier Post* of 19 June 1999 how self-defeating it was for the two countries to fight a war since the primary need for both people was to fight poverty, illiteracy, hunger and disease.[424] Another Pakistani journalist, Farhatullah Babar, was convinced that the ruling authorities in India and Pakistan alike used the Kargil episode to generate jingoism in an effort to divert public attention from crucial domestic issues.[425] In this context it is perhaps worth considering Cohen's suggestion for addressing the Kashmiri ethnic question:

> Ideally...the looser federation of the two 'Muslim' parts of Kashmir with their respective states, along with increased flow of goods and people between them, would create a 'soft' frontier where the boundaries between India and Pakistan were somewhat fuzzy, and the boundaries between a secular life and an Islamic one could be blurred.[426]

We can also think of considering the Kashmir question in the wider context of the politics of identity assertions by other South Asian ethnic groups like the Baluchs, Pakhtuns and Sindhis in Pakistan, the Sikhs and North-East tribal groups in India, Tamils in Sri Lanka, and Chakmas in Bangladesh.[427]

Many observers, however, believe that today's busy streets in Srinagar, greater control of militancy and increasing participation in elections cannot be taken as the disappearance of anti-Indian sentiments in Jammu and Kashmir. Anti-Indianism, asserts a recent survey, 'has become dormant, nowhere has it disappeared'.[428] The cause of self-determination, it is reported, 'hasn't decreased... it has lost focus and finds no rallying point'.[429] But I do not foresee Kashmiri insurgency heralding the breakup of the Indian federation. The Indian state has withstood the test of many centrifugal threats. In fact, the survival of Indian democracy against all odds testifies to Edward Ross's formulation: 'A society which is riven by a dozen opposition [parties] along lines running in every [political] direction may actually be in less danger of being torn with violence or failling to pieces than one split along just one line.'[430] One is also reminded of Ainslie T. Embree's perceptive comment that the divisions, 'divisive in isolation, are, in fact integrative in India's plural society'.[431] But to guarantee the resilience of the Indian polity a democratic resolution of ethnic aspirations of the people of Jammu and Kashmir within Indian federalism is indispensable. In the words of a Marxist commentator of Indian politics: 'There should be no feeling that everything is lost in Jammu and Kashmir. A positive turn can be given to the situation, though it will take time to fully fructify.'[432]

NOTES

1. *US & World Report*, 19 November 1990, p. 52.
2. S. Ganguly, *The Crisis in Kashmir: Portents of War, Hopes of Peace* (Cambridge: 1997), p. xiv.
3. ibid.
4. S. Widmalm, *Democracy and Violent Separatism in India: Kashmir in a Comparative Perspective* (Uppsala University: 1997).
5. ibid.; A Kohli, *Democracy and Discontent: India's Growing Crisis of Governability* (New York: 1990).
6. S. Bose, *The Challenge in Kashmir: Democracy, Self-Determination and a Just Peace* (New Delhi: 1997).
7. A. Jalal, 'A Terrible Beauty is Torn – Kashmir Scars', *The New Republic*, 23 July 1990, no. 4, vol. 203, pp. 17–20.
8. B. Buzan, *People, States and Fear: The National Security Problem in International Relations* (Sussex: 1983); E.E. Azar and C. Moon, 'Toward an Alternative Conceptualization' in Edward E. Azar and C. Moon eds., *National Security in the Third World: The Management of Internal and External Threats* (Aldershot: 1988). Scholars like K. Holsti argue that sources of European wars since 1945 have also tended to be 'predominantly internal'. See his *The States System and War* (Maharajah Sayajirao University, Baroda: 1989). Also see R. Chatterjee 'Ethnicity and Conflict in South Asia: A Study of Two Cases' in K. Bajpai et al, eds., *Essays in Honour of A.P. Rana* (New Delhi: 1995) for an interesting use of this analytical framework to analyze the Indo-Pak war of 1965 and India's role in Sri Lanka.
9. M. Ayoob, 'Regional Security and the Indian Ocean Littoral states: Lessons and Extrapolations' in R. H. Brucee ed., *Perspectives on International Relations in the Indian Ocean Region* (Hong Kong: 1987).
10. This situation is markedly different from what we see in the developed and industrialized West where with few exceptions ethnic conflicts do not necessarily 'pose a credible challenge to the integrity of the states'. See M.O. Heisler, 'Ethnic and Ethnic Relations in the Modern West' in J. Montville ed., *Conflict and Peacemaking in Multiethnic Societies* (Lexington: 1990). Other scholars have viewed the problem in the context of the internationalization of ethnic conflict. See R.R. Premdas, 'The Internationalization of Ethnic Conflict: Some Theoretical Explorations' in K.M. De Silva and R.J. May eds., *Internationalization of Ethnic Conflict* (New York: 1992). Premdas identifies the following links in the process of internationalization of an ethnic conflict: ethnic affinity link of diaspora groups; political power links associated with ideological support; economic link arising from common and endangered financial interests; ethnic linkages based on interest shown by governments and NGOs monitoring human rights violations.

11. In this context J.A. Vincent makes a comparison between resistance movements in the Valle d'Aosta of Italy with that in Kashmir. See his 'Differentiation and resistance: ethnicity in Valle d'Aosta and Kashmir', *Ethnic and Racial Studies*, vol. 5, no. 3, July 1982.

12. See A. Varshney, 'Three Compromised Nationalisms: Why Kashmir Has Been a Problem', in Raju G.C. Thomas ed., *Perspectives On Kashmir: The Roots of Conflict in South Asia* (Boulder: 1992), pp. 208–9.

13. Hari Singh belonged to the Rajput Dogra subcaste.

14. When the movement was first launched in 1931 the coordinating body was called the Muslim Conference. In 1939 it was renamed the National Conference. For an analysis of the mass upsurge of 1931 in Kashmir see U.K. Zutshi, *Emergence of Political Awakening in Kashmir* (Delhi: 1986).

15. Scholars like A. Lamb would stress the partisan role played by Mountbatten in ensuring Kashmir's accession to India. See his *Birth Of A Tragedy: Kashmir 1947* (Hertingfordbury: 1994) and *Kashmir – A Disputed Legacy 1846–1990* (Oxford: 1992).

16. For a first-hand account of Indian military operations in 1947–8 see *Defending Kashmir* (Publications Division, Ministry of Information and Broadcasting, Government of India, Delhi: 1949); Lt. Gen. E.A. Vas (Rtd), *Without Baggage: A Personal Account of the Jammu and Kashmir Operations October 1947–January 1949* (Dehradoon: 1987).

17. Henceforth, Kashmir will stand for Jammu and Kashmir. For an analysis of the first phase of the Kashmir dispute see R.P. Cronin and B.L. LePoer, *The Kashmir Dispute: Historical Background to the Current Struggle* (Congressional Research Service, Library of Congress, Washington DC, 19 July 1991); Wayne Ayers Wilcox, *Pakistan: The Consolidation of a Nation* (NY: 1963); J. Das Gupta, *Indo-Pakistan Relations* (Amsterdam: 1958); S. Gupta, *Kashmir: A Study in Indo-Pakistan relations* (Bombay: 1967).

18. Traditionally the USA and China have supported the Pak position on Kashmir, while the erstwhile USSR consistently stood by India. But currently both the USA and China are tending to be less favourable towards Islamabad. See *Afghanistan and Kashmir: Report of a Joint American-Russian Study Mission* (Asia Society, New York: 1993). In recent years the USA has tended not be involved in the Kashmir dispute, although individual officials were, like Robin Raphael, once an influential US Assistant Secretary of State, who went out of her way in 1993 to question the legality of Jammu and Kashmir's accession to India.

19. See Abdullah's speech before the Security Council, 5 February 1948, cited in A. Varshney, 'Three Compromised Nationalisms'.

20. J.N. Dixit, *My South Block Years: Memoirs Of A Foreign Secretary* (New Delhi: 1996) p. 330.

21. This is based on the 1981 Census.

22. It is believed that Kashur does not belong to the Indo-Aryan family of languages but has a Dardic base. See *Linguistic Survey of India*, vol. VIII, part II (Calcutta: 1910).

23. B. Puri, 'Kashmiriyat: the Vitality of Kashmiri Identity', *Contemporary South Asia*, 1995 4(1), pp. 55–63.

24. For instance, the practice of relic worship in Hazratbal shrine where the prophet's hair is believed to be preserved is connected to Buddhist influence. See O'Malley ed., *Modern India and the West* (1941).

25. Particular mention needs to be made of the contribution of such writers as Laleswari (popularly called Lal Ded), Habba Khatun and Shah Hamdan. For this eclectic Kashmiri culture see S. Dhar, *Jammu and Kashmir* (New Delhi: 1977)

and V.D. Chopra, *Genesis of Indo-Pakistan Conflict* (New Delhi: 1990), pp. 172–3.

26. G.M.D. Sufi, *Kashmir*, vol. I (1974), p. 19.
27. R. Choudhuri Tremblay, 'Kashmir: the Valley's Political Dynamics' *Contemporary South Asia*, 1985 4(1), pp. 79–101.
28. ibid.
29. See J.A. Vincent, 'Differentiation'.
30. B. Puri, 'Kashmiriyat'.
31. B. Puri, *Kashmir Towards Insurgency* (Tracts For Times 4, New Delhi: 1995 ed.), p. 9.
32. As late as 1990 the historian Gopal Krishna was venting similar feelings when he remarked: 'For our civilization, Kashmir is important. It is in Kashmir, that the seeds of Hinduism and Buddhism were sown. Don't tell us about self-determination – there are larger issues involved. There is no way I will give up Kashmir, even if a generation of people has to be sacrificed.' Cited in *The Herald*, July 1990.
33. Cited in V. Choudhary ed., *Dr Rajendra Prasad: Correspondence And Select Documents*, vol. 15 (New Delhi: 1991), pp. 361–2.
34. The RSS is a militant Hindu organization that stands for a Hindu nation in India.
35. Cited in P.N. Bazaz, *The History of Struggle for Freedom in Kashmir* (Ministry of Education, Government of Pakistan, Islamabad: 1976), p. 695.
36. Bharatiya Jana Sangh Central Working Committee's resolution of 20 April 1957, Bharatiya Jana Sangh Party Documents, 1951–72, vol. 3, Resolution on Defence and External Affairs (New Delhi: 1973) [hereafter BJSPD], pp. 46–7.
37. Central Working Committee resolution of 25 August 1964, BJSPD, pp. 108–112.
38. B.R. Madhok, *Jammu Kashmir and Ladakh: Problem and Solution* (Delhi: 1987).
39. For a graphic description of this episode see 'Flight of Fancy', *The Economist*, 1 February 1992, pp. 38–9.
40. *The Organiser* 21 September 1964.
41. Cited in *The Herald*, July 1990, p. 21.
42. A.M. Zaidi, *Congress Presidential Addresses*, vol. 5 (New Delhi: 1989) p. 183. The Congress Election Manifesto in the First General Election expressed this spirit when it maintained: 'We owe a duty to the people of the State [Kashmir] and we have to discharge it fully'. See *India – At a Glance* (New Delhi: 1953), p. 112.
43. See Nehru's address to the Indian Parliament on 17 September 1953, quoted in *Rise of Communism in Kashmir* (Kashmir Democratic Union, Delhi: 1952), p. 15.
44. P.N. Bazaz, *Kashmir in Crucible* (New Delhi: 1967), pp. 208–9. For Nehru's personal attachment with Kashmir see *Independence and After* (Ministry of Information and Broadcasting, New Delhi: 1949), p. 95.
45. Cited in P.N. Bazaz, *The History*, p. 695.
46. *Lok Sabha Debates*, vol. I, Part 2, 1957, Col. 678.
47. *The Statesman*, 1 and 20 September 1953; *The Times of India* 19 September 1953; *The Hindustan Times* 7 September 1953.
48. See Sundaraiya's statement of 6 June 1952, cited in *Rise of Communism*, p. 15. Also see CPI member Mrs Renu Chakravarti's speech in the Lok Sabha on 20 March 1957, *Lok Sabha Debates*, vol. I, Part 2, 1957, Cols. 121–2.
49. The CPI had supported the creation of Pakistan on the ground of the right of self-determination of Muslims.
50. Cited in B. Puri, *Jammu and Kashmir: Triumph and Tragedy of Indian Federalism* (New Delhi: 1981), p. 112.
51. S. Gupta, *Kashmir: A Study in India-Pakistan Relations* (Bombay: 1966), p. 450.

52. Cited in *The Herald*, July 1990, p. 20.
53. Quoted in M. Ahmar, 'Security Perceptions in the Indo-Pakistan Relationship', *Pakistan Horizon Quarterly*, vol. XXXVII, no. 1, 1984.
54. Quoted in ibid.
55. G.M. Nandurkar ed., *Sardar Patel in Tune with the Millions*, Birth Centenary, vol. II (Ahmedabad: 1975), p. 193.
56. M. Brecher, *The Struggle for Kashmir* (NY: 1953), pp. 53–4.
57. G.M. Nandurkar ed., *Sardar's Letters – Mostly Unknown*, Post-Centenary vol. I, Part Two (Ahmedabad: 1980), p. 176.
58. G.M. Nandurkar ed., *Sardar Patel in Tune with the Millions*, p. 73.
59. S.L. Poplai ed., *India 1947–50*, vol. 1, Internal Affairs (Oxford: 1959) p. 371. Also see A. De Mhaffe, *Road to Kashmir* (Lahore) p. 168.
60. *Caravan* (New Delhi) February 1950, Kashmir Issue, no. 41, p. 67.
61. *White Paper on the Jammu and Kashmir Dispute* (Ministry of Foreign Affairs, Government of Pakistan, January 1977), p. 45.
62. Events have, however, shown that the Indian ruling class perception of an expansionist China is largely misplaced.
63. M.C. Chagla, *Kashmir 1947–1965* (Government of India, New Delhi: 1965), p. 103. Also see *Kashmir: Text of Speeches by M.C. Chagla, Union Minister of Education and Leader of the Indian Delegation in the Security Council on February 5 & 10 1964* (Information Service of India, New Delhi, no date), p. 36.
64. That was how the Party Manifesto of National Conference was titled at the time of the 1951 election.
65. The Tenants (Stay of Ejectment) Ordnance, 1947; The Tenancy (Amendment) Act, 1948; The Realization of Debts (Temporary Stay) Ordnance, 1949; The Distressed Debtors' Relief Act, 1949; The Restitution of Mortgaged Properties Act, 1949. See A.P. Jain, *Kashmir: What Really Happened* (Bombay: 1972).
66. J. Korbel, *Danger in Kashmir* (Princeton: 1966) p. 212.
67. ibid. p. 216.
68. The Sheikh himself later realized this paradox when he recalled: 'Our plan affected Hindu and Muslim zamindars equally but… our measures were then labelled as anti-Hindu.' See *The Testament of Sheikh Abdullah*, (Dehra Doon: 1974), p. 37.
69. Balraj Madhok, the leader of the Bhaatiya Jana Sangh, reveals this in *Kashmir: Centre of New Alignments* (New Delhi: 1963). A cry was raised that Kashmir was being pushed to 'the road of radical left-wing totalitarian dictatorship'.
70. ibid. p. 38.
71. See A. Varshney, 'Three Compromised Nationalisms'.
72. Quoted in ibid., p. 213.
73. Cited in B. Puri, *Kashmir Towards Insurgency*, p. 30.
74. K. Singh, *Heir Apparent: An Autobiography* (Delhi: 1982); D.N. Raina, *Unhappy Kashmir: The Hidden Story* (New Delhi: 1990), p. 154; A. Varshney, 'Three Compromised Nationalisms'.
75. D.N. Raina, '*Unhappy Kashmir*', pp. 155–6.
76. S. Gopal, *Jawaharlal Nehru: A Biography 1947–56*, vol 2, (Delhi: 1979), p. 117.
77. B.N. Mullik, *My years with Nehru* (Delhi: 1971), p. 29.
78. K. Singh, *Autobiography*, p. 159. The New Delhi Agreement was the Agreement that Sheikh Abdullah concluded with Nehru in July 1952. On the strength of this Agreement Abdullah became the Prime Minister of Jammu and Kashmir. The Agreement also laid down the basic framework of future relations between Srinagar and Delhi.
79. Bakshi would exploit every opportunity to stress the irrevocability of Kashmir's

Accession to India and contend that 'the only problem facing the State was to liberate that part of the country which was in the occupation of Pakistan'. See P.N. Bazaz, *The Shape of Things in Kashmir* (New Delhi: 1965), p. 16.

80. Vallabhbhai Patel, for instance, had remarked: '...to the bewilderment and sorrows of the Nation, Panditji had Micawberian love and faith for the man [Abdullah]...' Cited in Patel's Foreword to *The Tragedy of Kashmir* (New Delhi: 1975). This book is an example of an anti-Sheikh tirade within the Congress rank.

81. Quoted in J. Korbel, *Danger*, p. 247.

82. See Nehru's speech in the Lok Sabha on 29 March 1956 where he justified his retreat from the Plebiscite offer due to 'changed circumstances'. He pointed out that the UN resolution on Plebiscite could not be implemented because Pakistan refused to withdraw its troops from 'occupied Kashmir', the Jammu and Kashmir Assembly had accepted the Indian Constitution, and Pakistan by signing the Western military pact had brought the Cold War to the subcontinent.

83. R. Brines, *The Indo-Pakistan Conflict* (London: 1989) and S.M. Burke, *Pakistan's Foreign Policy: A Historical Analysis* (London: 1973).

84. Cited in V.D. Chopra, *Genesis*, p. 228.

85. See S.M. Burke, *Pakistan's Foreign Policy*, p. 319.

87. By Presidential Rule is meant direct rule over a province by the central government of Delhi.

88. Any citizen could be imprisoned for five years without any show of cause; the press was heavily censored; public rallies could hardly be held. See P.N. Bazaz, *The Shape*.

89. Balraj Puri substantiates this by an opinion poll conducted on the implications of the dismissal of Sheikh Abdullah. See his *Jammu and Kashmir: Triumph and Tragedy*, pp. 132–3.

90. *The Testament of Sheikh Abdullah* p. 69. Also see p. 57 where Abdullah himself considers his first arrest in 1953 as 'the most unforgettable experience'. In an emotional speech before entering the prison he remarked: '...everyone... must die some day and must experience separation from his near and dear ones... I have full faith that our aims and objectives will be brought nearer fulfillment through this sacrifice.'

91. See G. Rizvi, 'India Pakistan and the Kashmir Problem 1947–1972' in R.G.C. Thomas ed., *Perspectives on Kashmir*. Rizvi also believes that Nehru's commitment to the Plebiscite was genuine. But he argues that the 'dispute was complicated by... domestic politics in both Pakistan and India, and... by the extension of the Cold War rivalry in South Asia'. See his 'Nehru and the Indo-Pakistan rivalry over Kashmir 1947–64', *Contemporary South Asia* 1995, 4(1), pp. 17–37.

92. *The Testament*, p. 79.

93. Cited in S. Gopal, *Jawaharlal Nehru: a Biography*, vol. III (Delhi: 1985 ed), pp. 261–2.

94. G. Rizvi, 'India', p. 67. Also see M. Ayub Khan, *Friends Not Masters: A Political Autobiography* (Oxford: 1967) for his extreme recalcitrance against India on the Kashmir issue.

95. G. Rizvi, 'India', p. 69.

96. See L. Ziring, 'The Rann of Kutch Arbitration' in M. Hasan ed., *Pakistan in a Changing World; Essays in Honour of K. Sarwar Hasan* (Karachi: 1978). The Indian authorities claimed that it had unearthed documents which proved that a training camp for infiltrators had been set up under Lt.-Gen. Akhtar Hussian Malik at Murree in West Pakistan. See M.C. Chagla, *Kashmir 1947–1965*, p. 59.

97. *The Hindustan Times* 2 April 1966; *White Paper on the Jammu and Kashmir Dispute*, p. 115.

98. Only in 1979 were Articles 11 and 12 of the Indian Constitution guaranteeing such rights extended to Jammu and Kashmir.
99. *The Testament of Sheikh Abdullah*, p. 70.
100. Cited in the *Indian Express* 31 March 1972.
101. Cited in *Kashmir Special Status* (All J & K National Conference Srinagar).
102. ibid. p. 218.
103. M.J. Akbar, *The Siege Within: Challenges to a Nation's Unity* (London: 1985), p. 275.
104. This refers to Sheikh Abdullah's aim to prevent Kashmir from becoming a colony of either New Delhi or Islamabad. See M. Faizili ed., *Kashmir Predilection* (Srinagar: 1988) and R.N. Kaul, *Sheikh Mohammad Abdullah: A Political Phoenix* (Delhi: 1985).
105. R. Punjabi, 'Kashmir; The Bruised Identity', in R.G.C. Thomas ed., *Perspectives on Kashmir*, p. 145.
106. No less a person than Sushil Silvano, a veteran police officer who had been Jawaharlal's Chief Security Officer and had raised the Border Security Force, admitted: 'The mistake that Indira Gandhi made in opting for communal politics in the State led to a steady decline in the faith of Kashmiris in us.' *Current*, 6–12 January 1990.
107. Farooq Abdullah, *My Dismissal* (Delhi: 1985) pp. 23–4. Farooq alleges that Mrs Gandhi even used the issue of the Bill to buttress Hindu support for her Party during the 1983 legislative elections.
108. B. Puri, 'Jammu and Kashmir: Congress (I)'s Short-Sighted Game', *Economic and Political Weekly* (hereafter EPW)/3, December 1983, vol. XVIII, no. 49.
109. See M. Weiner, *The Indian Paradox: Essays in Indian Politics* (New Delhi: 1989) chapter 3; Lloyd and Susanne Rudolph, *In Pursuit of Lakshmi: The Political Economy of the Indian State* (Chicago: 1987) chapter 4.
110. Farooq Abdullah, *My Dismissal*.
111. See S. Bose, *The Challenge in Kashmir*, pp. 42–3.
112. G.M. Shah was nicknamed 'Curfew Chief Minister' since 72 of his first 90 days in office saw the valley under curfew.
113. See S. Akhtar, 'Uprising in Indian-held Jammu and Kashmir, *Regional Studies*, vol. IX, no. 2, 1991.
114. J.A. Vincent, 'Differentiation'.
115. A.H. Suhrawardy, *Kashmir: The Incredible Freedom-Fight* (Lahore 1991), p. 51; see *Census of India 1981*.
116. *The Hindu*, 7 November 1990. Also see George Fernandes, 'India's Policies in Kashmir: An Assessment and Discourse' in R.G.C. Thomas ed., *Perspectives on Kashmir*. Unfortunately, the same George Fernandes, currently India's Defence Minister in the Vijpayee Government, now tends to express pro-Pundit views.
117. See B. Puri, 'Why Jammu goes restive', *The Tribune*, 10 December 1990.
118. *The Hindustan Times*, 25 April 1990. According to one estimate the Muslim share of employment in nationalized banks in Jammu and Kashmir is only 1.5 per cent, *EPW* 31 March 1990, pp. 660–61. Also see *India's Kashmir War: A Report* (Committee For Initiative on Kashmir, New Delhi, March 1990).
119. A.G. Noorani, 'The Betrayal of Kashmir: Pakistan's Duplicity and Indian's Complicity', in R.G.C. Thomas ed., *Perspectives on Kashmir*.
120. *India's Kashmir War*.
121. J. Clad and S. Ali, *Far Eastern Economic Review*, 26 April 1990, pp. 10–11.
122. S. Akhtar, 'Uprising'. Also see Mir Qasim, *My Life and Times* (New Delhi: 1993) for the emergence of a Muslim-educated group in the Valley.

123. See DN, 'Kashmir and India', *EPW* 24 August 1991, XXV, 34, p. 1961.

124. Many of the vital infrastructural projects suffered from inordinate delays. The most glaring example was the vital Dulhsti power project.

125. In 1968 90 per cent of the people in the state depended on land for earning their living. The rural/urban ratio of population was 83:17. See *Report of the Jammu and Kashmir Commission of Inquiry* (Government of Jammu and Kashmir, 1968), p. 19. The situation today is not that different.

126. M.J. Akbar, *Kashmir: Behind the Vale* (New Delhi: 1991).

127. DN, 'Kashmir and India'.

128. A. Maqsood, 'New Delhi and Kashmir: Integration or Alienation?', *The Kashmir Dossier* Feburary 1991, p. 11. Also cited in DN, 'Kashmir and India'.

129. A.P. Jain, 'Kashmir: What Really Happened'.

130. ibid.

131. Cited in A.A. Azmi, *Kashmir: An Unparalled Curfew* (Karachi: 1990), p. 71.

132. B. Puri, *Kashmir Towards Insugency*, p. 57.

133. R. Punjabi, 'Kashmir', p. 142. Also see A. Maqsood, 'New Delhi and Kashmir'.

134. S. Ali, 'Trouble in Kashmir', *Far Eastern Economic Review*, 18 May 1989.

135. Rs. 370 *crores* was the anticipated budget deficit and out of it Rs. 300 *crores* were for interest payments to Delhi. See A. Maqsood, 'New Delhi and Kashmir'.

136. A.J. Ganai, *Kashmir and National Conference Politics 1975–1981* (Srinagar: 1984), p. 103.

137. A. Maqsood, 'New Delhi and Kashmir'; DN, 'Kashmir and India', pp. 1959–61.

138. 'The demographic problem in Kashmir is not of ageing population but of a very young population expanding at a rapid rate.' J.A. Vincent, 'Differentiation', p. 322.

139. S. Ali, 'Trouble in Kashmir'.

140. Cited in *The Herald*, July 1990.

141. B.L. Kak, *Kashmir: The Untold Story of Men and Masters* (Jammu: 1974), p. 5.

142. G.B. Malik, 'Genesis of Kashmir Trouble', *The Statesman*, 29 March 1990.

143. D.E. Lockwood and B.L. LePoer, *Kashmir: Conflict and Crisis* (Congressional Research Service, Library of Congress, Washington DC, 8 August 1991).

144. Cited in A.G. Noorani, 'The Betrayal'.

145. For example Bose remarks: 'Poverty, corruption and unemployment in the sub-continent are not unique'. See S. Bose, *The Challenge in Kashmir*, p. 19.

146. See *India's Kashmir War*, p. 29.

147. Cited in ibid. p. 26.

148. Cited in *Surya India*, January 1990.

149. This is what a militant told the investigators who prepared *Indian's Kashmir War*.

150. Sher-i-Kashmir Sheikh Mohammad Abdullah, *Interviews and Speeches After his Release on 2 Jan 1968, Series 2*, pp. 12–13.

151. S. Bose, *The Challenge in Kashmir*, p. 44.

152. It needs to be remembered that the Islamic fundamentalist forces had polled about 32 per cent of the votes cast in the 1987 elections and the MUF won four seats, losing in three constituencies by a narrow margin. See B. Puri, 'Fundamentalism in Kashmir: Fragmentation in Jammu', *EPW*, 30 May 1987, XXIII, 22, pp. 835–7. In fact, it was in 1987 in prison that Yasin Malik, Ashfaq Wasi and others floated the idea of the Jammu and Kashmir Liberation Front.

153. The Indian Constitution has three Lists: the Union List, which covers subjects on which the Federal Government can alone legislate; the State List, which contains matters which the provincial governments can administer; and the Concurrent list, on

which both the central and provincial governments can legislate, although in the event of a clash between central and state legislation the former prevails over the latter.

154. Sher-i-Kashmir Sheikh Mohammad Abdullah, *Interviews and Speeches After his Release on 2 January 1968*, Series 2, pp. 12–13.
155. *The Indian Express*, 20 March 1993.
156. S. Akhtar, 'Uprising'.
157. Brig. (Retd) M. Shafi Khan, *Focus on Kashmir Sept 1989–Feb 1990* (Islamabad: 1989), p. 3.
158. ibid. P. Bhatia, 'The Kashmir Muslims' Psyche', *Amrita Bazar Patrika* [hereafter *ABP*] 3 September 1986; also see *The Telegraph*, 15 August 1985. See *Newsweek* (21–8 August 1989) for a vivid description of the celebration of Pakistan Independence Day in Srinagar.
159. Brig. (Retd) M. Shafi Khan, *Focus*, p. 2.
160. *The Muslim*, 29 May 1993.
161. R. Punjabi, 'Kashmir', p. 142.
162. See A. Cowshish's submission, *The Telegraph*, 24 September 1986.
163. See D. Lockwood and B.L. Lepoer, *Kashmir: Conflict and Crisis*.
164. Cited in *Peace Initiatives* vol. III, no. V, Sept–Oct 1997, p. 7.
165. A. Jalal, 'A Terrible Beauty is Torn'.
166. This is the estimate of the Indian government, *The Hindu*, 3 December 1990.
167. *ABP*, 7 February 1985.
168. ibid.
169. *Foreign Broadcast Information Service* [Hereafter *FBIS*]-NES-93-016, 27 January 1993, pp. 59–60.
170. T. Amin and N. Bajwa, *Kashmir Report* (Institute of Policy Studies, Islamabad, June 1990). On 24 April 1993 an Indian aircraft was hijacked from New Delhi to Srinagar. Delhi claimed that the Hizbul group was behind the plot.
171. *The Telegraph*, 20 April 1998.
172. S. Ganguly, *The Crisis in Kashmir*, p. 2.
173. S. Bose, *The Challenge in Kashmir*, pp. 72–3.
174. See *The Telegraph*, 7 August 1995, for a report of one such meeting.
175. See 'Hizb Confimation', *The Kashmir Times*, 14 September 1990.
176. Indian sources have published a map identifying JKLF training camps inside Pakistan. See V.D. Chopra, *Genesis*, p. 237. Western sources, too, admit that the JKJLF receives support from Pakistan in the same way as other militant groups do. See, for instance, *US News & World Report*, 11 June 1990.
177. S. Akhtar, 'Uprising'.
178. *The Economist*, 9 June 1990, p. 34. These young men are utilized to commit a variety of terrorist acts, including abduction of important officials or relatives of government functionaries. In 1990 the daughter of the Union Home Minister, himself a Muslim, was kidnapped and her release traded for freedom of jailed militants.
179. *Newsweek*, 30 April 1990.
180. Cited in D.N. Raina, 'Unhappy Kashmir', p. 196.
181. *The Indian Express*, 20 September 1989.
182. S. Akhtar, 'Uprising'.
183. See V.D. Chopra, *Genesis*, Appendix IV.
184. Khalistanis are the group which is fighting for an independent Punjab that would be called Khalistan.
185. This is what the Pak Prime Minister Nawaz Sharif explicitly stated. See *The Economist*, 15 February 1992, p. 36.

186. *The Indian Express*, 7 February 1990.
187. *The Indian Express*, 23 February 1999.
188. *The Economist*, 15 February 1992, p. 36.
189. *FBIS*-NES-90-088, 7 May 1990.
190. *Agence France Presse*, 5 February 1993.
191. H.R. Khan, 'The Kashmir Intifada', *Pakistan Horizon*, vol. 23, no. 2, April 1990.
192. ibid.
193. ibid.
194. See *The Nation*, 11 April 1988.
195. *FBIS*-NES-90-018, 26 January 1990.
196. Cited in H.R. Khan, 'The Kashmir'.
197. *India's Kashmir War*. Tehran is, however, exhibiting considerable restraint under the post-Khomeini regime.
198. *The Statesman*, 9 September 1992. An Afghan mujahid Akbar Bhai aged 26 told the correspondent of this newspaper that in one year he had killed more than a hundred Indian soldiers. Also see *The Times*, 30 January 1990, for a report on the connections between the Afghan mujahedin and Islamic militants in Kashmir. In an interview to the *Eyewitness* of June 1992 the spokesman of the new Afghan government openly lent support to the anti-Indian uprising in Kashmir. He remarked that for 14 years Mujahiddins had been looked after by Pakistan and now it was their duty to repay the debt by supporting the Pak-sponsored Kashmiri and Punjabi separatists. Also see *The Telegraph*, 8 August 1993, and *The Statesman*, 22 July 1994. L.K. Advani, the Union Home Minister in the Vajpayee cabinet, also admited in the Lok Sabha the presence of mercenaries from Sudan, Egypt, Lebanon, Bahrain, Chechnya and Bosnia, apart from Pakistan and Afghanistan. See *Outlook*, 7 June 1999, p. 28.
199. *Newsweek*, 30 April 1990.
200. Such a plan was unearthed in May 1993 when some of these militants in Jammu and Kashmir sought to go to Jeddah. The Indian government refused them the permission to leave the country, *The Telegraph*, 7 May 1993; also, see *The British Broadcasting Corporation Report*, 11 May 1993.
201. *Peace Initiatives* vol. III, no. V, Sept-Oct. 1997.
202. ibid.
203. *Ananda Bazar Patrika*, 1 June 1999.
204. Aunohita Mojumdar, 'A lost road map in J&K', *The Statesman*, 23 September 1999.
205. In recent times Fidayeen or death squad of local militants are mostly carrying on insurgency operations in Jammu and Kashmir.
206. U. Phadnis, 'Ethnic Dynamics in South Asian States', *South Asia Journal*, January–March 1990.
207. A. Jalal, 'A Terrible Beauty is Torn'.
208. *The Dawn*, 31 October 1947.
209. A. Beg, *Captive Kashmir* (Lahore: 1957)
210. See the statement by M.A. Gurmani, the Pakistani Minister of Kashmir Affairs, *Pakistan Times*, 14 January 1949.
211. *Al Barg*, 14 May 1944, see the report on the speech delivered by Jinnah at Srinagar, cited in S. Kaul, *Freedom Struggle in Jammu and Kashmir* (Delhi: 1990), p. 138.
212. *White Paper on the Jammu and Kashmir Dispute*, p. 16.
213. M. Brecher, *The Struggle For Kashmir*, p. 52.
214. S.L. Poplai ed., *India 1947–50*, p. 395.
215. Sardar M. Ibrahim Khan, *The Kashmir Saga* (Lahore: 1965), p. 176.

216. Quoted in M. Brecher, *The Struggle for Kashmir*, p. 47.
217. D. Lilienthal, 'Another Korea in the Making', *Colliers* (New York) 4 August 1951, p. 57.
218. A. Khan, *Raiders in Kashmir*, (Islamabad: 1970), p. 10.
219. See M. Brecher, *The Struggle for Kashmir*.
220. Cited in ibid., p. 49.
221. Sirdar Shaukat Hayat Khan, *The Nation that Lost its Soul: Memoirs of Sirdar Shaukat Hyat Khan* (Lahore: 1995).
222. They would argue that the very concept of Pakistan included Kashmir as its integral part, the letter K standing for Kashmir. See Maj-Gen. A. Khan, *Raiders*.
223. ibid.
224. ibid. p. 13. Besides, the Commander of the future Azad forces was himself a Pakistani officer. See A. Jalal, *The State of Martial Rule: The Origins of Pakistan's Political Economy of Defence* (Cambridge: 1990), p. 59.
225. N. Rahman, A.G. Soofi, *ABC of Kashmir's Bid for Freedom* (Azad Jammu and Kashmir Government, Muzaffarabad: 1956), p. 15.
226. ibid. pp. 4–5. Some scholars argue that the tribals who had traditionally been a source of disorder in the region were deliberately made to divert 'their interest and activity to Kashmir'. See R. Symonds *The Making of Pakistan* (London: 1950), p. 121.
227. See *Intelligence Reports Concerning the Tribal Repercussions to the Events in the Punjab, Kashmir and India* (Press, Lahore: 1948).
228. 'Even if it amounted to suicide the Azad Kashmir people will go to the help of their oppressed brothers', cited in P.N. Bazaz, *The History for Freedom in Kashmir* (Islamabad: 1976), pp. 701–2.
229. S. Munshi, 'Their feudal lords', *The Telegraph*, 28 June 1999.
230. *The Dawn*, 9 October 1963; *The Statesman* (Calcutta), 2 February 1964.
231. See Bhutto's speech before the Security Council on 3 February 1964, cited in *Bhutto: A South Asian View* (Information Division, Embassy of Pakistan, Washington DC: no date), p. 41.
232. See Bhutto's address to the Pakistan Islamic Council for International Affairs, cited in the *Pakistan Observer*, 22 June 1963. Also *The Patriot*, 21 February 1969; *The Mashiq*, cited in *The Patriot* (Delhi), 19 March 1970. Humayun Rashid Chaudhuri, once head of the Pak Chancery in New Delhi, but who later defected to Bangladesh in 1971, even testified to a move by Pakistan's military junta to attack Kashmir to balance the loss of the country's eastern half. See *The Hindustan Times*, 8 October 1971.
233. Cited in the *White Paper on the Jammu and Kashmir Dispute*, p. 127.
234. ibid. pp. 128–9.
235. V.D. Chopra, *Genesis*, p. 104; A. Jalal, *The State of Martial Rule*, especially Chapter 7.
236. *The Indian Express*, 12 February 1990.
237. H.R. Khan, 'The Kashmir Intifada', *Pakistan Horizon*, vol. 23, no. 2, April 1990.
238. *Middle East Newsweek*, 18 February 1993.
239. K. Callard had foretold this in 1957 in his *Pakistan: A Political Study* (Unwin, London: 1957) p. 309. Later on President Zia admitted this when he remarked: 'For 35 years Kashmir has got wrapped in its internal politics. I cannot unwrap it even if I had the intentions.' Cited in S.U. Kodikara, 'Strategic Dimensions of South Asian Politics: Emerging Trends' in *Perspectives on International Relations in the Indian Ocean region*, p. 24.
240. Cited in S.U. Kodikara, 'Strategic Dimensions of South Asian Politics'.
241. Quoted in J. Clad and S. Ali, 'Will Words Lead to War?' *Far Eastern Economic Review*, 26 April 1990, pp. 10–11. As the PM of Pakistan Bhutto had assured

the Kashmiri people that 'they have the support of a hundred million people of Pakistan', *FBIS*-NES-90-029, 12 February 1990.

242. *Newsweek*, 30 April 1990, p. 33.
243. *Time*, 4 June 1990.
244. *FBIS*-NES-90-024, 5 February 1990.
245. *The News*, 11 December 1998.
246. *Pakistan Parliamentary Debates 1957*. vol. I, p. 1086.
247. Quoted in *Times of India*, 23 September 1969.
248. Brig. (Retd) M.S. Khan, *Focus*, pp. 19–20.
249. S.P. Cohen, 'Kashmir: The Roads Ahead' in S.P. Cohen ed., *South Asia After the Cold War: International Perspectives* (ACDIS Conference Proceedings, University of Illinois at Urbana Champaign, 1992).
250. See for example how the Report of the Genocide Inquiry Commission presented to Azad Kashmir Government was cited in *The Dawn*, 8 August 1968. Newspapers such as *Jung, Anjam, Imroze, Nawa-e-Waqr* and *Nida-e-Milat* would spare no opportunity to raise the *jihad* cry for Kashmir. The state-run radio would also periodically broadcast the national pledge to liberate Kashmir from India's colonial rule.
251. *The Dawn*, 17 August 1953.
252. On 23 March 1940, the Muslim League formally passed the Pakistan Resolution to demand a separate homeland for the Indian Muslims.
253. *FBIS*-NES-90-063, 2 April 1990.
254. *FBIS*-NES-90-024, 5 January 1990, pp. 57–8; *FBIS*-NES-90-016, 24 January 1990; *FBIS*-NES-90-226, 29 January 1990; *FBIS*-NES-90-025, 6 February 1990, pp. 70–71; *FBIS*-NES-90-079, 24 April 1990, p. 58; *FBIS*-NES-90-080, 25 April 1990.
255. *FBIS*-NES-90-055, 21 March 1990.
256. *FBIS*-NES-92-207, 26 October 1992, p. 49.
257. *FBIS*-NES-93-024 8 February 1993, pp. 72–3.
258. Such scenes in Pakistan were reciprocated with anti-Pakistani demonstrations in different parts of India, especially at the initiative of the Youth Congress, the youth wing of the Indian National Congress(I) party. See *Ananda Bazar Patrika*, 6 February 1994.
259. B.L. Kak, '*Kashmir: The Untold Story*', pp. 70–79.
260. In 1947, 1965 and 1971.
261. R.G. Wrising, 'Kashmir Conflict: the new phase' in C.H. Kennedy ed., *Pakistan 1992* (Boulder: 1993); also see *Pakistan Abetting Terrorism in Jammu and Kashmir* (Govt. of India publication, no date and no place of publication mentioned) and *The Tribune*, 4 February 1993.
262. Cited in D.N. Raina, 'Unhappy Kashmir', p. 197.
263. *FBIS*-NES-92-240, 14 December 1992, p. 44; *FBIS*-NES-92-045, 6 March 1992, p. 61.
264. *Peace Initiatives*, vol. III, no. V, Sept–Oct 1997.
265. *FBIS*-NES-91-230, 29 November 1991, p. 6; *FBIS*-NES-92-072, 14 April 1992, p. 34; *FBIS*-NES-92-147, 30 July 1992, p. 34; *FBIS*-NES-92-178, 14 September 1992, p. 44.
266. See *The Hindustan Times*, 6 July 1969 and 3 June 1970; *The Northern India Patrika*, 8 July 1969; *The Times of India*, 10 April 1988.
267. Y. Lameel, 'Terror in the Valley', *The Telegraph*, 6 November 1986; K. Subrahmanyan, 'Kashmir', *Strategic Analysis*, vol. III, no. 2, May 1990; L.E. Rose, 'Indian Foreign Relations: Reassessing Basic Policies', in M.M. Boulton and P. Oldenburg eds., *India Briefing, 1990* (Boulder: 1970), p. 73.
268. *Times of India*, 31 May 1999.

269. *The Asian Age*, 4 June 1999.
270. ibid.
271. See the submission by S. Mustafa, *The Asian Age*, 26 June 1999.
272. ibid.
273. ibid.
274. ibid.
275. *Times of India*, 31 May 1999.
276. Cited in E. Desmond, 'The Insurgency in Kashmir', *Contemporary South Asia* 199, 4 (1).
277. ibid.
278. ibid. p. 8.
279. Cited in *Peace Initiaitves*, vol. III, V, Sept–Oct 1997, p. 10.
280. See the deposition, for example, by Zulfiqar Ali Shah, *FBIS*-NES-93-044, 9 March 1993, p. 62.
281. This was revealed by Hazi Adeel, the deputy leader of the Provincial Assembly of Pakistan's North-East Frontier Province. Cited in ibid., p. 19.
282. This was confided by an aide of Pak-based Khalistan Commando Force Chief Paramjit Singh Panjwar. See *The Statesman*, 21 April 1998.
283. *FBIS*-NES-93-016, 27 January 1993, p. 53. It is not uncommon to hear incidents of Indian security forces foiling attempts by the Pak army to push Kashmiri militants across the border, *FBIS*-NES-92-154, 10 August 1992, p. 47.
284. The Indian government faced the situation tactfully. It ordered a siege of the mosque and forced the militants to surrender. Among the Kashmiri militant groups engaged in the occupation of the mosque were JKLF, Ikhwan-ul-Muslameen, Al-Jehad, Allah Tigers, Jamayat-ul-Mujahideen and Hizbul Mujahideen.
285. *The Telegraph*, 7 August 1995.
286. *The Telegraph*, 25 October 1995, see the submission by O.N. Dhar.
287. All India Radio General Overseas Service in English cited in *International Intelligence Report*, 3 March 1993.
288. *FBIS*-NES-91-236, 9 December 1991, p. 68.
289. See the statement by M. Jacob, the Minister of State for Home Affairs, *The Statesman*, 18 August 1992.
290. P. Bhatia, 'The Kashmiri Muslims' Psyche', *ABP*, 3 September 1986.
291. *EPW*, 11 August 1990, XXV, 32, p. 1738. See the Letter to the Editor by Sukla Sen.
292. E. Desmond, 'The Insurgency in Kashmir'.
293. *The Economist*, 13 July 1991, p. 35.
294. *Peace Initiatives*, vol. III, no. V, Sept–Oct 1997, pp. 8–9.
295. According to one report the Jamaat-i-Islami raised in 1994 alone 25 million rupees (approximately one million dollars) for the militant cause in Kashmir.
296. *The Telegraph*, 17 May 1993.
297. Cited in *Peace Inititatives*, vol. III, no. V, Sept–Oct 1997, p. 5.
298. *The Telegraph*, 17 January 1994. An ISI officer, Brig. Mohammed Salim, is said to have been in charge of the training camps.
299. Cited in P. Gossman, 'An International Human Rights Perspective', in Robert G. Wrising ed., *Kashmir: Resolving Regional Conflict: A Symposium* (Meesrut: 1996) p. 153.
300. K. Nayar, 'Polls in Kashmir', *The Hindustan Times*, 31 January 1998. Nayar also refers to another similar group called the Lashkar-i-Taiba (army of the pure).
301. ibid., 30 May 1999.
302. Cited in the *Times of India*, 24 June 1999.

303. Quoted from *The Times* in *Ananda Bazar Patrika*, 1 June 1999.

304. *Times of India*, 31 May 1999.

305. *Asian Age*, 4 June 1999.

306. *Ananda Bazar Patrika*, 1 June 1999.

307. Cited in *Outlook*, 7 June 1999, p. 29. *The Washington Post* has also squarely blamed Pakistan for triggering off the current crisis. See *Times of India*, 29 June 1999.

308. Report of *The Observer* cited in the *Times of India*, 31 May 1999.

309. The membership of the Council is also designed to maintain the supremacy of Islamabad. It is presided over by the Prime Minister himself and includes five members of the Pakistan Assembly nominated by the Pakistani Prime Minister, the Federal Minister of Kashmir Affairs, the Prime Minister of Azad Kashmir and six Azad Kashmiris elected on a proportional basis. See L. Rose, 'The Politics of Azad Kashmir' in R.G.C. Thomas, *Perspectives on Kashmir*. In the words of a perceptive commentator: 'No genuine elections have been held (in Azad Kashmir), and the judicial system is rudimentary.' See S. Bose, *The Challenge in Kashmir*, p. 65.

310. L.D. Hayes, 'The Impact of US Policy on Kashmir Conflict', *International Studies*, no. 2; S. Ali, 'Line of Control', *Far Eastern Economic Review*, 10 May 1990.

311. P. Singh, 'An Indian Perspective II' in Robert G. Wrising ed.. *Kashmir: Resolving Regional Conflict: A Symposium*, p. 101.

312. *Azad Jammu and Kashmir Legislative Assembly Election Ordnance* 1970, Section 5, para 2, p. vii.

313. *Azad Jammu and Kashmir Interim Constitution Act 1974*, Section 4, para 7, p. 2. Cited in P. Singh, 'An Indian Perspective II'.

314. P. Singh, 'An Indian Perspective', pp. 102–3.

315. *The Economist*, 13 July 1991, p. 35. Leo Rose, however, refers to 'much less understood' disagreements between Islamabad and Muzaffarabad and argues that the Azad politicians are 'no more enchanted with…Islamabad than are Sindhis, Baluchis and Pathans…' See his 'The Politics of Azad Kashmir', p. 245. But this alleged tension between Azad Kashmir and the Government of Pakistan needs substantial simmering before it can become a factor to be reckoned with in Pakistani politics.

316. *The Economist*, 13 July 1991. Rathore belongs to the Pakistan Peoples' Party, which was opposed to the party then in power in Islamabad.

317. L. Rose 'The Politics of Azad Kashmir', p. 244.

318. Some scholars contend that Azad Kashmir itself is not socially homogenous. The Mirpuris, for example, are culturally more akin to the Potohari population in Pakistan proper than with Kashmiris of the Valley or Dogras of Jammu. Yet, they have become enthusiastic supporters of Kashmiri entity because of their 'strong… disillusionment about the way in which Pakistan has treated them'. See R. Ballard, 'Kashmir Crisis: View from Mirpur', *EPW*, 2–9 March 1991, XXVII, 90 and 91, pp. 513–17.

319. *The Statesman* 8 March 1998.

320. P. Singh, 'An Indian Perspective II'.

321. S. Bose, *The Challenge in Kashmir*, p. 70.

322. *The Telegraph* 28 April 1998.

323. ibid., 3 May 1998.

324. This view has been expressed, amongst others, by S. Bose, *The Challenge in Kashmir*.

325. *EPW*, 3 March 1990, XXV, 9, p. 423.

326. *The Statesman* 19 January 1990. Also cited in ibid.
327. *Inter Press Service*, 18 May 1993. According to a recent American report the number of Indian security personnel in Jammu and Kashmir has risen to 400, 000, R.P. Cronin and B.L. LePoer, *South Asia: U.S. Interests and Policy Issues* (Congressional Research Service, The Library of Congress, Washington DC: 12 February 1993), p. 18. In May 1993 *India Today* estimated the presence of at least 300 paramilitary companies in Jammu and Kashmir.
328. S. Ganguly, *The Crisis in Kashmir*, p. 2.
329. This term is borrowed from *EPW* 13 January 1990, XXV, 2, p. 64. There have been allegations of human rights violations by Indian security forces in Kashmir. Prisoners in Kashmir are allegedly tortured by electric shocks and sodomy and apparently 3,000 habeas corpus petitions on behalf of the incarcerated have been filed, but with no result. See *US News & World Report*, 19 November 1990; *Agence France Presse*, 8 May 1993; Report by Barbara Crossette, *New York Times*, 8 November 1992; S. Akhtar, 'Human Rights Violations in JK', *Regional Studies*, vol. XI, no. 2, Spring 1993; and reports of Indian voluntary organizations like the the People's Union for Civil Liberties, the Citizens for Democracy, the Radical Humanist Association and the Manav Ekta Abhiya. Asia Watch and Physicians for Human Rights have also charged the Indian forces in Kashmir with abduction, custodial deaths, summary executions of detainees and using rape as a 'war tactic'. Even accredited journalists have not escaped from the harassment of Indian security forces, *EPW* 9 June 1990, XXV, 3, p. 1228. In Sopore at one time all 22 members of the Bar Association had been imprisoned, *EPW* 15 Sept 1990, XXV, 37, p. 2023. The Indian government, however, denies allegations of human rights violations. But it has reportedly denied permission to international human rights groups to visit Kashmir, *FBIS*-NES-93-070 14 April 1993.
330. *The Telegraph*, 'Look', 13 August 1995.
331. *The Telegraph*, 13 August 1995; A.G. Noorani, 'A Pattern of Outrages in Kashmir', *The Statesman Weekly* 8 May 1993.
332. ibid.
333. *FBIS*-NES-93-002, 5 January 1993, p. 58. For instance, mention may be made of the complications caused by the Indian army's alleged desecration of the library of the Hazratbal mosque on 21 February 1992. See *FBIS*-NES-92-037, 25 February 1992, p. 50.
334. Popular belief in India's complicity in Farroq's assassination was evident from such cries during the funeral procession as 'Who killed Muhammad Farooq? Jagmohan! [the Governor of Jammu & Kashmir]'. See *Time*, 4 June 1990, p. 62.
335. See the interview by Abdul Kabir Sheikh, *Surya India*, January 1990. Also see *India's Kashmir War; Kashmir Bleeds: Report on the Kashmir Situation* (Srinagar: 1990); *Kashmir Under Siege* (1990); *Human Rights in India: Kashmir Under Siege* (NY & Washington: 1997); *Kashmir: A Land Ruled by the Gun* (Delhi: 1991).
336. *EPW* 7 July 1990, XXV, 27, p. 1428.
337. For example, on 4 July 1992 10,000 people from six localities in Srinagar were forced to come out of their homes in the dead of night and were then subjected to an identification parade. See A.G. Noorani, 'A Pattern'.
338. In a statement the Israeli Foreign Minister Shimon Peres supported India on the Kashmir issue and declared: 'We support fully and completely the territorial integrity of India', *Agence France Presse*, 18 May 1993.
339. *India Today* 5 May 1993; *The Reuter Library Report*, 10 April 1993, puts the figure at 10,000; R.Z. Khan, 'The Kashmir question and struggle for identity',

paper presented at a seminar on Kashmir, University of Sweden, 11–12 April 1992, cited in I. Ahmed, *State, Nation and Ethnicity in Contemporary South Asia* (London and New York: 1996), p. 157.

340. The *Asian Age*, 8 October 1995.
341. *The Telegraph*, 'Insight' 12 November 1995.
342. S. Hasan et al., *Kashmir Imprisoned: A Report* (Delhi: 1990); *Lawless Roads: A Report on TADA, 1985–1993* (New Delhi: 1993); *India: Torture, Rape and Deaths in Custody* (Amnesty International: 1991); *Kashmir Under Siege* (Asia Watch, New York: 1991); *Kashmir: Heaven on Fire* (British Parliamentary Human Rights Group, London: 1992); *United States Department of State Country Report on Human Conditions in India* (Washington DC: 1992). The US Department of State Country Reports on Human Rights Practice for 1992 cited the following figures for Kashmir: 1990: 1,214 civilians, 189 security forces and 890 militants killed.
1991: 900 civilians, 1,305 militants and 155 security forces killed.
1992: 1,106 civilians and 982 militants killed.
343. P. Gossman, 'An International Human Rights Perspective'. Gossman cites the evidence of Jammu and Kashmir Bar Association that of several thousand habeas corpus petitions pending before the High Court as of June 1994, 'the courts have responded to fewer than one per cent.'
344. Quoted from the *Sunday Times* by Public Opinion Trends Analyses and News Services, Pakistan Series, 18 December 1998, p. 4070.
345. *The Nation*, 12 December 1998.
346. *Crisis and Credibility* (Press Council of India: New Delhi, 1993).
347. E. Desmond, 'The insurgency in Kashmir (1989–91)', pp. 5–6.
348. Research and Analytical Wing. This is the intelligence wing of the Government of India.
349. M.J. Akbar, *Kashmir: Behind the Vale*. Bose in *The Challenge in Kashmir* also subscribes to the allegation that Jagmohan offered various incentives for the Hindu exodus, which was carried out under strictest press restrictions.
350. R. Manchanda, 'Kashmir's worse-off half', *Himal South Asia*, May 1999.
351. ibid.
352. See Teresa Joseph, 'Kashmir, human rights and the Indian press', *Contemporary South Asia* (2000) 9(1), pp. 41–55.
353. *FBIS*-NES-90-025, 6 February 1990; *FBIS*-NES-90-029, 12 February 1990, *FBIS*-NES-90-031, 14 February 1990. Indian and Pakistani troops were eyeball to eyeball in early May 1990.
354. *Newsweek*, 30 April 1990, p. 34.
355. A.H. Suhrawardy, *Kashmir*, p. 74.
356. S. Ali, *Line of Control*, pp. 18–19.
357. Y. Jamal, 'Terror in the Valley', *The Telegraph*, 6 November 1986.
358. See 'India's Kashmir War'.
359. See R. Manchanda, 'Loss of confidence: Both New Delhi and Militants Alienate Kashmiris', *Far Eastern Economic Review*, 3 September 1992, pp. 22–3.
360. *The Reuter Library Report*, 15 April 1993.
361. This was the incident in which Babri Masjid – an old mosque – in Ayodhya (Uttar Pradesh) was pulled down at the behest of Hindu sectarian forces on the plea that the site on which the mosque stood was the birthplace of the ancient Hindu epic hero Rama.
362. Cited in *The Muslim*, 14 January 1990.
363. S. Bose, *The Challenge in Kashmir*, Chapter 4.

364. *Times of India*, 31 May 1999.
365. *The Times*, 17 January 1990; Also see *Kashmir: A Land Ruled by the Gun*, for details of how Kashmiri women are made to strictly adhere to Islamic restrictions by militant outfits.
366. S. Viswam and S. Ali, 'Vale of Tears', *Far Eastern Economic Review*, 8 February 1990, pp. 18–19.
367. I.H. Malik, 'The Kashmir Dispute: A Cul-de-Sac in Indo-Pakistan Relations? in R.G.C. Thomas ed., *Perpectives on Kashmir*, p. 310.
368. N.Y. Dole, Kashmir: A Deep-rooted Alienation', *EPW* 5–12 May 1990. XXV, 18 & 19, pp. 978–9.
369. R. Manchanda, 'Loss of Confidence'.
370. See, for instance, the report in *The Statesman* 6 January 1990. *The Hindustan Times* particularly refers to activists of Hizbul Mujahideen working in such crucial departments as electricity. The Kashmiri Bar Association was one of the first professional associations to denounce the Indian Government's insensitivity to protestors in Jammu and Kashmir.
371. The Chaar-e-Sharief is a sacred spot venerated by both Muslims and Hindus. Militants sought to blow it up to provoke communal strife in Jammu and Kashmir.
372. General strikes in the Valley were provoked by the arrest of Hizbul leaders by the Indian army.
373. *The Telegraph*, 19 August 1995.
374. At the close of 1989 the militants had started targeting the followers of the Bharatiya Janata Party and a senior Vice President of the state unit of the Party, Tikka Lal Taploo, was gunned down. The non-Muslim population has virtually deserted the Valley. See *India's Kashmir War*. Balraj Puri had anticipated this as early as the 1960s and had advocated the separation of Jammu from Kashmir. See his *Jammu – A Clue to Kashmir Tangle* (Delhi: 1966). But once they became refugees these Hindus tended to be advocates of Hindu revivalist politics. See *EPW*, 24 November 1990, xxv, 47, pp. 2572–3 and N.Y. Dole, 'Kashmir: A Deep-rooted Alienation'.
375. S. Ganguly, 'The Prospects of War and Peace in Kashmir' in Raju G.C. Thomas ed., *Perspectives on Kashmir*.
376. David Welsh argues that this particular reconciliation is extremely difficult. See his 'Domestic Politics and Ethnic Conflict', *Survival* vol. 35, no. 1, Spring 1993, pp. 63–80.
377. Cited in B. Puri, 'The Challenge of Kashmir', *EPW*, 27 January 1990, XXV, 4, p. 191.
378. For a discussion of how 'the lower status accorded to regionalism, localism and religious, ethnic and linguistic specificities' by the Nehruvian integrationist bourgeois modernism has been largely responsible for ethnic politics in contemporary India, see Barun De and Suranjan Das, 'Ethnic Revivalism – Problems in the Indian Union', in K.S. Singh ed., *Ethnicity, Caste and People: India and the Soviet Union* (New Delhi: 1992). Many scholars argue this is the paradox of most Third World countries. See C. Thomas, *In Search of Security: The Third World In International Relations* (Hertfordshire: 1987).
379. Jay Prakash Narayan. 'The Need to Re-Think', *The Hindustan Times*, 15 May 1964.
380. See the submission by Nikhil Chakravarty, *The Pioneer*, 28 April 1993.
381. See Sheikh Abdullah's interview to *The Times*, 10 March 1972.
382. See the statement by M. Yusuf Tarigami, Secretary of Jammu & Kashmir state unit of the Communist Party of India (Marxist) *FBIS*-NES-90-005, 8 June 1990.
383. M.J. Akbar, *India: The Siege Within*, p. 228.
384. According to the Indian defence analyst K. Subrahmanyan, even a quick conventional

conflict would cost $2.5 billion, i.e. a dozen times more than India's bill for the 1971 war, *US News & World Report*, 11 June 1990.

385. Significantly, even after his undemocratic dismissal in 1984 Farooq Abdullah categorically stated: 'For us, accession of Jammu and Kashmir to India is complete, final and irrevocable. We will not allow this to be reopened in any case.' See Farooq Abdullah, *My Dismissal*, p. 84.

386. J.N. Dixit, *My South Block Years*, p. 337.

387. P. Singh, 'An Indian Perspective II', p. 111.

388. Balraj Puri's remarks are worth quoting here: 'The concept of an Indian nationalist devoid of all sub-national feelings is not real… [A] rigid and aggressive form of nationalism often provokes separatism while a healthy sub-nationalism contributes to integration.' See his 'Kashmir: Who Is Playing with National Interest?', *EPW*, 11 February 1984, vol. 19, no. 6.

389. *Peace Initatives*, May–June 1997.

390. D.L. Horowitz, 'Ethnic Conflict Management for Policymakers' in J.V. Montville ed., *Conflict* p. 115.

391. The BJP undertook this campaign on 23 June 1999. The RSS mouthpiece Panchajanya in its 23 June 1999 issue linked the 'martyrdom' of jawans killed in Kargil. It remarked: 'His [Mukherjee's] martydom was but a beginning in a series of sacrifices India has made to thwart the nefarious designs of our enemy. In the ongoing Operation Vijay at Kargil, hundreds of our valiant soldiers have made the supreme sacrifice.' On 20 June 1999 the paper even gave the irresponsible call for the use of the nuclear bomb on Pakistan to 'teach the country a lesson'. See the report on this RSS outburst in *The Telegraph* (Cal), 26 June 1999.

392. *Times of India* (Cal), 27 June and 4 July 1999.

393. D. Horowitz, 'Making Moderation Pay: The Comparative Politics of Ethnic Conflict Management' in J.V. Montville ed., *Conflict*, p. 453.

394. D. Horowitz, 'Ethnic Conflict', p. 119.

395. See J.V. Montville, 'Epilogue: The Human Factor Revisited' in J.V. Montville ed., *Conflict* for the necessity to emphasize the 'human factor' in any understanding of an ethnic conflict. After all, as *The Indian Express* (20 March 1993) remarks: 'India has to ask itself: why has Pakistan been able to recruit so many young men as militants and why do they get considerable popular sympathy? Why have the bulk of the people of Kashmir lost faith in their links with New Delhi? And what must be done to restore lost faith?' The then Indian Prime Minister Rao hinted at a new 'Kashmir package' on 31 October 1992, but nothing concrete followed.

396. A. Jalal, 'A Terrible Beauty is Torn'.

397. S.P. Cohen, 'Kashmir: The Road Ahead'. Kashmiri scholars like Ishaq Khan are firmly convinced that 'there is still an ample scope for the flowering of the idea of being a nationalist in J & K without indeed seeking the independence or division of the state on religions lines.' See Mohammad Ishaq Khan, 'Reflections on Kashmiri Nationalism', p. 8 (Paper presented in the seminar on 'Towards Understanding the Kashmir Crisis', Jamia Millia Islamia, New Delhi, 13–15 November 2000.

398. A delegation of Opposition parties like the CPI(M) and Janata Dal suggested this line of thought to the Union Home Minister on 30 June 1992. See A.G. Noorani, 'A Pattern'.

399. S. Mustafa, 'Why Kashmir is Still Hurting', *The Asian Age*, 25 September 1999.

400. See K. Bajpai et al., *Jammu and Kashmir: An Agenda for the Future* (Delhi Policy Group: Delhi March 1999), pp. 3–4, 50–51.

401. *People's Democracy*, 20 March 1994.

402. *The Hindu*, 18 January 1990, see the submission by O.N. Dhar.
403. The resolution demanded autonomy for Kashmir by a return to pre-1953 status. But this resolution was rejected by the Union Government. It has not also evoked much favourable reaction amongst the mainstream political parties.
404. ibid.
405. 'A conversation with Yasin Malik', *Peace Initiatives*, vol. 1, no. 1, July–August 1995.
406. Cited in B. Puri, *Kashmir Towards Insurgency*, p. 83. When the present book was in press the Hizbul Mujahideen declared a ceasefire with the Indian state as a prelude to a negotiation with New Delhi. But this cearefire was unilaterally withdrawn by the Hizbul Mujahideen following opposition from the Hizb leaders in Pakistan and subtle intervention from Islamabad.
407. *The Telegraph*, 30 September 1995.
408. S. Bose, *The Challenge in Kashmir*, p. 78.
409. See K.F. Rustamji, 'Do we have to live with terrorism forever?', *Delhi Midday*, 23 March 1999. Rustomji reckons that in today's Jammu and Kashmir 25 per cent would be for independence, 20 per cent for Pakistan, 45 per cent for India and 10 per cent undecided. He believes that if a full vote were obtained in the Hindu areas of Jammu, the Buddhist region of Ladakh and the border areas of Poonch and Rajaori, the percentage of votes for India would rise to 55 per cent.
410. Quoted in *Frontline* 21 May 1999, p. 40.
411. See Jamaat-e-Islami's leader Syed Ali Shaj's assertions as cited in ibid., p. 41.
412. Cited in K. Nayar, 'Polls in Kashmir'.
413. ibid.
414. *Peace Initiatives*, vol. III, Sept–Oct 1997, p. IV.
415. ibid. p. V.
416. ibid.
417. M. Ali Shah, 'The Kashmir Problem: A View from Four Provinces of Pakistan', *Contemporary South Asia*, 1995, 4(1).
418. I.H. Malik, 'The Kashmir Dispute'.
419. *EPW*, 2 June 1990, XXV, 22, p. 1173.
420. By this declaration India for the first time implicitly accepted Kashmir as a 'disputed question'.
421. See the report on Benazir's speech on 'Pakistan's Regression to an Authoritarian Past' at the Woodrow Wilson Center, Washington, in *India Abroad News* cited in *The Statesman*, 28 May 1999.
422. *Times of India*, 10 June 1999.
423. *Ganashakti*, 2 June 1999.
424. Cited in ibid., 4 July 1999.
425. ibid.
426. S.P. Cohen, 'Kashmir: The Road Ahead'.
427. This is what such organizations as the Center For Democratic Societies argue. See Arun Kumar's comment in *The Herald* July 1990, p. 21.
428. Aunohita Mazumdar, 'The Overbearing Past', *The Statesman*, 5 March 1998.
429. ibid.
430. Cited in D. Welsh, 'Domestic Politics', p. 75.
431. A.T. Embree, 'Pluralism and National Integration: The Indian Experience', *Journal of International Affairs*, vol. 27, no. 1, 1973, p. 47.
432. See the remarks by the Secretary General of the Communist Party (Marxist) Harkishen Singh Surjeet in the *Hindustan Times*, 6 December 1989.

Chapter 2

The Sindh Question in Pakistan's Polity

Sindh today is a powder keg for explosion. Those who are in any
mood to seek favours, to cajole or to please those in authority,
should better beware… The mood of Sindh under conditions of
anger and disillusionment might surge forth and burst into another and more disastrous explosion which will not be to the taste
and liking of our rulers and the Sindhi leadership.[1]

Nowhere has the state sanctification of violence been so pronounced as in Sindh, and nowhere have the wages of arms, drugs,
ethnicity, deprivation and despair been so great. Sindh's destiny
seems to have been written in blood, chapter after gory chapter,
by the custodians of the law, by the usurpers and wielders of
power, and the final tragedy, by those of its own soil.[2]

These are typical reactions of Sindhi intellectuals to spates of ethnic
clashes in Sindh, the second largest province in Pakistan. Sindh today is
an embattled province of Pakistan. Karachi, its capital city, is marred by
daily doses of intensifying ethnic violence between Sindhis and non-Sindhis.
To a large extent the Sindh problem is a manifestation of the unresolved
Sindh nationality question. For a long time Western, especially American,
social scientists considered Pakistan a 'homogeneous Islamic state',
ignoring its multinational character. It may be recalled how, as late as
1962 during his visit to Pakistan, the American diplomat Henry Kissinger
preferred not to take cognizance of nationalist insurgency in Baluchistan.[3]
But, as in Kashmir, the Sindh Question is connected with an imperfect
nation-building process that failed to strike a balance between Sindhi
and non-Sindhi ethnic aspirations within the broader framework of pan-
Pakistani identity. I propose first to delineate the historical context of the
Sindh Question and then to identify the main trends of Sindhi ethnonationalist politics.[4]

1. ROOTS OF CONTEMPORARY SINDHI
NATIONALISM

Sindh, the third most populous region at the time of Partition, lies in the south of Pakistan, bordering the Indian states of Rajasthan in the east and Gujrat in the south. Interestingly, it presents an economic paradox: a landlord-dominated backward rural sector coexisting with Karachi, the country's most thriving commercial city. But a striking feature of Sindh's history lies in its efforts to retain a distinct identity, the roots of which are often traced back to the Indus Valley Civilization. Studies have shown how tribal identity in Sindh evolved into a feudal state formation so that when the Arabs conquered the region early in the 8th century AD they could decipher a distinct Sindhi identity, different from that of Hind or India proper.[5] In 1592 the Mughal emperor Akbar extended his suzerainty over Sindh, but hardly succeeded in integrating it with Hindustan.[6] British colonialism also provoked a stiff resistance from Sindhis who rallied around the slogan of *murvesoon, Sindh na desoon* ('we will die but will not give up Sindh'). Although the Union Jack was planted on Sindh in 1843, the British recognized the region's advanced nationality development.[7]

Initially the Sindhis enthusiastically participated in Indian nationalist politics, reconciling their regional feelings with a pan-Indian identity in the face of the common enemy of colonialism. But when the Pakistan movement was developed, they rallied around it. The Sindhi support for Pakistan had, however, been predicated on 'autonomy' for Sindh, as envisaged in the 1943 Sindh Assembly resolution.[8] The Hur insurgency of the 1940s that aimed to establish an independent Sindh bears testimony to two parallel political trends in the region: support for Pakistan, and assertion of Sindhi identity.[9]

In the aftermath of the 'truncated settlement' of 15 August 1947 Sindh became one of the five provinces of Pakistan.[10] But the Pakistani polity was deprived of a consensual basis due to its strong centrist bias, the Punjabi dominance in bureaucracy, and intermittent doses of military dictatorship. The ruling elite's attempt to impose national unity through Islamic symbolism could hardly solve the national question in Pakistan. Not unnaturally, ethnic assertions tended to become an essential ingredient of Pakistani politics. The Sindh Question is a product of this ethnic politics.[11] One finds striking parallels in the articulation of Sindhi and Kashmiri ethnicities. There is, however, one point of difference. While Kashmir has remained a site of contest between India and Pakistan, the same is not true for Sindh, although Sindhi ethnic politics has demonstrated tendencies of cross-border ramifications.

Following recent studies it is possible to identify four basic ingredients in Sindhi ethnic resentment: (a) demographic; (b) economic; (c) cultural; and (d) political. But these are not mutually exclusive categories, there being constant overlapping of each other's boundaries.

1.1 The Partition, Transfer of Population and Threat to Sindhi Identity

Decolonization of South Asia resulted in the creation of two successor states along religious lines: a secular India, comprising the heartland of the subcontinent, and a Muslim-majority Pakistan consisting of two wings, the western part of which was separated from the eastern half by about 1,500km of Indian territory. This process was associated with a large-scale migration of people across the newly imposed frontiers – Muslims flocking to Pakistan and Hindus moving to India in search of safe haven. According to the 1951 Pakistan census 7.2 million Muslims migrated from India to Pakistan, although Western demographers push the figure to 10 million.[12] But this exchange of population had a differential impact within Pakistan itself. It contributed to ethnic homogeneity in the Punjab and North-West Frontier Provinces, virtually left Baluchistan unaffected, but rudely shook the demographic balance in Sindh. Although the Punjab was a much larger province and had a greater capacity to absorb the refugees from India, the Urdu-speaking Indian Muslims – except those from East Punjab – were primarily resettled in Sindh.[13] In the early 1950s, refugees from India represented 9.8 per cent of Pakistan's total population, but in Sindh they constituted 11.7 per cent of the inhabitants.[14] While 18 *lakhs* of Hindu Sindhis left for India following the Partition, 30 *lakh* Urdu-speaking Indian Muslims migrated to Sindh and 63.9 per cent of them settled in urban areas. By 1951 the predominance of Indian Muslims – the Muhajirs as they came to be called – in the major cities of Sindh becomes evident from the following table.[15]

City	Population	Muhajirs	Muhajirs as percentage of population
Karachi (Corporation)	1,064,557	612,680	57.55
Hyderabad	241,801	159,805	66.08
Sukkur	77,026	41,791	54.08
Mirpurkhas	40,412	27,649	68.42
Nawabshah	34,201	18,742	54.79
Larkana	33,247	11,767	35.39

In 1954 the number of Urdu-speaking Indian Muslims migrating to Sindh rose to one million, representing 20 per cent of the total population in the province.[16] In 1981 the linguistic ratio in the demographic profile of Sindh's prime city of Karachi was as follows: Urdu 54.3 per cent; Punjabi 13.6 per cent; Pushto 8.7 per cent; Sindhi 6.3 per cent; Baluchi 4.4 per cent; Hindko 1 per cent; others 11.7 per cent.[17] Significantly, although immigration to the Punjab virtually ended in 1948, the migration of Urdu-speaking North Indian Muslims to Sindh did not cease even after the visa system was introduced to curtail free travel between India and Pakistan.

Unlike the refugees settling in the Punjab who spoke the same language and shared the same culture and lifestyle, the North Indian Muslims seeking refuge in Sindh were socially, linguistically, culturally, politically and economically alien to the new environment. They failed to appreciate the cultural wealth of Sindh – its songs, its dances, its Susui Punhoon, its Shoni Mehwal, its Ho Jamalo, its Dhammal.[18] Instead, the newcomers to Sindh sought to project their distinct socio-political identity by propounding the superiority of their urban Mughal culture over indigenous Sindhi culture. They presented themselves as a non-assimilationist collective who stressed their 'refugee' or 'muhajir' status to separate themselves from the local Sindhis and claim special support from the state.[19] The primary concern for Muhajirs was to transform themselves from a migrant to a self-conscious native community and curve out a political space for themselves.[20] Their concentration in a geographical area certainly facilitated 'the formation of a cultural isolate – protected from local influences – in which the group could develop its ethnic identity'.[21] But equally important for the development of their 'group conscious-ness' was the internal structure of the Muhajir community itself.[22] For instance, the Muhajirs were marked out by an 'occupational characteris-tic'. The Muhajir labour force was overwhelmingly non-agricultural, 40 per cent of them being clerical and sales workers, 16.8 per cent service workers and 21.7 per cent skilled operatives. The community had a substantial educated middle class, detemined to avail of the opportunities for upward social mobility.[23] Besides, compared to other indigenous communities the proportion of poor and labouring class amongst the Muhajirs was considerably smaller.[24] In the words of a commentator: '…while the other groups were predominantly feudal, the Muhajirs were essentially middle class'.[25] This urban middle-class background of the Muhajirs had also exposed them to electoral and agitational politics in a greater way than other Pakistani nationalities.

The Muhajirs rallied around fundamentalist Islamic parties like Jamaat-e-Islami and Jamaita-ul-Ulema-e-Pakistan, finding in an Urduized Islamic Pakistan a protection against the new insecurity to which they had been exposed upon leaving their homeland.[26] Even in relation to Islam the Muhajir attitude contrasted sharply with the tolerant and Sufi-indoctrinated eclectic Islam of the Sindhis. Extremely conscious of their crucial role in the Pakistan movement,[27] the Muhajirs were determined to usurp the position of torch-bearer in the new Muslim homeland. Incidentally, both the first Governor-General and the first Prime Minister of Pakistan were Muhajirs. On the other hand, the Sindhis felt alienated by the 'occupier mentality' of Muhajirs,[28] and resented the Muhajir refusal to integrate with the larger Sindhi cultural and social milieu.[29] In the words of a Sindhi writer:

> Our compatriots from India brought a certain foreigness to Sindh and its soil and wanted to consolidate and perpetuate their habits and idiosyncrasies. They too were trying to challenge and change the order and the laws of nature.[30]

The demographic situation in Sindh was further complicated when the Muhajir influx was complemented by a considerable inflow of Punjabis and people from North-West Frontier Province in search of fortune.

Besides, after the formation of Bangladesh in 1971 several thousand Biharis who had been residents in erstwhile East Pakistan were settled in Sindh.[31] According to one estimate about 200,000 migrants were arriving every year in Karachi alone at one point.[32] These migrations generated a 'threat perception' amongst the Sindhis, a feeling of being reduced to a political, economic and, in some cases, demographic minority in their own homeland.[33] This fear psyche certainly had an empirical basis. In 1947 95 per cent of the population in Sindh were Sindhi speakers, but by the 1950s the urban populace in Sindh was pre-eminently Urdu-speaking, their ratio in cities like Karachi and Hyderabad rising to respectively 80 per cent and 66 per cent.[34] By 1989/90 Sindhis constituted less than half of the population in their own province and only about 5 per cent in the city of Karachi.[35] Sindhi nationalists thus alleged a deliberate plan of the federal government to convert 'Sindhis into a minority and... abolish their entity [in their own homeland]'.[36]

1.2 Economics of the Sindh Question

The Sindhis share a general resentment against their economic subordination to non-Sindhis in the province. Sindh's contribution to Pakistan's economy is considerable. Its share in the Gross Domestic Product is about 30 per cent, and Karachi continues to be the finance capital of Pakistan. But Sindhis are deprived of even a marginal share in this economic process.[37] Relatively more literate and skilled, the Muhajirs forged further ahead than the Sindhis in the race for employment both in private and public sectors.[38] As entrepreneurs, service groups, administrators, a petty bourgeoisie and a trained working class the Muhajirs represented, in the words of Zaidi, 'a more advanced urban capitalist culture which they had brought with them from the towns and cities of India'.[39] Not surprisingly, although representing only 3–4 per cent of the country's population, the Muhajirs rapidly established themselves in collaboration with the Punjabis as the 'ruling ethnic class' in Pakistan.[40] This had the tacit approval of the founding fathers of the Indian Muslim homeland – M.A. Jinnah and Liaqat Ali.[41]

The Muhajirs cornered 21 per cent of government jobs immediately after the Partition,[42] which gave them a hegemonic power in the 'overdeveloped and omnipresent' Pakistani state.[43] In 1968, 23 per cent of the ranks above Brigadier in the Pakistani military were held by Muhajirs;[44] in 1973 30.29 per cent of the top bureaucracy was manned by Muhajirs;[45] in 1974 50 per cent of the senior positions in the country's public enterprises were in Muhajir hands.[46] On the other hand, by the early 1970s the Sindhis held only 2.7 per cent of gazetted posts, 4.3 per cent of Secretariat offices and 3.6 per cent of executive positions in public enterprises.[47] No Sindhi was appointed till 1973 either to a provincial governorship or to ambassadorial and consular posts.[48] Between 1995 and 1970 amongst the 184 Deputy Inspector-Generals and Superintendents and 150 Commissioners and Deputy Commissioners of Police in Sindh only 53 and 41 respectively were native Sindhis.[49] The provincial capital city of Karachi was itself bereft of any senior Sindhi police official. A 1969–70 survey could not find in the private sector more than a thousand Sindhis amongst one million workers. In the same period only 250 Sindhis were found in every 10, 000 bank employees; the Sindhi share in federal and provincial services was respectively merely .02 and 40 per cent.[50] As late as the mid-1980s only 500 of the 2, 000 industrial units operating in Sindh were under Sindhi control.[51] In 1987 alone 7,000 doctors, 5,000 engineers, 4,000 agriculturists, 2,000 science graduates and 40,000 arts and science graduates remained unemployed in Sindh.[52] Sindh's share in the reserved quotas for the Civil Service in 1988 was 50 per cent for urban and 7.6 per cent for rural areas[53] – a mechanism which inevitable benefited the Muhajir community who were primarily urban dwellers. To quote a leading commentator:

In no other province have outsiders been Chief Secretary and Inspector-General of Police for 43 out of 45 years. In no other province was the Chief Executive an outsider for 30 out of 45 years. No province is ethnically more integrated, or economically dominated by outsiders as Sindh. No ethnic group in Pakistan has as negligible a representation in the armed forces as Sindhi.[54]

What emerged in Pakistan was a new Punjab-urban Sindh power axis, which dominated the Muslim League, the bureaucracy, army and the commercial sector.[55]

Sindhi frustration in the agrarian economy became equally marked. As in Kashmir, the economic structure in Sindh had strong communal

109

connotations: Hindu preponderance in landholding, moneylending and white-collar professions was juxtaposed by pre-eminently Muslim tenants known as Haris. On the eve of Partition the Hindus controlled as much as 2.5 million acres of cultivable land in Sindh.[56] A major impetus behind the enthusiasm of Sindhi Muslim peasants for the Pakistan cause was an expectation that the exit of Hindu landowners would lead to a redistribution of their estates. But this hope was dashed. The Pakistan government preferred to 'award' 800,000 of 1,345,000 acres of land left behind by erstwhile Hindu zamindars to the Muhajirs as a compensation for their loss of property in India. Even the million acres of new land brought under cultivation following the construction of the Kotri and Guddu barrages were made inaccessible to Sindhis. Part of it was 'officially awarded' to non-Sindhi army or civil officers and the rest passed to prosperous Punjabi farmers as a result of open auctions. By 1958, non-Sindhis had secured 153,620 of the 642,460 acres of land made fertile by the Sukkur barrage, while the Sindhis had to content themselves with 123,586 acres.[57] Out of the 1.48 million acres of land made cultivable by the Ghulam Muhammad Barrage, 0.87 million acres were allocated to defence personnel (largely synonymous with Punjabis), tribesmen of Quetta and the Frontier areas and settlers from East Pakistan.[58] The new non-Sindhi landowners were essentially absentee landlords, employing migrant labour for cultivation. A 1985 study estimated that Sindhi landowners occupied only 40 per cent of the province's prime agricultural land. Not unnaturally, this new agrarian scenario was perceived by the Sindhis 'as a threat to an already precarious ethnic balance'.[59] There are also instances – as in Pano Akil (Sukkur) – where Sindhi peasants had to 'vacate' their land in favour of a new cantonment without receiving any compensation.[60] The 1945 Punjab-Sindh agreement on the sharing of Indus water was also more violated than honoured, much to the detriment of the Sindhi peasantry. Even later irrigation works like the Mangla (1967) and Tarbela (1974) dams were widely believed by Sindhis to have been planned in a manner to reduce Sindh's quota of water.[61] Sindhis thus complained of a 'calculated perpetuation of regional inequality'.[62] Oil reserves have been recently discovered in Sindh. But there is an apprehension amongst a large section of Sindhis that they might not benefit from them at all. This fear is rooted in the particular developmental process, characterized by a concentration of the public sector in the

Punjab and the growth of a private sector under the aegis of the Muhajir mercantile community.

Nothing could be more revealing of this tale of economic deprivation that the Sindhis faced in their own province than an incident in the village of Piaro Goth of Dadu district. A typical village with hardly any non-Sindhi population, its character underwent a dramatic transformation when a sugar mill was established and when almost all employees – managerial and labourers alike – were recruited from the Punjab and North-West Frontier Provinces. Even the Imam of the new mosque was brought from the Punjab.[63]

1.3 De-Sindhization of Sindh's Cultural Identity and its Aftermath

Loss of demographic superiority and insufficient access to economic resources, which instilled a segregationist psyche amongst the Sindhis was further strengthened by deliberate attempts of the Pakistani government to undermine Sindhi cultural identity. Traditionally Sindhi culture had been eclectic and syncretic, shaped by Sufism and communal amity. Sindhi identity, as has been aptly remarked, 'is a mixture of different elements, a product of historical evolution'.[64] In the words of a Sindhi nationalist:

> Sindh is an ancient land. Home of some of the oldest of the world's civilizations, it has by its own right a place in the historical annals of the world. After long spells of Buddhist and Hindu periods, it became the home of Muslim Arab civilization in the 8th century AD and for many centuries people of these three faiths lived in relative peace and tranquility. Just as the Buddhist and Hindu cultures flourished together, so did Islam, Buddhism and Hinduism live side by side.[65]

Another Sindhi writer remarked in the same vein:

> Sindhi culture dominated by Muslim mysticism was a strong influence and some of the Hindus were among the best

exponents and interpreters of it. Nowhere else in India did Hindus of such status and calibre convert to Islam till so recently as they did in Sindh.[66]

Sindhi Hindus and Muslims celebrated Diwali together; the Shias and Sunnis in Sindh jointly mourned the martyrdom of Hasan and Hussain; Hindus of the province offered coconuts and 'patashas' to the *tazias* taken out during Muharram; wedding songs of Hindu and Muslim Sindhis were similar and sung in chaste Sindhi.[67] In fact, Sindhi Hindus still recall how many of their Muslim neighbours were unwilling to let them migrate to India.[68]

Spoken in 1947 by as many as 4.8 million, Sindhi is a mature language with a rich cultural heritage.[69] Sindh had a written script long before the arrival of Arabs and this largely contributed to the growth of a rich Sindhi literature.[70] Under the British Raj the Sindhis could retain their language both as a court language and medium of instruction in schools. Not only did all inhabitants of Sindh – Gujratis, Parsis, Christians, Hindus and Muslims – speak Sindhi, but Sindhi literature was itself enriched by contributions from Parsis, Christians and Boras.[71] This cultural efflorescence, unmatched in neighbouring provinces of British India, imparted a strong feeling of linguistic and cultural identity to the Sindhis. Sindhi pride in their language and literature was aptly expressed by one of their leading intellectuals, Sayid Ghulam Mustafa Shah:

It [Sindhi] is a language the existence of which was known to the Prophet of God. It is a language closest to the Quran... the traditions of the Prophet and the history of Islam. It was the first non-Arab language in which the Quran was translated. It is a language fundamentally drawing its strength, thought, content, and vocabulary and phraseology from the language of the Quran and is best epitomised in the Rasalo of Shah in which Auran is quoted in the most befitting context of Sindhi verse... [Shah Abdul Latif's] poetry in this regard is [a] most beautiful tessellation of philosophy, realism, faith and poetical rendering. To a Sindhi, Shah brings Sindhi verse and Quran as part of his life and faith.[72]

Unfortunately, the founding fathers of Pakistan failed to appreciate the rich legacy of Sindhi culture and language when they opted for

Pan-Pakistanism and adopted Urdu as the medium for cultural assimilation. Although spoken only by 7 per cent of Pakistanis, Urdu became the national language. Justifying this move the country's first Prime Minister Liaqat Ali Khan reiterated as early as February 1948: 'Pakistan is a Muslim state and it must have as its lingua franca the language of the Muslim nation... It is necessary for a nation to have one language and that language can only be Urdu and no other language.'[73] Urdu thus became the *sine qua non* of Pakistani identity. But till 1948 Sindh hardly had an Urdu newspaper worth its name. As late as the 1980s Urdu was the mother tongue of only 15 per cent of Sindh's population. Yet, in the new state of Pakistan, knowledge of Urdu was made mandatory for Sindhi students, although non-Sindhis in Sindh were not obliged to learn Sindhi. Recommending the introduction of Urdu in Sindh, the National Education Commission in its Report of 1959 emphasized:

> Urdu should be introduced as the medium of instruction from class VI from 1963 and should continue progressively in the higher classes. It is necessary to give Urdu the same position in Sindh as in the rest of West Pakistan.[74]

The Federal University of Karachi summarily abolished Sindhi as one of the languages in which examinations could be taken. The High School syllabus was revised in such a way that Sindhi children were left with no other option but to drop either English or their mother language as a subject of studies. In places like Karachi the old Sindhi-medium schools gradually disappeared.[75] While the federal government developed Karachi University as an 'Urdu-speaking University', a lower status was accorded to Sindh University in Hyderabad, which specialized in the cultivation of Sindhi culture. The Urduization policy amply suited the interests of the Urdu-speaking Muhajirs who already considered the Sindhis lesser Muslims and less civilized.

The doyen of Sindhi nationalism G.M. Syed suspected – not perhaps without reason – that the anti-Sindhi cultural policy of the federal government aimed to make the Sindhis 'lose their thousand-years-old language, which was the foundation for their unity... and thereby... forget their thousand years of old separate existence.'[76] The Sindhis naturally resented the Urdu-based unifying cultural process. They

113

ridiculed Urdu as 'Phurdu', which was considered to have 'no roots in Pakistan soil'.[77] To quote Sayid Ghulam Mustafa Shah: 'What we get in Urdu is borrowed thoughts, borrowed sentiments, plagiarized and jejune literature, commonplace and maudlin compilations, nostalgic poetry, sociological wailing and seductive pornography... In Urdu literature real sociological Pakistan does not exist.'[78] The Sindhi language now became for the Sindhis, especially for its middle-class intelligentsia, a symbol of cultural identity.

The feeling of disdain for Sindhi culture, shared by the first generation of Pakistani rulers, was revealed when Liaqat Ali told a delegation led by the Sindh Muslim League President Syed Ali Akbar Shah: 'What is Sindhi culture, except driving donkeys and camels?'[79] A typical Muhajir response to the Sindhi allegation of a systematic discrimination against their culture was assertion of the superiority of Urdu culture. The Muhajirs considered neither the Sindhi *waderas* (feudal lords) nor Sindhi *haris* (peasants) as competent for modern education and professions.[80] Studies have shown how the central government in Pakistan resorted to strict press censorship to stifle the Sindhi language. Officials ignored Sindhi writers and patronized Urdu scholars. Sindhi publications were denied official advertisements and Sindhi radio broadcasts were curtailed. The state controlled electronic media, too, deliberately undermining the use of Sindhi. For a long time Karachi TV allotted only a weekly one-hour slot to Sindhi programmes. Sindhi performing arts and traditional crafts were underrepresented on both TV and radio. Attainments of Sindhi national figures and folk heroes remained unrecognized in official discourses, while Karachi streets were named after Urdu intellectuals who did not even migrate to Pakistan.[81] Sindhi nationalist commentators alleged that while one-fourth of school texts covered indigenous Pakistani cultural attainments, three-fourths were concerned with 'northern India cultural symbols'.[82] All government records and registers – even at the municipality level – which were hitherto kept in Sindhi now came to be printed in Urdu. Even Sindhi signs in official buildings and bus and railway stations were replaced by Urdu. A Muhajir-oriented history of Pakistan was also imposed on the Sindhis. The success of the Pakistan movement was thus attributed to the Muslims of minority provinces in British India, ignoring the contributions of Muslim majority units like Sindh, which was among the first to endorse the demand for a separate Muslim homeland.[83]

Any text that could be interpreted as an expression of Sindhi cultural autonomy was a sufficient ground for its proscription by the federal government. Such prominent Sindhi writers as Amar Jaleel, Ibrahim Joyo, Shaikh Ayaz, Tanveer Abhasi, Najam Abassi, Tariq Ashraf and Rasheed Bhatti were subjected to ill treatment on charges of 'adulterating the ideology of Pakistan'. At one point in 1975 all leading Sindhi periodicals were forced out of circulation. The noted Sindhi analyst Feroz Ahmed himself testified to the difficulties he experienced in publishing his Sindhi monthly *Sanch*.[84] Islamabad's obsession with the fear that Sindhi cultural efflorescence would weaken pan-Pakistanism often reached the heights of absurdity. For instance, in 1975 the Sindh government was made to alter the theme of a conference from 'Sindh Through Centuries' to 'Sindh Through Centuries: a Province of Pakistan'. On this occasion even the list of participants required endorsement from federal intelligence officials. Even the then Prime Minister Zulfiqar Ali Bhutto – otherwise dubbed 'the lion of Sindh' – preferred to stay away from the inaugural ceremony of the conference.

Many scholars speak of a 'cultural genocide' perpetrated upon Sindh by the federal government of Pakistan.[85] This is perhaps an overstatement. But the central government's move to impose a cultural unity from the top was certainly perceived by the Sindhis as an affront to their cultural identity. The Sindhis felt that their language and culture were being made 'peripheral, not only in Pakistan but even in Sindh itself'.[86] In the words of a great Sindhi mind: 'Urdu as a language of Chawk, Aminabad, Channichowk, the battlefield and the mullahs has [a] problematical and uncertain future in Pakistan. The people of Pakistan and democracy will always suffer at its enforcement and currency.'[87] Confronted with this policy of Urduization, the Sindhis tended to fall back upon their 'historical national identification'. The Sindhi cultural spirit came to be well embodied in the opening lines of a popular song: *Sindh ahay amar, Sindh rahndi sada* ('Sindh is immortal, Sindh shall live forever').[88] Within days of the foundation of Pakistan, Jinnah's portraits were removed from Sindhi shops. The language of Muhajirs was ridiculed as 'Urdu-Phurdu' and they were dubbed 'red mouths' on account of their fondness for betel leaf (*pan*).[89]

1.4 The Political Dimension of the Sindh Question

For a variety of historical factors stable democratic institutions failed to develop in Pakistan in the way they did in India.[90] The ruling classes in Pakistan tried to acquire legitimacy in a multi-ethnic society not by creating democratic institutions, but by falling back on a strong and centralized political system. A viable nation-building strategy in Pakistan required 'an ethnic tightrope-walking' to satisfy the aspirations of less privileged ethnic groups. Instead, Pakistan was subjected to an authoritarian polity which sought to impose an Urduized and Islamized national political identity[91] by undermining regional, ethnic and local aspirations and responding to any ethnic dissent by strongarm measures.[92] While a small province like the NWFP had in 1949 two representatives in the federal cabinet, Sindh had only one. In 1993 only four out of 75 diplomats serving abroad were Sindhis; not till the beginning of 1994 could a Sindhi enter the Pakistani Foreign Office.[93] Even Radio Pakistan and leading Urdu and English newspapers were Muhajir-dominated. As early as 1947 Syed had warned:

> The prospect of a unitary Pakistan looms ahead as a terrible nightmare in which the people of Sindh [would be] trampled upon as mere serfs by the more numerous and aggressive outsiders; and it may involve Sindh into a desperately violent struggle, before it can shake itself free from this yoke of outside single domination.[94]

Syed's prophecy turned out to be true. The political roots of the current crisis in Sindh lie in repeated attempts by the federal government to injure Sindh's political identity.

Relations between Sindh and the federal government of Pakistan 'started on the wrong foot' from the very beginning.[95] The central government unhesitatingly ignored the voice of the Sindh legislature and either imposed its own rule or installed puppet governments, ostensibly to guarantee a living space for Muhajirs in the province. In the first two years after independence Sindh received from the federal government financial assistance of not more than Rs. 25 million, while the Punjab's share from the same source was approximately four times that sum. Sindhi identity received a further blow in 1948 when Karachi was

116

separated from Sindh to form the 'federal capital area'. G.M. Syed referred to Sindh's deprivation following this administrative measure:

> The capitalized and revenue assets comprising the financial aspect of Sindh's loss alone amount to more than a hundred *crore* of rupees. [Sindh] had to quit her own palatial Assembly Building, and move herself to the old, rickety Barracks after making them habitable at her own cost: and for being allowed this luxury of a barrack-roof she was called upon to pay and is actually paying rent to the Government of Pakistan. Nearly half of Sindh Chief Court's premises have been, without any consideration for the sanctity of that august institution, unauthorizedly occupied by the Ministry of Commerce, Government of Pakistan, who refuse to pay even their own monthly electricity consumption bills.

According to one estimate although the changed status of Karachi caused Sindh a financial loss of about eight hundred million rupees, federal compensation to Sindh was only around six million rupees. The leading Pakistani journalist M.B. Naqvi, himself a Muhajir resident of Karachi, admitted how Karachi's separation from Sindh was organized at the behest of 'no less a person than Qaid-i-Azam, which left an unhealable wound in Sindhi hearts'.[96]

In 1955 the survival of Sindh as a distinct federal unit was itself endangered when President Ayub Khan's 'one unit' scheme merged the Punjab, Sindh, North-West Frontier Province and Baluchistan into a single administrative unit. This measure benefited the Punjabis, who constituted 56 per cent of the country's populace, but adversely affected other nationalities. While post offices were instructed not to deliver any letter bearing the word Sindh, the Rs. 300 million surplus from the Sindh account was utilized to meet the one billion rupees deficit in the Punjab on the pretext of ensuring uniform national development. A tax was levied on Sindh to spread primary education in rural areas, and 20 *lakhs* of rupees collected in the process were appropriated by the One-Unit administration.[97] Even school and college curricula in Pakistan were framed in a way to convince the younger generation of the need for Islamic nationalism and a centralized state polity.[98] Besides, the Ayub regime (1958–68) – first based on martial law, and then on 'controlled

117

democracy' within a framework of military alliance with Washington – adopted a developmental strategy premised on 'functional inequality' and concentration of wealth, which aggravated uneven development both across regions as well as within provinces.[99] For instance, in Sindh the urban-rural divide was further entrenched when the state promoted investments in Karachi at the cost of schemes for rural uplift. At the same time when 80 per cent of the Pakistan Agricultural Research Council's budget was allocated for Punjab agriculture, Sindh's traditional cotton and fruit productions were made to suffer due to the lack of infra-structure support.[100] Ayub's rule also coincided with the final settlement of Muhajir property claims at the expense of Sindhi peasants.[101] The General even constructed 25,000 dwelling places in Karachi for the underprivileged sections amongst the Muhajirs.[102]

In the face of national resentment, the 'one unit' experiment was withdrawn in 1970, and Karachi once again became a part of Sindh.[103] But the pro-Punjabi and pro-Muhajir state policy continued to impair Sindhi interests. Between 1947 and 1990 the federal government sent abroad 380 Punjabi agricultural scientists for advanced training as against only three from Sindh. The Sindhi-Punjabi ratio in specialized federal offices like the Meteorological Department in 1985 was 5,000 to 23,000.[104] A systematic diversion of river waters for the Punjab handicapped fresh water fisheries and forestry schemes in Sindh, depriving about 1.6 million Sindhi villagers of their traditional occupation between 1980 and 1990. A 1985 incident aptly exposed how Sindh's legal rights were violated. In 1972 the Sindhi government had concluded the Chasma-Jhelum Link Canal (C-J Link Canal) Agreement with the Punjab, which permitted the Punjab government to withdraw the water of the canal only after securing the consent of the Sindh Chief Minister. But the Punjab government allegedly continuously stole water from the canal. Moreover, in 1985 despite water scarcity in Sindh, the Punjab Governor-General Ghulam Gilani and the federal water sharing body (WAPDA) 'forcibly had Sindh's water released for the Punjab', brushing aside Sindhi antagonism: 'To hell with Sindh.'[105] Sindhi anger against the first genera-tion of rulers in Pakistan is aptly expressed by the following quote:

Liaqat laid the foundation of Pakistan on sand. His lapses, fears and nightmares, his metaphysics of hate against the indigenous

118

[people] he eloquently and audaciously demonstrated in every action and decision. All subsequent events, episodes and disasters started with this suspicion and fear.[106]

Some analysts contend that the charge of Punjabi hegemony in Pakistan is a myth since a predominant section within Punjabi society is itself oppressed and exploited. But class exploitation within a nationality does not preclude the possibility of that nationality oppressing other nationalities. Even the exploited classes of the dominant nationality inadvertently benefit from such injustices.[107] It has also been argued that the Punjabi-Muhajir ruling clique that pushed through a distorted nation-building strategy received support from the White House, which found in dictatorial Pakistan 'an encirclement component against the Soviet Union'.[108] Eager to sustain a united Pakistan as a bulwark against Moscow, the USA preferred to share the Pakistani ruling class perception of any ethnic assertion as 'anti-Pakistani and Communist'.[109]

2. CONTOURS OF SINDHI ETHNONATIONALISM

Sindhi ethnonationalists may be categorized as those political actors in Pakistan who seek a cognisance of Sindhi collective identity. Their assertion of identity developed in four distinct phases: (a) from 1947 till the break-up of Pakistan in 1971; (b) 1972 to the execution of Zulfiqar Ali Bhutto in 1977; (c) 1977 to the death of General Zia-ul-Haq in 1988; and (d) from the post-Zia period to the present times. The following section identifies the shifts and turns in ethnic politics in Sindh.

2.1 The Initial Response

The first years of Sindhi ethnic politics was marked by what has been aptly described as 'the emergence of an 'us and them' syndrome' between the Sindhis and the Muhajir-Punjabi combine.[110] The period witnessed the emergence of a number of Sindhi ethnonationalist groups. But it was G.M. Syed's Jiye Sindh, established in 1967, which gave Sindhi ethnonationalism a sharp focus. Initially, the Jiye Sindh movement did not have a monolithic organization and represented a broad spectrum of organizations ranging from such cultural forums as Bazam-i-Soofyan-i-Sindh, Sindh Adabi Sangat, Sindh Students' Cultural Organization and Sindh Azad Students' Organization to leftist political bodies like the Sindh Hari Party. Syed's discourse was premised on the notion of a 'true federal Pakistan', which would ensure maximum provincial autonomy, restricting the authority of the central government only to national subjects like defence, foreign affairs and currency.[111] To undo the injustice perpetrated on his province Syed demanded recognition of Sindhi as the 'sole provincial language' and creation of a one-fourth quota for Sindhis in Pakistan's bureaucracy and army. During this period Sindhi ethnic politics developed primarily along constitutional lines with a decisively moderate tone.

2.2 Sindhi Politics 1971–1977: The Prelude to Militancy

The emergence of Bangladesh in 1971 occasioned a new debate in Pakistan on a restructuring of the national polity. The less developed regions of Sindh, Baluchistan and North-West Frontier Provinces now raised the demand for constitutional devolution of power to the provinces. At this juncture Zulfikar Ali Bhutto's Pakistan People's Party (hereafter PPP) stormed into the political centre stage of Pakistan with the slogan: 'Islam is our faith. Democracy is our polity. Socialism is our economy. All powers to the people.' Zulfikar's political agenda kindled new hopes of political justice for the dissatisfied ethnic groups in Pakistan. Himself hailing from Sindh, Bhutto adopted symbols and slogans of the Jiye Sind Movement,[112] admitted the legitimacy of Sindhi anger and sought to assuage it – first during his tenure as President and then as the Prime Minister of the country. Large estates of non-Sindhis in Sindh were confiscated and redistributed to landless Sindhi peasants; Muhajir commercial enterprises in the province were either placed under strict surveillance or nationalized. Sindhis were awarded crucial official posts; special federal grants were released for the development of villages in Sindh.[113] Bhutto also introduced a regional quota-system for recruitment to federal bureaucracy – 50 per cent for the Punjab, 11.5 per cent for NWFP, 7.6 per cent for urban Sindh, 11.4 per cent for rural Sindh and 3.5

per cent for Baluchistan. The distinction between the advanced predominantly Muhajir urban areas and the relatively backward Sindhi rural areas in Sindh was adopted to introduce a policy of positive discrimination in favour of Sindhis against the Muhajirs.[114] It seemed that Sindh 'was finally receiving its due share in terms of political power as well as resource allocation'.[115] But this was only a lull before the storm.

Zulfikar's image as the champion of provincial rights and aspirations was destroyed once he started toying with constitutional experiments. In 1973, Pakistan was given a new constitution based on parliamentary democracy and a fair degree of provincial autonomy.[116] In the new spirit of political toleration Bhutto had honoured the electoral mandate to allow the formation of governments by the two opposition parties – the National Awami Party (hereafter NAP) and the Jamiat-Ulema-e-Islam (JUI) – respectively in North-West Frontier Province and Baluchistan.[117] Unfortunately, this period proved to be for Pakistan only a short breathing space of political democracy. Haunted by a fear of increasing popularity of the NAP and JUI, Bhutto dismissed the opposition-run governments in Baluchistan and North-West Frontier Province on the pretext of their involvement with 'foreign conspiracy'.[118] The constitution itself was amended to disempower the judiciary and correspondingly to strengthen the executive. Bhutto's political opponents were silenced on charges of separatist politics. Pakistan was once again reverting back to a centralized polity.

Provincial aspirations ignited by Zulfikar's initial political pronouncements could not be, however, restrained by his own betrayal of the cause. Baluchistan and North-West Frontier Province came to be plagued by insurgency, and Sindhi ethnonationalists fraternized with these outbreaks as a part of the common struggle against overt centralization.[119] All these presaged in Sindhi politics an assertion of Sindhi identity over national identity. It was in this context that the Sindh legislature under the leadership of Chief Minister Mumtaz Ali Bhutto (a cousin of Prime Minister Bhutto) enacted on 7 July 1972 the Language Act to accord Sindhi the status of sole official language of the province. Government employees in Sindh were now required to learn Sindhi within a stipulated period of three months. To undo the underrepresentation of Sindhis in provincial education and civil service a quota system was also introduced.

Such measures, particularly the Language Act, struck at the root of

Muhajir pre-eminence in Sindh. The Muhajirs took the fight to the street, cities like Hyderabad and Karachi degenerating into sites of 'language riots' between the supporters (Sindhis) and opponents (Muhajirs) of the Language Act. A correspondent of *The Dawn* (11 July 1972) describes a typical scene:

> Karachi, normally a busy commercial and industrial centre, was virtually deserted today and barricades and bonfires blocked the streets. The few cars and taxis still circulating had to dodge through barricades of rubble and clusters of youths waving and screaming. Occasionally gunshots rang out. Cars were flying black flags and drivers wore tags of black cloth.

Muhajir students ransacked and burnt the library of the prestigious Institute of Sindhology.[120] On 8 July 1972 the Urdu newspaper *Jang* carried provocative articles, condemning the Language Bill as a proclamation for the death of Urdu.[121] The Muhajir resentment was such that it was not 'an uncommon scene in the Muhajir homes in Karachi to see parents shouting at their children to turn off that *bakvass* (nonsense/rubbish)' if they watched a Sindhi television programme.[122] Meanwhile, the Jiye Sindh activists made bonfires of Urdu newspapers and defiled pictures of Iqbal. Sindh Sujag Jathas (Sindh Awakening Squads) were formed to carry the message of Jeya Sindh to the rural areas.[123] The following quote aptly reflects the Sindhi perception of the language controversy:

> If Urdu is accepted as an official language of Sindh, the rights of Sindhis will be undermined. As soon as Urdu is accepted as the second language of Sindh, it would amount to accepting the [existence] of two nationalities in the province. And if this is accepted then the Sindhis' claim that Sindh belongs to them is wrong... In this manner Urdu-speakers will create a Muhajirstan.[124]

Some leftists suspected that 'Urdu extremism' was being fomented by Muhajir industrialists to keep the working class in Sindh divided.[125] The government estimated that there were two deaths and 319 people wounded from Sindhi-Muhajir clashes. Property was damaged to the tune of Rs. 1,671,427.[126]

Bhutto's intervention to stem the tide of violence assumed the form of an ordinance prohibiting discrimination of government servants on grounds of language, and recognizing both Urdu and Sindhi as official languages of Sindh for the next 12 years.[127] This action was perceived by many in Sindh to be a compromise with the Muhajirs.[128] Zulfiqar now even dismissed some of his senior Sindhi officials and resorted to such repressive laws as the Defence of Pakistan Rules to stifle Sindhi dissent.[129] All these inevitably disheartened Sindhi nationalists who were subsequently driven along the extremist path.

Perhaps the first manifestation of Sindhi militancy was seen in June 1972 with G.M. Syed renaming his erstwhile Sindh United Front – established to confront Ayub's One-Unit Scheme – as the Jiye Sindh Mahaj.[130] Disillusioned with attempts to mitigate Sindh's miseries by working within Pakistan's political system, Syed now called for the creation of a separate Sindhu Desh (Land of the River Indus). The fundamentals of Sindhu Desh laid out by Syed were:[131]

(a) Recognition of the principles of secularism, socialism, democracy and nationalism.

(b) Redistribution of agricultural land from non-Sindhis to Sindhis.

(c) Control of trade, commerce, banks, insurance and government agencies by 'Sindhi speaking and permanently settled people in Sindh'.

(d) Checking of immigration to Sindh and expulsion of all those resisting absorption into Sindhi society.

(e) Quotas for Sindhis in government jobs.

(f) Recognition of Sindhi as the sole national and official language and cancellation of citizenship for those having no knowledge of the language.

(g) Depriving non-Sindhis of the property left behind by Hindus and Sikhs and its distribution to Sindhi Muslims or those Sindhi Hindus who would prefer to return to their motherland.

(h) Prohibition of the institutions of Pirdom and tribal headmanship.

(i) Guarantee for a strict legal separation of religion and state.

(j) Nationalization of all means of production.

(k)   Stress on heavy industries.

(l)   Implementation of an equitable land reform scheme.

(m) Provision of greater role for women in public life on a footing of equality with men.

(n)   Official patronization of Sindhi culture.

(o)   Promotion of friendship with India, Afghanistan, the Arab world and the Soviet Union.

Syed was probably contemplating a re-enactment of another Bangladesh drama.[132] To quote him:

> The reason was the continuous struggle to get the rights of Sindhis accepted by the authorities. When they were neglected, we went on escalating our demands… We said Sindhis were a separate nation. We insisted that we have a separate culture. We were not given proper rights. So we demanded the right of self-determination. So from the idea of Jiye Sindh, we have reached the conclusion that without the breaking up of Pakistan and the formation of Sindh as an independent country and a member of the United Nations, no other solution is possible.[133]

In an interview with Mary Ann Weaver, Syed categorically stated: 'There is no room for compromise. Sindh must become an independent State.'[134] Syed reminded his followers that even under Zulfikar Ali Bhutto Sindh contributed three-fourths of national revenues, but not more than 1 per cent of it was spent for the welfare of the province.[135] For Syed, Bhutto was nothing more than an 'agent of the Punjabi-Muhajir imperialistic domination of Sindh'.[136] Syed was astonished: '… President Bhutto, in his eagerness to retain the Presidency, has joined hands with the enemies of Sindh and other vested interests whose prime object is to perpetuate exploitation of Sindh.'[137]

In 1976, he even contemplated the waging of a guerrilla war to establish Sindhu Desh. Thanks to the campaigns of Jeya Sindh Student's Federation and Sindh Graduates' Association, the popularity of Syed amongst the Sindhi youth and students soared to such heights that it was virtually impossible to criticize him in any campus in Sindh. This was the time when Sindh's young generation was captivated by Syed's treatises.

They included *Struggle for New Sindh, A Nation in Chains* and *Jeen Ditlo Ahe Moum* ('As I have seen'), which criticized religious funda-mentalism, *Paighaam-e-Latif*, which reintroduced Shah Abdul Latif Bhitai's ideals of humanistic nationalism, *Naye Sindh Jaye Jiddojehad* ('Struggle for a new Sindh'), which recaptured the author's parliamentary struggle in pre-Partition India, *Heenyar Pakistan Khey Tuttan Khappey* ('Now Pakistan should disintegrate'), which advocated dismemberment of Pakistan, and *Sindhu Desh*, which outlined the blueprint of an inde-pendent Sindh.

Of course, Syed's organization was not alone in crusading for Sindhi rights. Rasool Bux Paleejo's Sindh Awami Tehreek was, for example, a significant force in Sindhi subnational politics. But the difference between this organization and Syed's Jiye Sindh Mahaz was essentially strategic. While Paleejo argued for combining the political movement for greater Sindhi autonomy with an agrarian struggle for land reforms, Syed preferred to work for socio-economic reconstruction only after attaining the desired political change. One is reminded of the debate between Gandhi and the Left during India's freedom movement.

2.3 1977–1988: The Years of Sindhi Separatist Turmoil

The overthrow of the Pakistan People's Party (PPP) government by a military junta led by the Punjabi General Zia-ul-Haq on 5 July 1977, and the subsequent execution of Zulfikar Ali Bhutto, presaged wide-spread ethnic violence in Sindh. For the popular Sindhi psyche the military coup was a Punjabi-Muhajir affront on Sindh. In the words of a perceptive Pakistani journalist: 'When Zia overthrew, imprisoned, and executed him, Bhutto became in Sindhi eyes a monument to Punjabi injustice.'[138] Ironically, the same Bhutto who had incurred the wrath of Sindhi nationalists in the later part of his regime now became the new symbol of Sindhi resistance to Punjabi-Muhajir hegemony. A minister in Zia's cabinet himself acknowledged this fact when he 'saw Bhutto in the face of every Sindhi'.[139]

General Zia's anti-Sindh activities – provoked by a general Sindhi sym-pathy for the Bhutto cause – added fuel to the fire of Sindhi ethnic poli-tics. High-ranking Sindhi government officials were either marginalized or removed to make way for followers of Jamaat-e-Islami, who happened to be Muhajirs. Preferential quotas were introduced in the bureaucracy, the military and the public sector for the benefit of Punjabis and Pakhtuns. According to one estimate the Sindhi presence in the federal bureaucracy under Zia was only 4 per cent.[140] Meanwhile, the Punjab won most of the new industrial investments.[141] While the central government during Zia's tenure reportedly earned 80 per cent of its revenue from Sindh, hardly 2 per cent of it was diverted for developmental schemes in that province.[142] Besides, the move to construct the Kalabagh dam on the river Indus incited anger in Sindh and North-West Frontier Province.[143] Sindh – already discriminated against by the Mangla, Tarbala, Chasma and Rawal irrigation projects – now suspected that the Kalabagh dam, too, had been designed to provide additional water and electricity for the Punjab at the cost of converting two million acres of arable land in southern Sindh into a desert.[144] These years also witnessed a substantial rise of unemployment among the Sindhi youth who ascribed their economic plight to the non-Sindhi monopoly over their provincial resources.[145]

General Zia-ul-Haq introduced, to use a Gramscian term, a 'Bonapartist-Caesarist type' of authority.[146] He won the confidence of Pakistan's traditional feudal class by putting into storage Bhutto's proposed agricultural income tax, and advocating the idea of partyless elections. Simultaneously, his policy of selective denationalization assured the industrialists that they were in 'safe hands'.[147] For Sindhi ethnonationalists, the last straw on the camel's back came with Zia's policy of Islamization.[148] The General's idea of Nizam-i-Islam[149] was incompatible with Sindh's Sufi-based syncretic Islam. Sindhis now increasingly perceived the Punjabis, Muhajirs and Pakhtuns more as agents of 'domestic colonialism' rather than as a member of the same Islamic *ummah* (community).[150] Zia's drive for Islamization thus impelled the Sindhi literary, cultural and social organizations to demonstrate the uniqueness of Sindhi language, literature and culture.[151] To quote a contemporary comment:

> The youth and the people of Sindh will not condone or stand any nonsense of prevarication and progression. The youth and the people of Sindh are charged with anger, bitterness and even

revolt... Today the Sindhi leadership both in office and out of office is under examination and on trial. There is no place for pusillanimous collaborators and quislings in Sindh any more.[152]

Sindhi women, too, became involved in the new struggle to retain Sindhi identity.[153] The first ever Sindhi Women's Conference was held in 1982.

Contradictions between the military regime and Sindhi consciousness was also manifest in the enthusiastic Sindhi response, especially in the rural areas, to the Movement for the Restoration of Democracy (MRD) that had been initiated by the PPP and other democratic parties in 1983 to demand the holding of national elections under the 1973 constitution.[154] Many analysts describe Sindhi support for the Movement as 'largely spontaneous' over which the traditional Sindhi leaders had little control.[155] While the Movement in cities generally assumed the form of protest marches and boycott of law courts, it sparked off considerable radicalism in villages.[156] Militant expressions of ethnic and regional sentiments in rural Sindh naturally invited intense military reprisals. General Zia mobilized about 45,000 troops in whose hands between 300 and 600 Sindhi civilians lost their lives.[157] By September 1986 the number of Sindhi political prisoners rose to 10,000.[158] Student leaders owing allegiance to the PPP like Iqbal Hisbani became victims of unprovoked police shooting.[159] Often the army worked in close cooperation with Zia's political supporters.[160] In the words of M.J. Akbar:

> Within days the whole [of] Sindh was on fire, with villagers in the interior challenging often violently any image of martial authority they could find. Politicians were lynched, soldiers attacked, in one symbolic gesture, dogs were let loose with 'Zia' painted on their bodies. It was a spontaneous and even inspiring display of the people's disgust.[161]

Camps established for what was widely perceived as the 'Punjabi army' remained in Sindhi eyes 'colonial outposts in defence of distant interests'.[162] Writing about the intensification of Sindhi anger against Islamabad following the military crackdown, the noted Pakistani journalist Irshadul Haque Haqani was confident that: 'If a referendum was restored in Sindh, probably 95.8 per cent [of] Sindhis would prefer to opt out of Pakistan.'[163]

Order could be restored in Sindh only after four months, but only by driving Sindhi nationalists underground. The period occasioned a new spate of Sindhi nationalist literature and the rise of a number of political groups whose goals ranged from provincial autonomy to independence for Sindh.[164] Such organizations as the Sindhi Adabi Conference, Sindh Sujan Sabha and Sindhi Boli Sath kept alive the demand for increased use of Sindhi language for official purposes. Mention may be also made of Sujag Bar Tahreek ('Movement for the Awakening of Children'), which 'carried banners in support of Sindh'.[165] Benazir Bhutto was not wide of the mark when she admitted: 'The army does not realize the depth of the people's resentment. The whole of rural Sindh has been revolutionized.'[166]

It is, however, important to note that the legendary Sindhi nationalist G.M. Syed distanced himself from the MRD, arguing that the agitation was designed to reinstate the Bhutto dynasty in Islamabad. Syed noted in this connection: 'PPP has no principle, while Mahaz is not ready to give up its own line of action whatever may be the circumstances.'[167] After losing the 1970 elections Syed is said to have lost his faith in parliamentary democracy[168] and even came to prefer imposition of martial law since oppressive military regimes would ultimately strengthen the separatist movement in Sindh.'[169]

Syed's opposition to the MRD, was not shared by his colleagues like Hamida Khuro, who, with the help of the Jeya Sindh Students Federation and Sindh Graduates Association, mobilized a considerable section of the Sindhi middle class to join the struggle against the junta.[170] Besides, Rasool Bux Paleejo's Sindh Awami Tehreek developed a parallel support base amongst Sindhi ethnonationalists. Unlike the Jeya Sindh this party propounded the idea of a socialist Sindh, aiming to telescope the political and social transformations in Sindh. Its main constituency comprised the peasantry, working class and students; it condemned G.M. Syed as a 'representative of the feudal class'.[171] Another party formed in this period to voice Sindhi identity was the Sindhi-Baluchistan-Pakhtun Front. Established in 1985 by Mumtaz Bhutto and Hafeez Pirzada, it campaigned for a confederal system in the country.[172] Three other Sindhi nationalist groups also need to be mentioned: the Jamiat-e-Ulema-e-Sindh, Sindh Sagar Party and the Jamhoori Tehrik formed by the former Communist Jam Saqi. But their influence was limited. An international platform for Sindhi nationalists was also created through the organization of World Sindhi Congress.[173]

Nevertheless, Zia promptly took advantage of divisions within Sindhi nationalists to counteract the challenge to his authority. He foiled the MRD movement, imposed an agricultural tax (*Usher*) upon anti-Islamabad Sindhi landlords and ousted pro-PPP Sindhi officials from central and provincial governments. He then held a referendum in support of the Islamic character for Pakistan and in January 1985 called for partyless elections to the National Assembly. To demonstrate an apparent concern for Sindh, the General even appointed a little-known Sindhi, Mohammed Khan Junejo, as the Prime Minister. Zia, however, later fell out with Junejo, which caused the latter's dismissal in May 1988. In August of that year the General himself died in a plane crash.

Incidentally, the days of the MRD coincided with an abnormal rise of rural banditry in Sindh, which was widely believed to be a political ramification of the ethnic strife. *The Herald* of July 1986 reported 250 cases of abduction by dacoits during the last three months in the districts of Nawabshah, Dadu and Larkana. The victims of dacoities belonged to a broad social spectrum – landowners, politicians, civil servants, judges and ordinary villagers. A leading journalist noted how 'well-known names in Karachi city and interior Sindh are in constant fear of being kidnapped. Traders of the rural areas, government officers, doctors, lawyers, engineers, et al., let alone the tycoons of industry and business, are potential victims, as are zamindars.'[174]

Opinions differ about the social background of the bandits. But they generally comprised disgruntled political activists and educated unemployed youth.[175] Most of these dacoits are believed to have been Sindhi activists in the MRD who took refuge in jungles to escape from military repression and eventually resorted to banditry. Dacoits who had become household names such as Kashmir Khan, Karri (Blacki) Machhi, Nadir Jaskani, Mitho Kasai and Haider Khoso, Janu Arain, Alam Choliani, Hassan Chandio, Dadan Chano and Noor Jehan Magsi allegedly had strong Sindhi nationalist connections.[176] Political escapees from jails, too, fuelled the ranks of dacoits.[177] Easy availability of arms following Zia's conversion of Pakistan into an American front-line in the Afghan war, the presence of armed mujahedin and widespread drug traffic in cities like Karachi were further contributing factors in sustaining the climate of violence in Sindh.[178] But in many instances the dacoits received political patronage from the military junta to meet a dual objective: (a) to keep

Sindhis preoccupied with local disorders so as to leave them with little time to join anti-state political agitations; and (b) to maintain a climate of political disorder which could be used as a pretext for maintaining the federal military presence in the province.[179] The Sindh Hari Committee reported how: '...innocent villagers in the name of anti-dacoit operations had been maltreated. Villagers had been involved in false and fabricated cases.'[180] The Indian observer M.B. Naqvi also agreed that Islamabad's deployment of the army against dacoities 'was a political ploy... intended to brutally suppress the opposition in the province'.[181] Not unnaturally, army actions against dacoits were largely perceived by Sindhis as a Punjabi-Pathan plot against them.[182]

The other aspect of ethnic politics in Sindh during the Zia period was open clashes between Sindhis and Muhajirs. The accentuation of this conflict was partly related to the establishment of the first political organization of Muhajirs – the Muhajir Qaumi Mahaj (MQM) on 18 March 1984. While the Muhajirs previously worked either through the Jamaat-e-Islami or Muslim League, the MQM now provided them with their own platform for organized politics. The institutional origin of MQM lies in the All Pakistan Muhajir Students' Organization, which had been formed in 1978 to safeguard the interest of Muhajir students in the face of 'perceived tyranny and violence'.[183] It was the initiative of these student leaders that led to the formation of the MQM.[184] Some Sindhi observers suspected that the MQM was actually sponsored by the federal government to foil the possibility of a united opposition in Sindh against Islamabad.[185] Many even found in the establishment of the MQM the joint hand of General Zia and the US Central Intelligence Agency to accelerate 'the ethnic polarization of Pakistan's politics, as a part of a larger strategy of disorienting the political process in the country'.[186] Strong links between the MQM and Inter-Services Intelligence (ISI) were also hinted at.[187]

Led by the charismatic Altaf Hussain, the MQM called for recognition of Muhajirs as the fifth nationality in Pakistan and demanded a separate province for Muhajirs with Karachi as its capital.[188] The Muhajirs now replaced their earlier emphasis on Islamized nationhood by an exclusive preoccupation with Muhajir interests.[189] 'We want our own province, our own chief minister, our government, our own police' – this became the main slogan of the MQM.[190] That the MQM's political objective increasingly turned sectarian was exemplified by Altaf Hussain's own admission: 'we do not support anything which doesn't contain the word Muhajir'.[191]

Some commentators have cited the 'non-elite character of the MQM leadership', and refer to the party's bid to present itself as an organization of the poor.[192] Yet, the fascist nature of the MQM has been widely commented upon. Composed mostly of middle and lower middle classes (petty bourgeoisie, self-employed and service workers) the party has a 'clear hierarchical order', sanctified by a strong notion of 'order and discipline'.[193] In the words of an observer:

> the MQM tried to raise a strictly disciplined organization with an unambiguous chain of command. Its hierarchy was purposely kept highly centralized and openness in policy decisions was strongly discouraged. Internal criticism was discouraged, a tendency which is also reflected in its politics outside the organization.[194]

Altaf Hussain is presented as 'a cult figure (*pir* or religious divine, *quaid* or leader) who demands absolute loyalty'.[195] Currently in exile in London, he uses satellite technology to address his supporters. The organization 'is populist and uses terror and appeases its people interchangeably'.[196]

With an estimated ten to twelve thousand trained cadrs, the MQM has a three-tier organizational structure: the Markaz (centre), the zones and sectors. All members – however important in public life – have to follow party dictates. Membership of the party is granted after considerable scrutiny and, once someone is a member, he or she remains bound by party decisions even on such private matters as family feuds or marriage. The MQM's financial support comes primarily from the Muhajir middle class and commercial elite. It organizes an effective propaganda campaign through rallies, posters and pamphlets. The party also has an armed wing – the Black Tigers – described by many as 'a death squad' for the Muhajir cause. The MQM maintains a strong connection with religious fundamentalist parties like Jamaat-e-Islami and Jamiata-ul-Ulema-e-Pakistan.[197] *Bhattas* (forcible donations) are collected from business units, multinational corporations and business magnates to ensure financial solvency for the party. The MQM's first success in institutional politics was recorded in 1987 when it swept the municipal elections in Karachi, enabling the 28-year-old MQM activist Farooq Sattar

131

to become the youngest mayor of the city. The next national elections elevated the MQM's position to the country's third largest party.

Rapid growth of the MQM is often linked to its adoption of the politics of violence. But this causal connection appears too far-fetched.[198] For the anti-MQM formations could be as violent as the MQM itself. Indeed, the MQM gained part of its respectability amongst its constituency by performing an effective social role. Through a range of institutional networks it helped the Muhajir community in such matters as admissions to educational institutions, access to credit agencies, financial assistance for widows, construction of dwelling units and improving sanitation facilities for the needy, and even arranging marriages for the poor. The MQM advocated land reforms and organized free bazaars and eye hospitals for the disadvantaged sections of the Muhajir community.[199] The MQM thus began performing for its members many of the functions that the state was technically supposed to discharge.[200]

The deepening Muhajir-Sindhi cleavage found expression in a series of open confrontations. On 30 September 1988 alone 250 Muhajirs were allegedly gunned down in Hyderabad by the followers of the Jiye Sindh leaders Qadir Magsi and Janu Araon.[201] In two days of October of the same year at least 400 lives were lost in clashes between the two communities.[202] April 1989 witnessed a major Muhajir-Sindhi conflagration – erupting first in Hyderabad and then spreading to Karachi and Nawabshah. About 50 people reportedly died from this spate of violence. 'Unfriendly press' was a favourite target of MQM violence. Offices of *Jang* were ransacked and 'partial' journalists assaulted. Suspected traitors to the Muhajir cause were abducted and tortured. To quote a contemporary observer:

> The recurring violence of the last month has had a highly negative effect on the forces of reason. The moderates among the various political groups or in the Sindhi- and Urdu-speaking communities appear to be losing ground, and the new wave of chauvinism appears to be creating more extremist pressure groups within already militant ethno-political organizations.[203]

Protesting against the anti-Muhajir bias of the provincial police force, Muhajir leaders demanded the imposition of martial rule in Sindh.

Slogans like *Martial law lagao, humain bachao* ('impose martial law and save us') were raised and pictures of General Zia displayed. *The Herald* (June 1990, p. 38) identified the 'new disturbing aspect' of this outburst:

> the use of even more sophisticated weaponry by the rival sides – including the use of rocket launchers – and more grisly methods of killing, such as by strangulation, lynching and hanging. There was also a chilling pattern to most of the killings: people were killed not for their involvement in the violence or because they came in the way, but for the simple reason that they happened to be Sindhi or Muhajir.

2.4 The Post-Zia Era Imbroglio

The elections following General Zia's death in the plane crash of 11 August 1988 returned the PPP to power both in Islamabad and Sindh. Legislative elections in Sindh, however, confirmed the ethnic polarization in Sindhi politics: the PPP retained Sindhi votes and the MQM maintained its appeal in the Muhajir-dominated urban areas like Karachi and Hyderabad. Benazir Bhutto seemed to have appropriated the Sindhi cause. Bhutto herself had condemned the Muhajirs as 'traitors' and 'anti-nationals', remarking: 'they [Muhajirs] do not have the tears you have in your eyes, they do not have the same blood you have in your veins and they do not have the love for Pakistan which you have in your heart.'[204] She now appointed Sindhis to crucial government offices and relegated prominent Muhajir civil servants to the backbench.[205]

Nevertheless, functioning under the careful eye of the army and the strong opposition front of Islami Jamhoori Ittihad (Islamic Democratic Alliance, IJI) led by Nawaz Sharif, the Benazir Bhutto government in Islamabad could not afford the risk of restructuring the country's political system.[206] Besides, Bhutto lost her credibility amongst sections of Sindhi politicians when she struck an alliance with the MQM in the National Assembly in a desperate bid to retain power. This alliance did not survive long, largely because Bhutto was unable to meet such Muhajir demands as repatriation of the remaining Biharis from Bangladesh, and

introduction of Muhajir quotas for civil service jobs.[207] Meanwhile, the
MQM openly expressed its 'sympathy' for Punjabi and Pakhtun settlers
in interior Sindh. Amidst heightening tensions between the PPP and MQM,
the latter withdrew from the provincial government in May 1989. This
was widely perceived as a 'grim indicator of the ethno-political division
of Sindh which may ultimately lead to an administrative bifurcation of
the province'.[208] Many commentators believe that the army actually
conspired to cement an MQM-IJI front.[209]

In the aftermath of the breakdown of the PPP-MQM alliance, street
violence between Muhajirs and Sindhis once again became common.
Sindhi-Muhajir outbreaks assumed many forms:

> Sometimes a traffic accident triggers off [a] clash between
> two communities, at other times one group fires on the other
> who retaliates. An incident in Shah Faisal Colony echoes in
> Liaquatabad and a minor fight in Banaras Chowk may reverber-
> ate in Ajmer Nagri or Orangi Town. Universities and Colleges
> invariably respond with violence and trigger-happy students are
> let loose.[210]

Karachi and Hyderabad particularly degenerated into ethnic enclaves,
the communally segregated slums or Katchi Abadies constituting the
focal points of violence.[211] In May 1990 ethnic violence in Hyderabad –
provoked by the federal government's arrest of the Sindhi nationalist
leader Dr Qadir Magsi – took a toll of at least 130 lives.[212] Sindhis retaliated by attacking the Muhajirs. It became unsafe for Muhajirs to even
travel on the highways in Sindh. On 27 May 1990, an apparently
peaceful demonstration of Muhajir women and children in Hyderabad
to demand restoration of the water supply was brutally crushed by the
Sindh government police. This in turn incited Muhajir violence against
Sindhis living in Karachi. An observer recounted:

> The once-thriving mandis are all but deserted. Houses owned by
> Sindhis in Muhajir-dominated areas like the Pucca Qila are licked
> and abandoned; political parties compete with each other to dem-
> onstrate that their side has the larger refugee camps, consisting
> of displaced people either from the city centre or the smaller

towns around Hyderabad. Army and police check-posts at every major intersection and all entry-exit points of the city hold up traffic to search for weapons. Gossip and rumour-mongering dominate everyday life… the air of tension and apprehension is almost palpable… [The residents] recall times when Resham Gali and other bazars were alive with lights and noise till late at night, as if remembering some distant past. Today, only the occasional stray dog or army patrol stirs in the city centre's main streets after nightfall.[213]

The following quote recaptures similar incidents of violence in riot-torn Karachi:

In less than a decade Karachi has evolved from a bustling, developing metropolis to a city wrecked by violence and crime. And no one, nowhere is safe. A six-year-old girl plays in Clifton Park with her parents one evening; within seconds, a random bullet from a sniper irrevocably changes the family's life. The bullet hits the little girl and she becomes yet another statistic in the city's hydra-headed war with itself.

A nine-year-old boy is kidnapped. His parents cannot pay the ransom. He returns home weeks later, ostensibly unharmed. But there is a jagged scar on his midriff. A doctor's examination reveals that one of the boy's kidneys has been removed. The ransom has been paid.

In Defence Society, two teenage sisters are doing their home-work on one lazy Friday afternoon as their parents take a siesta upstairs. The front door is suddenly wrenched apart as three armed men enter. One of the girls screams and is soundly beaten by one of the intruders with the butt of his rifle. She falls uncon-scious. The other girl is grabbed by two other men who proceed to rip her clothes off, their intent clear. Providence is in the girl's favour. Their father awakens to the noise, grabs his gun and charges downstairs, bellowing his outrage. The intruders flee.

Eight women are engaged in an amicable conversation one evening… The focus of conversation is crime and violence. Every single woman… has a horror story to relate: burglary, street

violence, rape. If it hasn't happened to her, it's happened to a
sister, a neighbour, a friend.[214]

Ethnic polarization in Sindh reached such heights that elected parliamentary representatives of one ethnic group had no 'legitimacy' for people
of another community. Clashes in Sindh also occasioned considerable
demographic unsettlement, although no reliable data is readily available.
But the following report is illustrative:

> Each violent incident in Hyderabad or the interior of Sindh only
> speeds up the process of migration. Family after family belong-
> ing to Sindh's Urdu speaking community has moved from
> Larkana, Dadu, Thetta, Badin and other areas and a substantial
> Sindhi-speaking population has left Latifabad and parts of
> Hyderabad in search of safer abodes.[215]

Ethnic strife also resulted in a significant upsurge in crime. In Karachi
the number of kidnapping cases for ransom rose from only two in 1985
to 91 in 1990, the incidence of murders increased from 220 in 1985 to
585 in 1990, and instances of motor vehicle thefts surged from 1,553 in
1985 to 8,091 in 1990.[216] Even G.M. Syed referred to the 'criminalization
of Sindhi nationalist movement'.[217] Amidst deteriorating law and order
the PPP government was dissolved in August 1990.

Parliamentary elections held in October 1990 were widely believed
to have been rigged by the IJI. Under the new IJI ministry Pakistan
once again reverted to a Punjabi-dominated polity, betraying pro-
military leanings and a commitment to an 'amalgative' policy of ethnic
management. Meanwhile, in Sindh, too, the IJI-MQM combination
formed the government, although the PPP had emerged as the single
largest party in the legislature. The new regime in Sindh used the
Punjabi-dominated security agencies to curb Sindhi nationalist dissent
and ensure Sindhi underrepresentation in government offices. But this
coalition government in Sindh lost power in June 1992 in the wake
of MQM leader Altaf Hussain's bid 'to operate independently of his
erstwhile military mentors'.[218] 'Street politics' of the MQM reached a
climactic point when party workers assaulted and kidnapped an army
officer, Major Kaleem Ahmad. The incident presaged the Pakistan

army's 'Operation Clean-up Sindh' on 19 June 1992. An estimated
30,000 military and paramilitary personnel were inducted in Sindh who
committed atrocities on the civilian population on the pretext of
combating insurgency. Leading MQM personnel were declared 'proclaimed offenders'; many other activists of that party went underground
to escape arrests. MQM supremo Altaf Hussain himself was implicated
in some 32 criminal cases, which made him seek exile in London. The
army claimed to have unearthed 22 MQM torture cells and an MQM
map of proposed independent Urdu Desh to be curved out of parts of
Sindh, comprising Karachi, Hyderabad and some coastal areas.[219]

Meanwhile, such events as the celebration of the 89th birthday of
G.M. Syed on 17 January 1992 in Karachi's historic Nishtar Park over-
looking Jinnah's mausoleum evoked strong Sindhi nationalist sentiments.
In this rally 7,000 Jiye Sindh activists waved the hatchet-bearing red
Jiye Sindh flag, and the Sindhi nationalist veteran cut a cake representing a map of Pakistan out of which he carefully detached Sindh amidst
the chanting of *Sindhi Desh ji dharti totay pahanjo cees newayan,
mittee mathey layaon – Sindhu Desh jee dhanti*[220] and *G.M. Syed
rebbar abi, Sindhu Desh muqaddar abi* ('G.M. Syed is our leader,
Sindhu Desh is our destiny').[221] Two Jiye Sindh women volunteers sang
Sindhu Desh's national anthem – a poem by Sheikh Ayaz.[222] Addressing the audience, Syed went beyond the notion of Sindhu Desh, and
spoke of 'independent states of Baluchistan, Pakhtunistan and Seraiki
Desh', which would 'see the boundaries of present-day Pakistan shrink
to less than half of the Punjab province'.[223] He also condemned the
Muslim League as a 'communal organization', emphasising that 'since
Sindh was a separate entity when the British colonialists occupied this
region, it has a right to choose the path of independence'.[224] Among
the leaders of Jiye Sindh present at Nishtar Park were Gull Muhammad
Jhakhram, Hussain Bux Narejo, Bashir Ahmad Qureshi, Syed Ahmad
Langa and Riffat Sindhi. Recalling the day a journalist wrote: 'At Nishtar
Park G.M. Syed was undeniably at his best, demonstrating that even at
the age of 89 – when he can't even stand on his own feet – he is still
capable of causing a furore throughout the country.'[225] The strength of
Sindhi nationalist sentiments at that moment was revealed when a Jiye
Sindh Mahaz leader, asked if he would accept more autonomy within
the framework of Pakistan, remarked: 'It is like selling a mild painkiller

to assuage the injuries wrought by an earthquake.'[226] This was the time when the Sindhi press also experienced an efflorescence 'like never before'.[227] Its extensive coverage of events in the province rekindled nationalist aspirations amongst the Sindhi intelligentsia and literate villagers.

A perturbed Islamabad fell back upon the army to confront the challenge of Sindhi ethnonationalism. What followed was the perpetration of military savagery. For instance, during a village raid soldiers picked up 10 poor peasants on charges of sheltering Sindhi nationalists and shot them dead.[228] To silence political dissent the security forces did not hesitate to sexually assault Sindhi nationalist women volunteers.[229] The life of detainees in detention camps was one of 'horror'.[230] Photographs of Sindhi student and nationalist activists were distributed to airports and railway stations to enable the security forces to apprehend them if they tried to escape from the province. The state-run electronic media suppressed the news of arrests and killings of thousands of Sindhi nationalists by the military.

Following the parlimentary elections of October 1993 the PPP formed the government in Islamabad with a slender majority. The MQM had boycotted this poll in protest against state repression, although it participated in the Sindh Assembly elections three days later and won 27 seats. To maintain her precarious parliamentary strength the Prime Minister Benazir Bhutto had to pursue a cautious policy, remaining careful not to affect the military's 'institutional interests'.[231] But she did not hesitate to adopt a policy of 'coercion rather than negotiation' in dealing with the MQM. As the ruling party in both Islamabad and Sindh, the Bhutto-led PPP now projected itself as representing the interests of the Sindhi-speaking population and dubbed the MQM 'a bunch of terrorists' who deserved a 'cleansing operation'.[232] Despite a strong presence in the provincial Assembly and controlling the municipal bodies in the two cities of Karachi and Hyderabad,[233] the MQM was largely left outside the decision-making process in Sindh. This frustrated the MQM's agenda of improving civic amenities in Muhajir areas and creating additional openings for the Muhajirs in academic institutions and government employments.[234] In the commercial sector, too, the Muhajirs rapidly lost ground to the Punjabis. The army – still predominantly Punjabi – itself developed 'lucrative business interests'.[235] The Muhajirs faced competition from the Pathans even for jobs and opportunities on the factory floor. Meanwhile, a decline in the inflow of Gulf money from the late 1980s meant a setback for the urbanized consumerist culture in Pakistan, the chief beneficiary of which had been the younger generation of Muhajirs. As Zaidi remarks: 'Sindh was no longer the domain of the Muhajirs: the Punjabis began to dominate industry, land, services and also displaced local labour in both the rural and urban areas of the province'.[236] Altaf Hussain was himself convicted by the Suppression of Terrorist Activities Court and sentenced to a 27-year jail term.

In the new political scenario of the country the MQM was thus pushed to the receiving end of state power. Frustrated by the loss of their entrenched position in Pakistani society and polity, the Muhajirs were gradually driven to an 'open display of arms' in the transformed political climate[237] both against Sindhi ethno-nationalists and the Pakistan state. To quote a commentator: 'the Muhajir community is gripped by paranoia about its future. There is a feeling that if Muhajirs do not stand united, they will be victimized and picked off individually by the Sindhi-dominated bureaucracy and government of Sindh.'[238] Altaf Hussain went into exile in London to escape from prosecution and urged the Muhajirs rather 'to die than... live under this subjugation'.[239] The Muhajir leadership increasingly found a political panacea in the creation of a separate province for Muhajirs to be curved out of southern Sindh comprising Karachi, Hyderabad, Badin and Thatta.[240] This naturally provoked a Sindhi nationalist retort: '...if any one calls himself a Muhajir after 40 years it means Pakistan has not suited him. Someone comes from another country and settles in a country. The problem ends there. If they are still refugees after 40 years, the United Nations has set up a Commission for them.'[241] The MQM filed a petition in Pakistan's Supreme Court against Benazir Bhutto's government for denying constitutional and human rights to the Muhajirs.[242] Many analysts felt that the media – especially the vernacular press – should share the responsibility for generating the climate of ethnic animosity in Sindh.[243]

An issue that kept the Muhajirs in an agitated mood during the first half of the 1990s was the question of the repatriation of Biharis stranded in Bangladesh to Sindh. While the Muhajirs supported the repatriation move, Sindhi nationalists opposed it, fearing it would further reduce the Sindhi percentage in the demography of the province.[244] The extremist Muhajir leader Dr Salim Haider warned that if the Sindh Assembly passed any resolution against the repatriation of the stranded Biharis his organization would not allow the legislators to return home. Sindhi politicians protested against the arrival of 321 Biharis in Lahore by hurling bombs at a Bihar colony in Kotri near Hyderabad on 10 January 1993.[245]

By the end of 1994, ethnic violence in Sindh had claimed at least 2,823 lives and caused serious injuries to 10, 524 people in 7,420 incidents.[246] There were instances where people were blindfolded and shot to death in Karachi.[247] The working-class movement in Karachi, too, was affected by ethnic conflict.[248] In 1995 the MQM organized at least 34 general strikes.[249] A working day lost by strike in Karachi was estimated to have cost 1.3 billion rupees or $38 million.[250] This inevitably caused a decline in the commercial activities of cities like Karachi and Hyderabad.[251]. The guerrilla war that the MQM fought with the security forces on the streets of Karachi throughout 1995 often occasioned the use of sophisticated weapons by both sides. Custodial deaths and extra-judicial killings of MQM activists were not uncommon. Humiliating searches of Muhajir households, monetary extortion from Muhajir notables and torture of ordinary Muhajir citizens had become the order of the day.[252] The government announced cash awards to those rendering help in apprehending leading MQM personalities. Referring to police brutalities against MQM detainees, the chairperson of the Pakistan Human Rights Commission Asma Jahangir admitted: 'Police brutality is an unpardonable act of crime and it has crossed all limits. Our policemen… arrest a man, assume the role of judge, jury and executioner and mete out instant justice.'[253] Mohammad Anwar of the MQM even called for a UN investigation of the violation of human rights of Muhajirs.[254]

Meanwhile, the traditional Sindhi ethnonationalists experienced a significant erosion of their political strength. After the 1992 Nishtar Park rally the doyen of Sindhu nationalism, G.M. Syed, was instantly put under house arrest. He died in house custody in Karachi in April 1995 at the age of 92, having suffered 29 long years of imprisonment. But the fire of Sindhi ethnonationalism could not be completely extinguished. This was evident when only three months after Syed's death the Secretary-General of the World Sindhi Congress Dr Munwar Q. Halepota emphatically asserted in August 1995: 'The people of Sindh have lost faith in the present political system in Pakistan', and spoke in favour of Sindh's 'right of self-determination'.[255]

3. ETHNIC POLITICS AND THE POLITICIZATION OF SINDHI WOMEN

Recent studies refer to the politicization of both Sindhi and Muhajir women in the context of ethnic tensions in the province.[256] The Sindhiani Tehrik – established in May/June 1982 – has been at the forefront of mobilizing Sindhi women against Muhajirs. Initially formed to aquaint Sindhi women with the idea of Sindhi nationalism, it rapidly developed as a forum for discussing gender implications of Islamization, illiteracy, early marriage and polygamy, as well as such subject as stultification of social progress under feudalism, essentials of socialism and works on Russian and Chinese women. With a core of 4,000 activists and 50,000 members, the organization is today a well-knit body. A chain of command links a 22-member elected Central Committee with multiple district and *tehsil* units. The group draws its membership from a broad social segment, ranging from professionals, students and educated housewives to peasants. But the leadership comes from the land-owning class and petty bourgeoisie. Since 1992, however, women from the lower social strata have started gaining entry into the upper echelons of the organization.[257] The Sindhiani Tehrik holds rallies and publishes pamphlets, leaflets and newsletters to make its voice felt. It uses religious occasions for propaganda purposes. Lives of such illustrious Sindhi women as Mai Bakhtawar are celebrated to enthuse the Sindhiani Tehrik's constituency. The organization was prominent during the 1983 Movement for the Restoration of Democracy. Since 1988 it has been enthusiastically participating in parliamentary election campaigns. In 1992 members of the organization joined a march from Sukkur to Karachi, which the Awami Tehrik had organized to strengthen Sindhi consciousness.

Partly as a response to the Sindhiani Tehrik, the MQM constituted its women's wing in 1986. It first came to prominence through its involvement in the MQM campaign for the 1987 elections to local bodies in Sindh. Much of the MQM's electoral success in Karachi and Hyderabad can be attributed to large-scale participation of Muhajir women, particularly from the traditional families. Women Muhajir volunteers are trained to keep the doors of party offices open when their male colleagues get arrested or go underground.[258] Muhajir women have also demonstrated in large numbers, demanding the dropping of charges against their leader

Altaf Hussain. On this issue they organized in July 1988 a mammoth rally, attended by a crowd 'anywhere between 50,000 to 100,000'.[259] During that occasion armed female guards controlled the gathering. Another evidence of the militancy of Muhajir women was found on 27 May 1990 when in Karachi they defied a police ban and led a procession with Quran in hand to demand restoration of the supply of drinking water. This march resulted in 12 women succumbing to police firing, which provoked a national outcry.

The nature of the women's wing of MQM is, however, qualitatively different from the Sindhiani Tehrik. Unlike the latter, it has no social agenda, but functions as an adjunct to the MQM. It is a closed organization whose members – like their male counterparts – are subjected to strict party discipline. The MQM women have to wear Islamic dress; their marriages require the prior sanction of the local party unit. Even differences within the families of MQM activists are settled by the party. In 1991 11 MQM legislators are believed to have proclaimed their loyalty to Altaf Hussain, declaring 'betrayal with the Chief of MQM is more shameful than raping our own mother, sister and daughter'.[260] But there was hardly any disapproval from MQM women activists of such sexist expressions. The women's wing of the MQM was also not reportedly vocal against the 1991 Shariat Bill. Its influence in the party hierachy is minimal, if not absent.

Nevertheless, ethnic conflict in Sindh has provided both Sindhi and Muhajir women with an enlarged space in the public realm. This, of course, might not constitute a step forward in their emancipation from traditional gender oppression. For, this politicization of women in Sindh has been essentially on male terms, the women playing a supportive role either for Sindhi or Muhajir identity politics whose leadership remains pre-eminently male. As has been remarked: '...the role of women is basically to serve as 'propagandists' and their participation is based on 'order and authority' – with no, or at best token, inclusion in decision-making bodies.'[261]

Many commentators have considered the social orientation of Sindhiani Tehrik to be relatively more progressive than the MQM's women's wing. Yet, it is doubtful if the current political involvement of women in Sindh would be 'a link' in the process of Pakistani women's struggle for a better social status.[262]

4. THE QUESTION OF INDIAN COMPLICITY
IN THE SINDH CRISIS

The period between 1977 and the death of Zia witnessed Sindhi ethnic politics developing a tendency to look beyond its domestic borders for support. The veteran Sindhi nationalist G.M. Syed apologized to his community for having proposed the Pakistan resolution in the Sindh legislature.[263] To make amends for his 'mistake' he now toyed with the idea of either an independent Sindhu Desh or making Sindh a confederate partner of India.[264] Syed himself confessed his plan to create an independent Sindhu Desh.[265] He even met the Indian Prime Minister Rajiv Gandhi in 1987 and exhorted India's moral and material support. To quote Syed: 'If we cannot be free, we would rather be part of India. Even if the Indian Government is like Pakistan's Government, our condition would be no worse than what it is at present. But at least we shall have been rid of Punjabi dominance.'[266] In *Sindh Galbai Thee* ('Sindh speaks') he wrote: 'If in this regard it's a crime in the eyes of your [state's] law, then I have not only committed this crime today but will be committing such crimes the rest of my life.'[267] Sheikh Ayaz, the outstanding poet of Sindh, also proclaimed, 'Jai Sindh! Jai Hind!'[268] Sindhi nationalist resentment against Islamabad reached such proportions that on the occasion of Jinnah's birth centenary posters were distributed denouncing the Father of Pakistan as *Qadu Hajam* ('Silly Barber'), *Qatil-e-Azam* ('Great Murderer'), *Kafir-e-Azam* ('the Great Heathen') and *Ghadar-i-Sindh* ('Traitor to Sindh').[269] Sindhi intellectuals settled abroad have also endorsed the idea of either a 'Sindhi-Baluchi and Siraiki confederation with India or an independent Sindhi-Baluchi and Siraiki state having a defence pact with India'.[270] A leading organizer of North American Sindhis asserted: 'The historical experiences of partition has taught them [Sindhis] that ethnic and socio-cultural bonds are more important than religious bonds. Religions can be changed by conversion, but not so ethnicity.'[271]

On India's part, too, events in Sindh had always evoked considerable public response. Leading Indian political personalities had strong connections with pre-independence Sindh. Mahatma Gandhi was himself proud of his close relations with the people of Sindh.[272] At the same time Dr Hedgewar, the founder of the Hindu militant organization

RSS, was particularly active in Sindh during pre-Partition days. The current BJP leader L.K. Advani himself is a Sindhi. As early as 1950 Pandit Jawaharlal Nehru had perhaps Sindh in mind when he admitted:

> We are also interested in the future of many of the Frontier areas and the people who inhabit them. We are interested in them whatever the political and international aspects may be, because we had close bonds with them in the past and no political change can put an end to our memories and to our old links.[273]

Not surprisingly, New Delhi accorded diplomatic support to the Movement for the Restoration of Democracy in Sindh in 1983. The then Premier Mrs Indira Gandhi herself noted with concern: 'We cannot shut our eyes to any inhuman conduct which we have always condemned.'[274] She did not lose the opportunity of attending the 1983 New Delhi session of the World Sindhi Conference, which demanded immediate withdrawal of Pakistani military forces from Sindh and restoration of constitutional rights for the people of the region.[275] Her External Affairs Minister, Narasimha Rao, assured the Parliament that the Government was watching 'with uneasiness and distress the recent happenings in Pakistan'.[276] Such statements were received by G.M. Syed with 'unabashed delight'.[277] In 1983 the All India Radio started Sindhi broadcasts which invited Pakistani reproof as attempts to feed the Sindhis with 'inflammatory disinformation'.[278] Not unnaturally, support for a Sindhi ethnic outburst was also forthcoming from non-official Indian sources. Materials published in Bombay reportedly continue to be smuggled to Sindh; Sindhi nationalist pamphlets are allegedly printed in Delhi.[279]

In the wake of the 1972 Urdu-Sindhi language riot the Governor of Sindh alleged that 'those who were raising the language controversy to create dissension in the province were enemy agents, having their links with persons across the border'.[280] On that occasion *The Jang* referred to an 'unidentified third country' informing Pakistan 'about the alleged Indian plot (in Sindh), which included bombings, missile attacks and shootings'.[281] Once Sindhi ethnic assertions gained in strength in the 1980s, the Indian intelligence agency – RAW – was charged with opening training camps for both Jiye Sindh and Al-Zulfiqar Sindhi groups.[282] Pakistani political commentators like Malik Saeed Hasan alleged that 500 to 600

Indian commandos were operating as Sindhi *dacoits* 'in a scientific manner'.[283] *The Jang* (25 August 1986) specifically cited the arrest of an Indian who had been sent to help 'terrorism in Sindh'.

Islamabad officially alleged in the 1990s an 'Indian hand' behind the ethnic conflagration in Sindh. Pakistani Home Secretary S.K. Mahmud reported in February 1990 'clear indications of an Indian abetment in the recent trouble in Sindh', which has a sizeable Hindu minority.[284] When an express train was bombed near Lahore in May 1990 Prime Minister Bhutto remarked: 'Those who want to distract attention from what is happening inside India have a motive to do something in Pakistan.'[285] In May 1992 the Pakistan Defence Minister Ghaus Ali Shah publicly reiterated the charge of Indian involvement in Sindh.[286] *The Frontier Post* reported on 20 March 1993 the arrest of 11 RAW agents who had 'sneaked' into Pakistan to create disorders in Sindh.[287] At a press interview of October 1995 Prime Minister Bhutto directly indicted New Delhi for 'fomenting violence in Pakistan'.[288] The reported Indian intervention on behalf of Sindhi nationalists was widely interpreted in Pakistan as a revenge act against 'Pakistani troubles in Jammu and Kashmir'. Pakistan imputed Indian complicity in 2,444 acts of terrorism between 1982 and 1992, which killed 1,354 and injured 5,088 Pakistanis.[289] In March 1998 the Pakistan Information Minister Mushahid Hussein claimed to have 'conclusive and irrefutable evidence of India's Research and Analytical Wing's (RAW) involvement' in as many as 30 terrorist acts perpetrated in Pakistan in the first nine weeks of the year, killing 86 and wounding 27.[290] In the words of Hussein: 'The acts of terrorism are attempts to divert attention of the Indian people from the political instability at home and to create a scare and destabilize Pakistan.'[291]

A 1998 April Pakistani press report charged the RAW with organizing 40 camps in Rajasthan, Delhi, Punjab, Madhya Pradesh, Maharashtra, Karnataka and Jammu and Kashmir to train volunteers to carry out subversive activities in Pakistan.[292] Two months later on 7 June at least 23 people were killed and 32 injured by a powerful time bomb that 'tore through' the Khyber Mail travelling through Sindh. The Islamabad government placed the blame squarely on the RAW.[293] Assertion of an Indian hand in Sindhi politics received a new impetus when on 6 September 1998 an Indian flag with inscriptions of Jiye Sindh and Bharat was hoisted on a building in the city of Hyderabad.[294] Significantly, the incident occurred on the day that Pakistan's annual Defence Day was being celebrated. The Pakistan government also alleged the formation of a special cell within the RAW, codenamed 'Establishment 2000', to organize operations in Sindh.[295]

Interestingly, Islamabad's allegation of New Delhi's intervention in Sindhi politics was not confined to Sindhi outbursts against the Pakistani state. Pakistan also accused India of encouragement for the MQM violence of August 1995. The Interior Minister Naseerullah Babar claimed on the basis of intercepted signals that India's Zee Television network was used to communicate secret information to Karachi terrorists.[296] The MQM leader Javed Langra was reportedly provided with a secret refuge in Bombay.[297] The MQM was charged with running training camps in India.[298] It is certainly not without significance that the then Indian Minister of State of External Affairs, Salman Khurshid, expressed concern at the Karachi crisis, which he characterized as a factor in regional instability.[299] He admitted 'mounting pressures' from Muhajir relatives in India for Delhi's patronization of their cause, and hinted at the possibility of India taking up the Karachi issue with friendly Islamic countries.

Nevertheless, the Indian allegation of Pakistani involvement in Kashmir and the Punjab appears to be more substantial than the Pakistani tirade against an Indian hand in Sindhi ethnic politics. For instance, the former Pakistan Prime Minister Junejo refused to provide details of an Indian reportedly apprehended for inciting subversive politics in Sindh.[300] On the other hand, G.M. Syed himself stated that the former Indian premier Rajiv Gandhi neither promised him any support nor was favourably disposed to the Sindhi claim for recognition as a distinct nationality.[301] Many analysts praise Indian restraint on the Sindh Question. Perhaps the Indian inhibition against intervention in Sindh is dictated by fears of Pakistan's retaliation in the Punjab and Kashmir.[302] At the same time a section of Sindhi nationalists would prefer to stay clear of India and concentrate on gaining support from other deprived nationalities within Pakistan itself.[303] India's policy of restraint in Sindh has not, however, led analysts to completely discard chances of covert Indian support for Sindhi separatism. But it is also true that India has always been the whipping boy for the ruling power in Islamabad. It is thus not surprising that while Zia dubbed Benazir as an Indo-Soviet agent, Benazir later castigated India for intervention in Sindh. Some have even suggested that the USA operated through an organization called Friends of Pakistan to destabilize Pakistan by seeking to divide the country into small states: Pakhtunistan, Baluchistan, Punjab and Sindh.[304]

5. THE PRESENT STALEMATE

Sindhi ethnic assertion – a forceful presence during the Zia days – is today fragmented and weak. The breakdown of the Sindh National Alliance, an umbrella organization formed in May 1988 to voice Sindhi aspirations and once considered as a 'milestone in Sindh's troubled history[305], is a significant pointer to this fact. As one commentator remarked: 'Jiye Sindh was once a junction for most leftist and progressive nationalists – who had joined Syed after being inspired by his writings – but left on being disillusioned with his lack of interest for organization and future programme.'[306]

A significant number of Sindhi politicians have now reconciled themselves to resolving their identity issue within the structure of Pakistani politics. The Sindhi middle class, too, is accepting the PPP as an outlet to enter mainstream national life.[307] In the words of a leading commentator:

> Despite the use of all forms of state and street terrorism against them, most Sindhis still do not buy the idea of national liberation as the solution to their problems. The merchants of these dreams are the Sindhi nationalists, groups of disorganized middle class young men who have got more clout than is their due because of Sindh's peculiar political situation.[308]

As early as 1986 G.M. Syed had himself admitted his isolation in Sindhi politics: 'Jeaye Sindh Mahaz was engaged in an ideological struggle instead of power politics. Chances [of success] of the Mahaz struggle are remote as 90 per cent of the Sindhis are with the PPP.'[309] When Zulfikar Bhutto became a martyr in many a Sindhi eye, Syed lamented: 'These brainless Sindhis worship Bhutto who was hung by the Punjabis after he had served their purpose... I have served Sindh all my life. But these people are senseless; they are nothing.'[310]

What was once G.M. Syed's Jiye Sindh Tehrik is thus today split into four major groups: (a) the Jiye Sindh Tehrik, led by Gul Muhammad Jakhrani and Bashir Khan Qureshi, whose members are loyal to Syed, believe in armed struggle and are particularly active on campuses in interior Sindh; (b) the Jiye Sindh Mahaz under Syed Ghulam Shah and Abdul Wahid Aresar, which primarily consists of moderate socialists and advocates the cause of an independent Sindh, but is opposed to a confrontation with the Muhajirs; (c) the Jiye Sindh Taraqqi Pasand led by Qadr Magsi, which is the most strident critic of Syed and enjoys considerable grass-roots support and regards the Muhajirs as the prime enemy of Sindhis; (d) the Hamida Khusro group, which perhaps wields least influence amongst the Sindhi nationalists.[311]

Some observers ascribe the present weakness of Sindhi ethnonationalism to Syed's 'personalized and enigmatic approach' and his 'refusal to prepare a blueprint for an alternative socio-economic structure', which restricted the appeal of the Jiye Sindh movement largely to landed and educated elites. Feroze Ahmed, a leading commentator on contemporary Sindh, thus refers to Syed's 'class collaborationist' character of Sindhi ethnonationalism which exposed the injustices committed against the Sindhis by other communities, but conveniently overlooked 'the humiliation…meted out every day to Sindhi peasants by the Sindhi landlords'.[312] Qadir Magsi, the leader of Jiye Sindh Taraqqi Pasand, acknowledged that they were the products of 'intellectual activity inspired in part by Syed', but regretted:

> Syed has been involved with the politics of Sindhu Desh for 22 years, but Sindhis – the educated middle class, lower middle classes and the toiling masses – have gained nothing except destruction and death. The Sindhi feudals and *wederas*, meanwhile, have continued to mortgage the rights of Sindh and barter their conscience for privileges and ayasbi… His [Syed's] reliance on palace conspiracies has totally distanced his politics from grassroots.[313]

Leftist Sindhi nationalist leaders like Rasul Bux Palejo underlined some 'structural' factors behind the weakening of the Sindhi ethnic challenge to the centralized Pakistani polity. Such aberrations within Sindhi society as the absence of a strong Sindhi Muslim middle class and discord between *waderas* (absentee landlords) and *haris* (landless nomadic farm workers) enabled the federal government to play one group of Sindhis against another.[314] Studies have shown that Islamabad, particularly under Zia-ul-Haq, tried to drive a wedge amongst the Sindhis with the help of *pirs* (saints of tightly organized local sects) who owned large estates, wielded considerable local influence and were traditionally associated with the Muslim League.[315] Rasul Bux Palejo's pro-Maoist Sindh Awami Tehrik and Communist Party of Sindh are currently seeking to provide a new dynamism to Sindhi politics by combining Sindhi ethnic politics with an anti-feudal programme. Two long marches to highlight the cause of human rights, and the language and culture of Sindh received considerable popular support.[316] But such socialist groups still have a limited presence in Sindhi politics. Meanwhile, the problem of Sindhi nationalism remains 'one of organization, where no single party has emerged as a representative of his consciousness'.[317]

In recent years a new complication has been added to Sindhi politics. It started when Benazir Bhutto's estranged brother Mir Murtaza Bhutto organized the Pakistan People's Party (Shaheed Bhutto) and contested the 1993 parliamentary elections against the PPP candidate. Since then Murtaza has developed close ties with Sindhi nationalist organizations and rallied considerable rural support against Benazir's submission to the Punjabi establishment. Benazir retaliated by arresting and prosecuting Murtaza's supporters. The climactic point in the Benazir-Murtaza strife was reached on 20 September 1996 when the latter was gunned down by police. Although Benazir dubbed the incident a conspiracy against her government, the event provoked widespread anti-PPP sentiments in Sindh. Amidst such intra-Sindhi tensions and allegations of 'extra-judicial killings' of MQM activists, President Farooq Leghari dismissed the PPP government. In the ensuing 1997 elections the Punjab-based Nawaz Sharif's Muslim League swept to power in Islamabad. Meanwhile, the elections reconfirmed ethnic polarization in Sindh. While the PPP retained most of its constituencies in rural Sindh, the MQM won in all Muhajir-majority areas of the province. In the aftermath of elections the PML (N) leader Liaquat Jatoi formed a ministry in Sindh with the help of a motley coalition of MQM, Pir Pagara's PML (Functional), the Shaheed Bhutto group, National People's Party and Sindh National People's Party. This regime had a distinct pro-MQM orientation. As the price for extending its support to Jatoi, the MQM reportedly extracted from him a secret deal which included (a) release of all detainees and withdrawal of cases against MQM leaders, workers and sympathizers; (b) the disarming and flushing out of all 'armed terrorists' in areas identified by the MQM; (c) the appointment of a judicial commission to investigate extra-judicial killings; (d) financial compensation to victims of judicial killings on the basis of a list prepared and authenticated by the MQM leadership and a duly constituted government committee; (e) scrapping of such measures of the previous PPP government as the creation of the Malir District and Lyari Development Authority which the MQM considered 'discriminatory' for the urban populace; (f) upward revision of urban Sindh's federal quota from 7.5 per cent to 11.5 per cent; (g) repatriation of Pakistani Biharis stranded in Bangladesh; (h) appointment of MQM nominees as Governor of Sindh, Speaker of the Provincial Assembly and eight ministers in the provincial cabinet.[318] Sindh's MQM-Muslim League ministry thus tried to undo the measures undertaken by the Benazir government to assuage Sindhi discontent. To quote a perceptive comment: 'Sindhis once again have little voice in their own province and virtually none in the centre'.[319] The subsequent Nawaz Sharif regime witnessed a continuation of this trend.

In some ways, however, hopeful signs of the improvement of the Muhajir-Sindhi relationship can also be seen. The Muhajirs are increasingly feeling the brunt of economic competition from Punjabis, Pathans and Lahandas, which might in the long run soften their hatred towards the Sindhis.[320] While in 1951 80 per cent of the Karachi populace consisted of Muhajirs, the 1981 demographic breakdown in that city was as follows: Muhajirs 54.3 per cent, Punjabis 13.6 per cent and Pakhtuns 8.7 per cent. The end of the 1980s registered a sizeable presence in Karachi of Iranians, Sri Lankans and Bangladeshis.[321] At one point between December 1986 and January 1987 clashes between Muhajirs and Pakhtuns became more frequent than between Muhajirs and Sindhis.[322] Muhajir-Pathan tensions in Karachi in February 1998, following the marriage of a Muhajir boy and Pathan girl, testified to hardened relations between the two communities.[323]

There also appears to have been a change of emphasis in the MQM's political discourse from 'ethnic terminology' to an 'idiom of social classes'.[324] Perhaps realising that reliance upon a simple politics of ethnicity would restrict the organization only to urban Sindh, sections in the MQM in 1991 sought to present themselves as the champion of the oppressed within all ethnic groups. The MQM renamed itself the Muttahada Qaumi Movement and has reportedly proclaimed its determination to replace the present rule for the privileged 2 per cent of the population by a polity geared to the interests of 98 per cent of the people of the country.[325] Such broadening of the political discourse of the MQM has opened up new possibilities of understanding with Sindhi nationalists to work in the interest of the underprivileged social groups in both communities. A section within the MQM also appears to be gradually distancing itself from Islamic fundamentalism.

Moreover, the MQM – like Sindhi nationalists – is today a divided house, the Altaf Hussain group fighting open gun battles with the Haqiqi faction.[326] In the words of an observer, 'the Muhajir Qaumi Movement has been reduced to a shattered, confused and divided body struggling to find a new identity'.[327] During the first six months of 1997 Muhajir infighting took a toll of 400 lives.[328] In two days of internecine violence amongst MQM factions in March 1998, 21 people lay dead.[329] Between the third week of May and the end of June 1998, 180 fell victim to intra-MQM clashes.[330] Recounting one such scene of violence a press correspondent wrote: 'People in the area called it a war zone as bands of heavily armed activists from both sides ran through the maze of narrow lanes choosing their targets and killing them. Activists from both factions were pulled from their homes and taken out on the street and killed…'[331] The crisis brought 'entire neighbourhoods under siege'.[332] To quote from a vivid report on incidents of violence:

> Neighbourhoods like Orangi, Korangi, Mahe, Landhi, Shah Faisal Colony and Liaquatabad are veritable battlegrounds as rival groups of militants freely display their arms and engage in full scale war games. It is not just vendetta and crimes of attrition that Karachi's citizens are witnessing: it has now become a numbers game, as each group competes with its rival to win the corpse tally. Even more gruesome is the pride the killers take in recounting the gory details of each murder they have committed.[333]

Again, Karachi has been recently torn apart by Shia-Sunni discord which prompted the provincial government to institute a state of emergency.[334]

In such circumstances it is not unnatural to find moves for a peaceful resolution of the Sindhi-Muhajir conflict. S. Sultan Anwar represents an emerging trend within the contemporary Sindhi educated community when he writes: 'The Muhajirs should not be organized as a Muhajir party which is allied to the Punjabi elite in Islamabad... On the contrary, their best bet is to join a liberal democratic party like the PPP and take part in mainstream politics.'[335] Dr Qadire Magsi of Jiye Sindh Taraqqi Pasand Party remarked in a similar vein: '...the Muhajirs must join the struggle for the national rights of the Sindhi people. They must give up calling themselves Muhajirs and recognize the reality that they have to live here and die here so they should merge with the Sindhis.'[336] An increasing segment within both the Sindhi and Muhajir communities is becoming aware that the conflict between the two communities 'does not promise them salvation'.[337] Instead, they have realized the need to 'shift their focus from Sindh to the national framework'.[338] It is thus not without significance that a two-day nationalist conference of Sindhis, Pushtoons, Balochs and Seraikis at Islamabad in early October 1998 resolved to launch 'the Pakistan Oppressed Nations Movement', aiming to create a true federal polity and restore to all ethnic nationalities the fundamental rights so long enjoyed only by the Punjabis.[339]

Any process of normalization of ethnic relations in Sindh is, however, unlikely to be welcomed by the army, intelligence agencies and bureaucracy, which had thrived on the policy of divide and rule to forestall a united front in the province to fight federal injustice against Sindh. Powerful business interests, too, are believed to have a stake in Sindhi-Muhajir ethnic contradictions since it helps them to keep the working class in Sindh divided.[340] A Sindhi intellectual complains:

> Since the inception of Pakistan, vested interests and classes have tried their utmost to damage unity of the people. Whenever there is trouble, tension or some unhappy incident in Karachi or Hyderabad, politicians from other provinces rush in, and, instead of helping solve problems, incite one group against other, thus adding fuel to the fire and enjoy[ing] fishing in troubled waters.[341]

6. SINDHI ETHNICITY AND NATION-BUILDING IN PAKISTAN

The irony of Pakistan's history lies in the fact that a separatist movement developed in the province whose legislature was the first to adopt the Pakistan resolution. Since the mid-1980s 15,000 were killed by Sindhi-Muhajir ethnic strife. In 1995 alone 2,000 were injured by internecine clashes.[342] Post-colonial India, too, has been plagued by ethnic strife. But scholars like Hamza Alavi identify a qualitative difference in the nature of ethnic assertions in the two successor states of South Asia.[343] While ethnic politics in Pakistan assumes the form of subnationalism since it is directed against what is perceived by the underprivileged ethnic groups as the Punjabi-dominated central government, the ethnic conflict in India tends to be confined to the 'local level' because no single ethnic group wields absolute power. But in India ethnic assertions also usually assume an anti-Delhi posture because they are premised on the demand for a restructuring of centre-state relations.[344]

The foregoing discussion has indicated that a resolution of the Sindh Question requires an accommodation of Sindhi ethnic aspirations within the Pakistani federal polity as well as an assuaging of the Muhajir sense of insecurity. To ensure this a stable democratic political system is of prime necessity. But Pakistan was unfortunately subjected to intermittent doses of military dictatorships which inevitably took advantage of 'fragmentation and weakened legitimacy of political forces'.[345] The power structure in Pakistan, as it has evolved, tends to be 'oligarchic' in composition, though the state elite plays a crucial role in operating it.[346] The nationalist Muslim Maulana Abul Kalam Azad anticipated the difficulties in the nation-building process for Pakistan when he warned the Indian Muslims migrating to their new home:

> You know where you are going? You are not going to any Pakistan different from Sindh, Punjab, Baluchistan, Frontier and East Bengal, all full of people having their own cultures, languages, literature, traditions and ways of lives, different from one another. If, at about 25 years from today, local nationalism springs up amongst them, what will be your fate and where will you go?[347]

In fact, the failure to create a democratic polity in Pakistan was largely related to the nature of the Muslim League movement itself. While the Indian National Congress had local and regional networks and was connected to a wide range of popular protest politics, the Muslim League lacked the institutional structure of a mass-based party, which made it rely on an appropriation of regional political organizations around the slogan of a separate Muslim homeland. Besides, the Muslim League did not initially enjoy popular support in the very areas that now constitute Pakistan. In such circumstances, the political establishment in Pakistan – unsure of sustaining itself with continuous popular support – fell back upon the bureaucracy and army for survival. In Pakistan the military holds the 'political veto', even when the country has the 'trappings of a democratic regime'.[348] Capitalist modernity itself has developed in Pakistan a symbiotic relationship with precapitalist formations based on language, religion, caste, kinship and locality. As Hamza Alavi aptly remarks:

> The history of the Pakistan movement does not have the depth and character to provide the substance of national memories. It has manifestly proved to be incapable of providing over-arching national bonds for it is tied too closely with the fortunes of a fragmented and discredited political party. This fact is compounded by the even more significant and paradoxical fact that the Pakistan movement was at its weakest in the Muslim majority provinces of India that today make up Pakistan.[349]

Besides, more than that of India, the modernization programme in Pakistan has rested on a centralized and overcrowded state.[350] Under Zia-ul-Haq Islam was particularly used to buttress this state control.[351] But in a multi-ethnic state with strong regional imbalances, this centralization carried with it a danger of the marginalization of sections of population who were perceived by the ruling power as unsuitable for the nation-building process.[352] Instead of appreciating the genuine grievances of Sindhi ethnonationalists, Islamabad responded negatively to the assertion of Sindhi identity, an attitude aptly expressed when General Tikka Khan, the erstwhile Governor of East Pakistan, remarked:

We failed in East Bengal because it was too far away; there were too many people there, and it was helped by India. If 'Sindhu Desh' raises its head, we can easily crush it because it is near at hand, not very populous, and not likely to be helped by any foreign power. We will then offer the Sindhi Pirs and Zamindars, who are fattening now, as a sacrifice (*qurbani*) in celebration of our victory, *Jashne-e-fateh*.[353]

Here is a classic example, of what Anderson calls, 'official nationalism' where national identity is not 'spontaneously generated from below', but imposed from the top to subvert subnational movements that appear to wield considerable popular support.[354] When the need was to recognize Pakistan as an ethnically diverse unit, the 'central elite' of the country opted for a 'viceregal system' that failed to integrate 'the existing social structures... into the political and economic mainstream'.[355] The ethnic imbroglio in Sindh was a fall-out of this process. As a Sindhi analyst notes:

Problems of national unity in Pakistan stem from the very philosophy of the country – as prophesied by those who wield power. The philosophy and ideology of the state negates the reality, i.e. the existence of nations that together formed Pakistan. The policies and practices based on philosophy and ideology of the creation of Pakistan have obviously damaged the problems of national unity.[356]

The commentator in *The Herald* (February 1992) was not wide of the truth when he remarked:

Even if the Sindhu Desh idea does not gain ground, conditions that gave rise to the... movement will continue to create new recruits to the cause. What unites all the disparate groups is deep insecurity about the future, a fear about the Sindhi's very survival as an entity.

Although Sindhi nationalists are today hopelessly divided, they still feel their deprivation from 'inalienable historical rights'. This was clear when at the December 1996 Calcutta meeting of Pakistan-India People's

Forum for Peace and Democracy the leader of the Jamait-e-Ulema-Sindh Maulana Ubaidullah Bhutto asserted:

> In the constitution of our organization… we have clearly stated that Sindh for us is a separate nation and that is the political goal towards which we are working… In Sindh, we have an alliance of nationalists all fighting together for an independent, free Sindh. We have an alliance with them. Jiye-Sindh-Muttahedu Mahaz, Jiye-Sindh-Mahaz… Jiye-Sindh-Tarakki Pasand Party, Sindh Sagar Party, Jamiat-e-Ulema Sindh, Mazdoor Kisan Party and Pakistan Tarakki Kaumi Movement, which are fighting for those border areas within the Punjab that they argue should be a separate state. Our alliance is called the United National Alliance whose chairman is Mumtaz Ali Khan Bhutto who is currently Chief Minister in Sindh.[357]

The following warning from a Sindhi intellectual still true in many a Sindhi ear: 'The foundations of this nation need honest effort to stabilize. No storytelling, no fibs and fantasies, no slogans, no religiosity and bunkum and jargon of verbosity and ideology are any longer acceptable and workable.'[358] Echoing the same feeling a perceptive Pakistani scholar also finds the resolution of the ethnic question in Pakistan in the 'structural transformation' of the national polity to ensure 'tangible' regional autonomy and administrative decentralization.[359]

Some Western and subcontinental scholars[360] have expressed pessimism about the possibility of reconciliation between centralism and ethnic pluralism. A public opinion poll conducted by *The News* in September 1997 also found a substantial section of Pakistanis despondent about the ability of the state to curb lawlessness, and apprehensive of the breakdown of Pakistan itself.[361] In the wake of the post-nuclear economic crisis the then Prime Minister, Nawaz Sharif, firmly fell back on 'Punjab-centred policies', causing resentment amongst other ethnic groups.[362] His surprise decision announced on 11 June 1998 to begin construction of the Kalabagh dam – shelved for the past four decades because of opposition from Sindh, Baluchistan and NWFP – won him political suport in the Punjab, but turned Sindh and the Frontier provinces against Islamabad.[363] The federal government's decision to deprive the smaller provinces of the right to collect taxes has also evoked tensions within the Pak polity. Significantly, the present Punjabi leadership did not take into confidence the federal units either on the nuclear tests or on the drafting of a new post-nuclear national agenda. Nawaz Sharif fell back on the old belief: 'since Punjab alone knows what is best for Pakistan, whatever it says, must be accepted as such by every other province'.[364] This dictatorial posture evoked considerable protest in Sindh. Interestingly, this outburst in Sindh was organized jointly by the MQM and the PPP. Nawaz Sharif's government resorted to a large-scale crackdown, involving thousands of political imprisonments.[365] Such political trends are certain to generate new and resurrect old ethnic tensions in Pakistan.

Nevertheless, as in Kashmir, so in the case of Sindh, I decipher new signs of hope.[366] While there is an increasing realization of 'ethnic segmentation of markets' in Sindh due to internecine clashes, the younger generation of Sindhis and Muhajirs are more interested in curving out their own space in the national economy instead of engaging themselves in ethnic conflict.[367] Expansion of pan-Pakistani market forces, building of national alliances across ethnic and regional lines for electoral gains, declining importance of religious fundamentalist forces in representative political institutions, a critical press, vigilant human rights groups, a women's movement, repeated attempts by the judiciary to break its 'conformist traditions' – all these demonstrate, in the opinion of a commentator, a move to go beyond existing parameters of national and provincial politics that has, 'entered a cul-de-sac'.[368] Pakistan was unfortunately once again brought under military dictatorship on 12 October 1999. Yet, we have now better possibilities for the growth of a civil society in Pakistan, which could foster closer co-operation amongst the four major nationalities of the country. This alone could be a prelude to a new phase of constructive nation-building in Pakistan.

NOTES

1. S.G. Mustafa Shah, 'Sindh: The Causes of Present Discontent, Sindhi Leadership, Its Hopes and Hazards', *Sindh Quarterly*, vol. XII, no. 1. 1984.
2. *Newsline*, October 1991, p. 9.
3. S.S. Harrison, 'In Afghanistan's Shadow: Baluch Nationalism and Soviet

Temptations' (Washington DC: Carnegie Endowment for International Peace) cited in A.A. Kazi, 'Ethnic Nationalism and Super-Powers in South Asia: Sindhis and Baluchis', *Journal of Asian and African Affairs*, vol. 1, July 1989.
4. B. Ali, 'The National Question in Pakistan', *Economic and Political Weekly* (hereafter *EPW*), vol. 21, no. 43, and 'Sindh and Struggle for Liberation', *EPW*, vol. 22, no. 10; S. Harrison, 'Ethnicity and Political Stalemate in Pakistan' in A. Banuazzui et al. eds., *The State, Religion, and Ethnic Politics* (Lahore: 1987); S.A. Zaidi, *Regional Imbalances and the National Question in Pakistan* (London: 1992).
5. F. Ahmed, 'Pakistan's Problems of National Integration' in M.A. Khan ed., *Islam, Politics and the State: The Pakistan Experience* (London: 1985).
6. While Mughal rule in Sindh was constantly challenged by sporadic revolts, the Mughal governors here were no more than farmers-general of revenue. According to one estimate at least forty Sindhi clans continuously revolted against Akbar's *satraps*. Later Mughal rulers had to recognize the sovereignty of Sindh. See S.J. Burki, *Pakistan: The Continuing Search for Nationhood* (Boulder: 1991).
7. F. Ahmad, 'Pakistan's Problems'.
8. ibid.
9. In fact, the Hur rebellion posed so serious a challenge to the Raj that it imposed martial law in 1942 which was lifted only a few months before the Transfer of Power.
10. The five provinces were Punjab, Sindh, North-West Frontier Province, Baluchistan and East Bengal.
11. Other deprived ethnic groups in Pakistan like the Baluchs, Pukhtuns and eastern Bengalis were also involved in ethnic politics. But while the Bengalis developed themselves into a sovereign state in 1971, the Baluch and Pakhtun ethnic assertions expressed themselves in the form of sporadic revolts. On the other hand, Sindhi ethnicity has assumed a relatively long-drawn organized form.
12. One in 10 people in Pakistan is a refugee from India. The total population of Pakistan is about 120 million, out of which more than 20 million have migrated from India. See M.G. Chitkara, *Muhajir's Pakistan* (Delhi: 1996).
13. H. Alavi, 'Nationhood and Communal Violence in Pakistan', *Journal of Contemporary Asia*, vol. 21, no. 2, 1991, p. 165.
14. Cited in T. Rahman, *Language and Politics in Pakistan* (Karachi: 1996), p. 111.
15. *Census of Pakistan*, Karachi, 1951, vol. 6. See the Statement 3-R, p. 36.
16. *Census of Pakistan*, Karachi, 1951, vol. 1, Statement 5-C, p. 87. Of course, not all who came to Karachi were Urdu speakers. Among non-Urdu speakers were Memons, Gujratis, Bohras and Kathiawaris. But they developed an identity of interests with Urdu speakers. See S.A. Zaidi, 'Sindhi Vs Muhajir: Contradiction, Conflict, Compromise' in S.A. Zaidi ed., *Regional Imbalances*. As a result of this migration the religious composition of the population in Sindh also changed overnight. While in 1941 Muslims constituted 42 per cent of total population, their share rose to 96.1 per cent in 1951. On the other hand, the proportion of caste Hindus and Scheduled Castes declined from a little above 50 per cent in 1941 to 1.6 per cent in 1951. See *Census of Pakistan* 1951, Chapter 5, Statement 5-B.
17. 1981 Census Report of Karachi Division (Islamabad: 1984), p. 10. Also see B. Ali, 'Political Forces in Sind' in S.A. Zaidi ed., *Regional Imbalances*. Also see A. Rashid and F. Shaheed, *Pakistan: ethno-politics and contending elites* (Geneva: 1993), p. 7. In 1991 the Census operations were postponed, following attempts by Sindhis and Muhajirs to inflate their respective numbers.
18. G.M. Mehkri, 'Random thoughts on Sindh: Some Painful and Ominous Realities – Sindh and the Immigrants From India', *Sindh Quarterly*, vol. XVI, no. 1, 1988, p. 15.

19. In Islamic terminology 'Muhajir' implies migration in the cause of Islam. The term is derived from the Arabic word 'Hijra', used to describe the flight of prophet Muhammad and his followers from Mecca and Medina to avoid persecution by enemies of Islam. Interestingly, children of refugees born in Sindh after 1947 also call themselves Muhajireen, refusing to identify themselves with Sindhis. See I.H. Malik, 'The Politics of Ethnic Sindh: Nation, Region and Community in Pakistan' in S. Mitra and R.A. Lewis eds., *Subnational Movements in Asia* (Boulder: 1996).

20. M. Waseem, 'Ethnic Conflict in Pakistan: Case of MQM', p. 1 (paper presented at the conference on Communalism and Migration: South Asians in Diaspora, University of Edinburgh, June 1997).

21. F. Ahmad, 'Ethnicity and Politics: The Rise of Muhajir Separatism', *South Asia Bulletin*, vol. 8, nos. 1 & 2 (1988).

22. F. Ahmed, *Ethnicity and Politics In Pakistan* (Lahore: 1998), pp. 96–8.

23. ibid.

24. According to a 1959 study of the Pakistan Institute for Development Economics 'the social condition measured by the unemployment rate, percentage of children attending school, houses built with proper material and equipped with electricity, running water, toilet and bathroom, were marginally better than those of the immigrants from the North and substantially better then those of the local people', ibid., p. 105.

25. ibid. p. 99.

26. Hamza Alavi contends that in this way political loyalties in Pakistan were externalized in the name of religion. See H. Alavi, 'Nationhood and communal violence in Pakistan', *EPW*, 24, 27, 1989.

27. The Muhajirs dominated the All India Muslim League in British India.

28. A.T. Tahir, Political Dynamics of Sindh 1947–1971' (unpublished M.Phil thesis, Pakistan Study Centre, University of Karachi, 1990), cited in S.A. Zaidi 'Sindhi Vs Muhajir'.

29. E. Ahmed, 'Behind the Crisis in Sindh', *The Friday Times*, 19–25 July 1990.

30. S.G. Mustafa Shah, 'Sindhi Society and Sindh Tomorrow: The Resurgence and the Revolt of The Indigenous in Pakistan', *Sindh Quarterly*, vol. XV, no. 4, 1987.

31. F. Ahmed, 'Pakistan's Problems': Ethnicity and Politics in Pakistan (Karachi: 1998).

32. I.H. Malik, 'The Politics of Ethnic Sindh'.

33. Interview with Hafeez Pirzada 16 April 1989, cited in K.R. Khory, 'Separatism in South Asia: The Politics of Ethnic Conflict and Regional Security' Ph.D. thesis, University of Illinois at Urbana Champaign, 1991.

34. *The Dawn*, 14 December 1989; S. Kardar, 'Polarisation in the Regions: The Roots of Discontent' cited in A. Rashid and F. Shaheed, *Pakistan: Ethno-Politics*. In none of the cities in Sindh do the Sindhis have a clear majority.

35. M. Ispahani, 'Pakistan: Dimensions of Insecurity', Adelphi Papers no. 246, winter 1989/90.

36. See the interview with G.M. Syed in *Pakistan Times*, 5 June 1986.

37. F. Ahmed, 'Pakistan's Problems', p. 235.

38. 40 per cent of Muhajirs were clerks and sales workers, 16.8 per cent were service workers and 21 per cent were skilled operatives. See F. Ahmad, 'Ethnicity and Politics'. While the literacy rate for Mahajirs was 23.4 per cent, the figure for Sindh as a whole was 13.2 per cent. See T. Rahman, 'Language and Politics in Pakistan' p. 112. For Sindhi backwardness compared to the Muhajirs also see F. Ahmed, 'Agrarian Change and Class Formation in Sindh', *EPW*, vol. 19, no. 39; M.H. Khan, *Underdevelopment and Agrarian Structure in Pakistan* (Boulder:

159

1981); C.H. Kennedy, 'The Politics of Ethnicity in Sindh', *Asian Survey*, vol. XXXI, no. 10, October 1991; T.P. Wright, Jr., 'Indian Muslim Refugees in the Politics of Pakistan', *Journal of Commonwealth and Comparative Politics*, July 1974; and 'Centre-Periphery Relations and Ethnic Conflict in Pakistan Sindhis, Muhajirs, Punjabis', *Comparative Politics*, April 1991.

39. S.A. Zaidi, 'Sindhi vs Muhajir'; K.B. Sayeed, *Politics in Pakistan: The Nature and Direction of Change* (Praeger: 1980).
40. S. Mahmood, *Sindh Report* (Lahore: 1989), p. 15.
41. Even before the establishment of Pakistan Jinnah had visualized economic development of the 'Muslim homeland' along capitalist lines with the help of an 'entrepreneurial class' migrating from India. See K.B. Sayeed, *Politics in Pakistan*.
42. M. Waseem, *Politics and the State in Pakistan* (Islamabad: 1994); C. Kennedy, 'Managing Ethnic Conflict: The Case of Pakistan', *Regional Politics and Policy*, vol. 3, no. 1. Spring 1993.
43. H. Alavi, 'Class and State in Pakistan' in H. Gandezi et al. eds., *Pakistan: The Roots of Dictatorship: the political economy of a practosian state* (Delhi: 1986); see also his 'Nationhood and Nationalities in Pakistan', *EPW*, 24, 27, 1989.
44. See S.J. Burki, 'Twenty Years of the Civil Service of Pakistan: A Reevaluation', *Asian Survery*, vol. 9, no. 4, April 1969; B. Hashmi, 'Dragon Seed: Military in the State' in H. Gandezi et al. eds., *Pakistan: The Roots of Dictatorship*.
45. Fourth Triennial Census of Central Government Employees of Pakistan (Islamabad: 1973).
46. C. Kennedy, 'The Politics of Ethnicity in Sindh', *Asian Survey*, vol. XXXI, no. 10, October 1991.
47. ibid. In 1968 there was not a single Sindhi general in the military. Also see S. Ahmed, 'Centralisation, Authoritarianism and the Mismanagement of Ethnic Relations in Pakistan', in M.E. Brown and S. Ganguly eds., *Government Policies and Ethnic Relations in Asia and the Pacific* (Massachusetts: 1996).
48. *Sindh Quarterly* vol. XII, no. 1, 1984.
49. G.M. Syed's communication to the Governor of Sindh in 1949.
50. F. Ahmed, 'Pakistan's Problems'.
51. Cited in S. Mahmood *Sindh Report*, p. 15. In the country as a whole the Gujarati-speaking Muhajirs owned seven of the 12 large industrial houses. H. Papnek, 'Pakistan's Big Businessmen', *Economic Development and Cultural Change*, 21, 1972.
52. Sangat (Sindhi Association of North America, vol. 3, no. 4, December 1987) cited in A.A. Kazi, 'Ethnic nationalism'.
53. *The Herald*, January 1988.
54. E. Ahmed, 'The Challenge in Sindh', *The Dawn* (Karachi), 21 June 1992.
55. M. Waseem, *Politics and the State in Pakistan* (Islamabad: 1994), p. 34.
56. G.M. Syed, *Sindhoodesh Chho ain Chha Lai* (Ulhasnagar: 1974), p. 125. Quoted in ibid. According to one estimate in 1936 only 13 per cent of Sindhi Muslim agriculturists were free from debts. See P.A. Ahmed, *Kaya Hum Ikhatry Reh Saktay Hein*, cited in I. Ahmed, *Nation, State and Ethnicity in Contemporary South Asia* (London: 1996).
57. I. Ahmed, *Nation, State and Ethnicity*, p. 192. The Sukkur Barrage was constructed by the British in the 1930s.
58. Cited in K. Mumtaz, 'The Gender Dimension in Sindh's Ethnic Conflict', in K. Rupesinghe and K. Mumtaz eds., *Internal Conflicts in South Asia* (New Delhi: 1996).
59. See Z. Hussain, 'Sindh: Day of the Nationalist', *The Herald*, June 1988, pp. 44–5.
60. S. Mahmood, *Sindh Report*, p. 98.

61. The Kalabagh dam – proposed for construction about 120 miles downstream from the Trabela dam – incited the most stringent Sindhi criticism. It allegedly will result in a net loss of 12.86 MAF of water for Sindh. Experts in Sindh have also estimated that the dam would threaten Sindh's 1.9 million acres of thick riverine forest, 1.3 million acres of rich grazing land, 600,000 acres of cultivated land and 650,000 acres of mangrove forests. Even towns like Nowshera in NWFP are likely to be submerged by the dam,. See *Newsline*, July 1998, p. 43.

62. R.G. Wrising, 'Ethnicity and Political Reform in Pakistan', *Asian Affairs*, vol. 15, no. 2, summer 1988. Such discontent was voiced by the Baluchis and Pukhtuns too.

63. F. Ahmed, 'Pakistan's Problems', p. 243.

64. H. Alavi, 'Nationhood and Communal Violence', p. 165.

65. M.A. Khan, 'Thoughts on Sindh', *Sindh Quarterly*, vol. XII, no. 2, 1984.

66. K. Hussain, 'Sindh: The Rise and Growth of Nationalism', *Sindh Quarterly*, vol. XVI, no. 3, p. 26.

67. See K.R. Malkani, *The Sindh Story* (Delhi: 1984) pp. 150–59. The first recorded Hindu-Muslim communal conflict was in 1927.

68. ibid. See Malkani's own experience, pp. vii–viii.

69. M.A. Khan, 'Thoughts on Sindh', *Sindh Quarterly*, vol. XII, no. 2, 1984.

70. F. Ahmed, 'The Language Question in Sind' in S. Akbar Zaidi ed., *Regional Imbalances*.

71. S.G. Mustafa Shah, 'Sindhi Literature and Sindhi Society', *Sindh Quarterly*, vol. X, no. 1, 1982.

72. ibid. p. 11.

73. Cited in K. Callard, *Pakistan: A Political Study* (London: 1977), p. 24.

74. Cited in T. Rahman, *Language and Politics in Pakistan*.

75. F. Ahmed, 'Pakistan's Problems'.

76. Cited in T. Rahman, *Language and Politics in Pakistan*, p. 119. See also G.M. Syed's communication to the Governor of Sindh in 1949 cited in *Sindh Quarterly*, vol. XII, no. 1, 1984.

77. A.A. Kazi, 'Ethnic nationalism and Baluchis'.

78. S.G. Mustafa Shah, 'Sindhi Literature', p. 14.

79. F. Ahmed, 'Pakistan's Problems', p. 130. Another way of ridiculing Sindhis was to say: 'How is a Sindhi Muslim born? From the urine of Hindus.' Cited in M.G. Chitkara, *Muhajir's Pakistan*, p. 87.

80. See *Jang*, 31 October 1987.

81. For instance, Ram Bagh and Achal Singh Park in Karachi have been renamed respectively as Aram Bagh and Iqbal Park. See K.R. Malkani, *The Sindh Story*.

82. A. Kazi, 'Ethnic Nationalities, Education and Problems of National Integration in Pakistan', *Sindh Quarterly*, 1989, no. 1, pp. 21–7.

83. ibid.

84. T. Rahman, *Language and Politics in Pakistan*, p. 118.

85. F. Ahmed, *Pakistan's Problems*.

86. T. Rahman, *Language and Politics*, p. 118.

87. S.G. Mustafa Shah, 'Sindhi Society And Sindh Tomorrow', pp, 34–5. Among other Sindhi writers who advocate the cause of Sindhi ethno-nationalism are Shaikh Ayaz, Abdul Wahid Aresar, G. Allana, Hamda Khuro and Fahmida Riaz.

88. F. Ahmed, 'Pakistan's Problems'.

89. M.G. Chitkara, *Muhajir's Pakistan*, p. 8.

90. Hamza Alavi explains this as a typical post-colonial dilemma 'where the usual process of becoming a nation before becoming a country has been reversed'. See his 'Nationhood and Nationalities in Pakistan', *EPW*, XIV, 8 July 1989.

91. K.B. Sayeed calls this 'civil-military oligarchy'. See his *Politics in Pakistan*, p. 28.
92. S. Ahmed, 'Centralization, Authoritarianism, and the Mismanagement of Ethnic Relations in Pakistan'. At the time of independence the respective shares of Punjab, North-West Frontier Province, Sindh and Baluchistan were 77 per cent, 19.5 per cent, 2.2 per cent and 0.6 per cent. See S.P. Cohen, *The Pakistan Army* (Berkeley: 1984). The greatest irony was the fact that even the Sindh Regiment remained overwhelmingly Punjabi. According to another analyst about 70 per cent of senior officers and 80 per cent of the NCOs are estimated to be from the Punjab. See F. Ahmed, 'Pakistan's Problems'. As late as the early 1980s only 2 per cent of the country's army were Sindhis, see S. Mahmood, *Sindh Report*.
93. M. Ali Shah, *The Foreign Policy of Pakistan: Ethnic Impact on Diplomacy 1971–1994* (London and New York: 1997).
94. Quoted in T. Amin, *Ethno-National Movements of Pakistan: Domestic and International Factors* (Islamabad: 1988), p. 70. Commentators like Iftikhar H. Malik ignore fears such as Syed apprehended. See his 'The Politics of Ethnic Conflict in Sindh'.
95. F. Ahmed, 'Pakistan's Problems'.
96. Cited in S. Harrison, 'Ethnicity and the Political Stalemate in Pakistan' in S. Akbar Zaidi ed., *Regional Imbalances*, p. 240.
97. *Awami Awaz*, 31 July 1991.
98. A.A. Kazi, 'Ethnic Nationalities'.
99. A. Hussain. 'The Dynamics of Power: Military, Bureaucracy and the People', cited in A. Rashid and F. Shaheed, *Pakistan: Ethno-Politics*, p. 16. Also see R.B. Rais, 'Building State and Nation in Pakistan', paper presented in ICES seminar, August 1993, Colombo. In the words of Rais: 'Pakistan's fledging bourgeoisie class emerged as the staunchest supporter of petty bourgeoisie state dominated by the bureaucratic-military elite' (p. 14). Rais also aptly remarks (p. 15): 'The storm of agitational politics that erupted with the celebration of the 'developmental decade' in 1968 was a manifestation of the inequitable distribution of rewards of economic development and reflective of political frustration.'
100. A Hussain, 'The Dynamics of Power'.
101. F. Ahmed, *Ethnicity and Politics in Pakistan*.
102. ibid.
103. Z.K. Maluka, *The Myth of Constitutionalism in Pakistan* (Karachi: 1995). Sindhi literature was enriched during the days of the anti-One Unit Movement. Poets like Sheikh Ayaz shot to fame; Haider Bux Jatoi composed the famous poem entitled *Jiye Sindh*, which ignited nationalist feelings of Sindhis.
104. M.H. Panhwar, 'The Economic Plight of Sindh Under Pakistan', *Sindh Quarterly*, vol. XVIII, no. 2, 1990.
105. *Newsline*, July 1998, pp. 43–4.
106. S.G. Mustafa Shah, 'Sindh: Conflagration of Martial Laws and its Resurrection from Ashes', *Sindh Quarterly*, vol. XV, no. 1, 1987, p. 12.
107. F. Ahmed, 'Pakistan's Problems', p. 173.
108. A.A. Kazi, 'Ethnic nationalism', p. 10.
109. ibid. p. 11.
110. K.R. Khory, 'Separatism in South Asia'
111. Cited in T. Amin, *Ethno-National Movements of Pakistan*, p. 75.
112. For example the Sind PPP ceremoniously observed 4 March to honour the students killed during the anti-One Unit riots in 1967.
113. L. Ziring, *Pakistan: The Enigma of Political Development* (Folkstone: 1980), pp. 146–7.

114. C. Kennedy, 'The Politics of Ethnicity'.
115. K.R. Khoray, 'Separatism In South Asia', p. 221.
116. A bicameral legislature was introduced and spheres of authority between the centre and provinces were carved out.
117. Bhutto's Pakistan People's Party retained power at the centre, Punjab and Sindh.
118. T. Amin, *Ethno-National Movements of Pakistan*, pp. 126–9.
119. The feeling for a Baluch-Sindhi front against Islamabad was expressed by a Baluch politician to Seling Harrison when he asserted: 'if the worst should ever come to the worst and Pakistan should disintegrate the Baluch and Sindhis would be together. They like each other and might well create a federated state of Sindh and Baluchistan...', cited in S.S. Harrison, 'Ethnicity and the Political Stalemate in Pakistan' in S. Akbar Zaidi ed., *Regional Imbalances*.
120. F. Ahmed, *Ethnicity and Politics in Pakistan*, p. 56.
121. The following line from the poet Rais Amrolivi – although written in another context – was printed as headlines: '*Urdu ka janaza hae zara dhoom say niklay*' ('This is the funeral procession of Urdu; let it go out with fanfare'), cited in T. Rahman, *Language and Politics in Pakistan*, p. 125.
122. A. Rashid and F. Shaheed, *Pakistan: Ethno-Politics*, p. 18.
123. *The Dawn*, 25 March 1972.
124. Cited in T. Rahman, *Language and Politics in Pakistan*, p. 127.
125. ibid. p. 126. Unofficial statistics put the death toll much higher. See D. Mukherjee, 'Pakistan's Growing Pains: Language Riots in Sindh', *Times of India*, 17 July 1992.
126. *The Dawn*, 29 August 1972. But according to some studies the number of dead was at least 55. See C. Kennedy, 'The Politics of Ethnicity', p. 944.
127. K.B. Sayeed, *Politics in Pakistan*, pp. 154–5.
128. When the 12-year period lapsed the country was under the military dictatorship of Zia-ul-Haq who preferred to ignore the Act.
129. *Newsline*, February 1992, p. 44.
130. The fronts in the Jiye Sindh Supreme Council were: Jiye Sindh Mahaz (Political Front); Jiye Sindh Students' Federation; Jiye Sindh Girls' Front; Latif Students' Sangat (Children's Organization); Nari Tehreek (Women's Front); Poreet Sangat (Labour Front).
131. See G.M. Syed, *Sindhu Desh: a Study in its Separate Identity Through the Ages* (Karachi: n.d.); G.M. Syed, *A Case for Sindhu Desh* (Bombay: 1985); I. Ahmed, *State, Nation and Ethnicity in Contemporary South Asia*, pp. 213–14.
132. *Times of India*, 24 July 1972.
133. Interview with Syed, *The Herald*, August 1989, p. 178.
134. M.J. Akbar, *India Siege Within: Challenges to a Nation's Unity* (Harmondsworth: 1985), p. 65.
135. *Times of India*, 24 July 1972.
136. See A.H. Syed, 'Political Parties and the Nationality Question in Pakistan', *Journal of South Asian and Middle Eastern Studies*, vol. XII, no. 1, autumn 1988, p. 52.
137. *The Dawn*, 1 August 1972.
138. E. Ahmed, 'Zia's Hand in Sindh's Agony', *The Friday Times*, 26 July–1 August 1990.
139. S.G. Mustafa Shah, 'Sindhi Society and Sindh Tomorrow'.
140. S. Kandar, *The Political Economy of Pakistan* (Lahore: 1987).
141. K.R. Khoray 'Separatism In South Asia', Chapter 5; M. Ispahani, 'Pakistan: Dimensions of Insecurity'.

142. Allegation by G.M. Syed, *Pakistan Times*, 5 June 1986.
143. The dam is located at Kalabagh in Punjab, 100 miles southwest of Islamabad
144. J.R. Langhari, 'The Kalabagh Dam and the Loss of Water to Sindh', *Sindh Quarterly*, vol. XIV, no. 4, 1981. Also see J.R. Laghari, 'Environmental concerns: Kalabagh dam and Sindh: Punjab water dispute in Pakistan', *Journal of Asian and Affrican Affairs*, vol. 1, no. 1, 1990.
145. L. Ziring, 'Public Policy Dilemas and Pakistan's Nationality Problem: The Legacy of Zia-ul-Haq', *Asian Survey*, vol. XXVIII, no. 8, August 1988, p. 806.
146. A. Gramsci, *Selections from the Prison Notebooks* (ed. and tr. Quintin Hoare and Geoffrey Nowell Smith, London: 1990).
147. A. Hussain, 'The Dynamics of Power'; O. Noman, *Pakistan: A Political And Economic History Since 1947* (London: 1990).
148. Music, sport, arts and culture had to conform to an Islamic code. This was buttressed by military might. See O.A. Khan, 'Political and Economic Aspects of Islamisation' and Z. Haque, 'Islamisation of Society in Pakistan' in A. Khan ed., *Islam, Politics and the State: The Pakistan Experience* (London: 1985). Also see Z. Haque, 'Islamic Processes: Realities and Trends', *South Asia Bulletin*, 8, 1988.
149. For an analysis of Zia's bid to Islamize Pakistan see J.L. Esposito, 'Islam: Ideology and Politics in Pakistan' in A. Banuazizi et al. eds., *The State, Religion and Ethnic Politics*.
150. L. Ziring, 'Public Policy Dilemmas and Pakistan's Nationality Problem: The legacy of Zia-ul-Haq'.
151. For instance, 1981 was celebrated as the year of Sindhi literature. See S.G. Mustafa Shah, 'Sindhi Literature', op. cit. Another important Sindhi cultural society was Shah Abdul Latif Cultural Society. This was also the period when Sindhology developed as a distinct branch of intellectual exercise in Sindh. See S.G. Mustafa Shah, 'Sindhology – Its Meaning and Scope', *Sindh Quarterly*, vol. X, no. 3, 1982.
152. S.G. Mustafa Shah, 'Sindh: The Causes of Present Discontent', p. 1.
153. S.G. Mustafa Shah, 'Sindhi Society and Sindh Tomorrow'.
154. See F. Ahmed, 'Sindh: Another Bangladesh', *Pakistan Democratic Forum*, November 1983; V. Ahmed and A. Rashid,*The Management of Pakistan's Economy 1947–82* (Karachi: 1984).
155. A. Rashid and F. Shaheed, *Pakistan: Ethno-Politics*, p. 20.
156. See the analysis by H.A. Rizvi, *Asian Survey*, vol. XXIV, no. 5, May 1984.
157. Estimates of people killed by the army vary widely. For instance see *Far Eastern Economic Review*, 17 July 1986 and M. Ali Shah, *The Foreign Policy of Pakistan*.
158. *The Frontier Post*, 1 September 1986.
159. *The Muslim*, 1 June 1986.
160. *Times of India* (Delhi), 20 August 1986.
161. M.J. Akbar, *India: The Siege Within*, p. 65.
162. ibid.
163. *The Jang*, 31 August.
164. S. Harrison, 'Ethnicity and Political Stalemate in Pakistan'.
165. T. Rahman, *Language and Politics in Pakistan*, p. 128.
166. Cited in ibid., p. 66.
167. Interview with G.M. Syed, *Pakistan Times*, 5 June 1986.
168. 'Syed's Last Stand', *Newsline*, February 1992, pp. 40–41.
169. *Pakistan Illustrated Weekly*, vol. 3, nos. 7 and 8, 12 April 1991.
170. A.H. Syed, 'Political Parties and the Nationality Question in Pakistan'.
171. K.R. Khoray, 'Separatism In South Asia' pp. 239–40.

172. But its tenure was short-lived. Disbanded in February 1989, it was replaced by Mumtaz Bhutto's Sindh National Front.
173. The World Sindhi Congress has its headquarters in the UK.
174. M. Rashdi, 'Sindh Malaise', *Pakistan Illustrated Weekly*, 30 June 1991, p. 12.
175. See M. Ali, *In the Shadow of History* (Lahore: 1993) pp. 191–2. *The Herald*, July 1986 reported how several student hostels had been converted into dacoits' sanctuaries.
176. *Newsline*, February 1992, pp. 44–5.
177. See the statement of the Inspector General of Police of Sindh, *The Dawn*, 24 June 1986.
178. For the role of the arms and drugs trades in maintaining the violent temper see M. Ispahani, 'Pakistan: Dimensions of Insecurity'. He writes: 'Along with the arms sent into Pakistan through pro-Kabul Pakhtun tribesmen by the Afghan regime, an estimated 40 per cent of the weapons destined for the war effort... have "leaked" into Pakistan...' Also see O. Noman, *The Political Economy of Pakistan 1947–85* (London: 1988) and J. Rashid, 'Ethnic Conflicts', *The Friday Times*, 9–15 July 1992, p. 8.
179. See the Sindhi nationalist leader Rasul Baksh Paleejo's statement in *The Muslim*, 8 July 1986. A.H. Jatoi also voiced a similar opinion in *The Dawn*, 20 June 1986. During this period there were also incidents of the burning of Hindu temples in Sukkur and Jacobabad. This was the first communal incident reported in this region since independence and was widely believed by the PPP to have been fomented to frustrate the MRD. See *The Frontier Post*, 6 March 1986. Again, other observers have cited how senior police and civil officers of Sindh government were 'hand in glove' with dacoits. See H. Mujtaba's submission in *Newsline*, November 1995. Also see M. Ali Shah, *The Foreign Policy of Pakistan*, p. 56.
180. *The Dawn*, 18 July 1986.
181. *The Daily Jang*, 18 July 1986.
182. S. Mahmood, *Sindh Report*, Chapter 1.
183. I. Farooq, 'Imperatives of Discipline and Organisation' (MQM Urdu Document) cited in M. Waseem, 'Ethnic Conflict in Pakistan'.
184. The MQM supremo Altaf Hussain was himself prominent in the Muhajir student body. See F. Ahmed, 'The Rise of Muhajir Separatism', *South Asia Bulletin*, vol. 8, 1988; Arif Hasan, 'The MQM Factor', *Herald*, March 1987. Also see Reply Statement of the Government of Pakistan and Government of Sindh in the Supreme Court of Pakistan, 5 June 1995, no. 46/94, cited in M. Waseem, 'Ethnic Conflict in Pakistan'.
185. Statement of Hamida Khuro of Jeay Sindh and the Sindh National Alliance quoted in K.R. Khoray, 'Separatism In South Asia', p. 234. One need not forget that although in 1979 Zia had jailed Altaf for anti-national activities he relased him at the height of the MRD to mobilize the Muhajirs against Sindhi nationalists.
186. F. Ahmed, 'Ethnicity and Politics', p. 33.
187. I. Ahmed, *State, Nation and Ethnicity*, pp. 202–3.
188. Altaf Hussain, *Safr-e-Zindagi and The Journey of Life* (autobiographical account of Altaf Hussain, Lahore: 1988). The MQM claims that Muhajirs contitute 60 per cent of the population in Sindh, although the 1961, 1972 and 1982 Census estimates present a substantially lower ratio. See MQM Constitutional Petition in the Supreme Court of Pakistan Part I (Boston: 1994), pp. 4–5. Also see Altaf Hussain, *Safr-e-Zindagi* (Lahore: 1988); I. Ahmed, *State, Nation and Ethnicity*, p. 215.
189. H. Alavi, 'Nationhood and Nationalities'.

165

190. *The Herald*, May 1994.
191. Altaf Hussain's interview, *The Herald*, September 1987.
192. 'MQM is the Symbol of Being Oppressed' (MQM Urdu document), cited in M. Wasim, 'Ethnic conflict in Pakistan', p. 11.
193. S. Akbar Zaidi, 'Sindhi vs. Muhajir'.
194. M. Mirza, 'Rise and Fall of the MQM', *The Friday Times*, 25 June-1 July 1992, p. 3.
195. A. Rashid and F. Shaheed, *Pakistan: Ethno-Politics*, p. 28. Altaf has been given the title of *Quaid-e-Tehrik* (leader of the movement) and is called *pir sahib* (spiritual leader).
196. S. Akbar Zaidi, 'Sindhi vs Muhajir', p. 340.
197. See B. Ali, 'Political Forces in Sind' in S. Akbar Zaidi ed., *Regional Imbalances*.
198. O. Verkaaik, *A People of Migrants: Ethnicity, State and Religion in Karachi* (Amsterdam: 1994).
199. I.H. Malik, 'The Politics of Ethnic Conflict in Sindh'.
200. The social role performed by the MQM fits in with the theory of 'pillarization' developed for post-colonial Indonesia where the vacuum in the realm of emancipation and social mobility caused by the weakness of a successor state is filled by a political party.
201. M. Ahmar, 'Ethnicity and State Power in Pakistan: A Case Study of Karachi Crisis', unpublished paper, 30 May 1996.
202. *The Friday Times*, 25 June–1 July 1992, p. 3.
203. Z. Hussain, 'Sindh: A Province Held to Ransom?', *Newsline*, August 1988.
204. Quoted in P.C. Singh, 'Muhajirs and Ethno-Nationalism in Pakistan', *Journal of Peace Studies*, vol. II, 12–13, September–December 1995.
205. C. Kennedy, 'The Politics of Ethnicity', p. 951.
206. M. Hussain and A. Hussain, *Pakistan: Problems of Governance* (New Delhi: 1993).
207. Z. Hussain, 'Sindh: A Province Held to Ransom'.
208. Z. Abbas, 'Sindh: Falling Apart?', *The Herald*, May 1989.
209. S. Ahmed, 'Centralization, Authoritarianism, and the Mismanagement of Ethnic Relations', p. 113.
210. *Sindh Quarterly*, vol. III, no. 3, 1990, p. 40.
211. ibid. p. 46.
212. *The Herald*, June 1990.
213. *The Friday Times*, 25 June–1st July 1992, p. 61.
214. S.I. Khan, 'Living with Violence', *Newsline*, October 1991, pp. 20–22.
215. *The Herald*, May 1989, p. 28.
216. *Newsline*, October 1991, p. 30.
217. *Newsline*, February 1992, p. 44. Addressing a rally in Karachi in 1991, Syed remarked: 'Unfortunate are the organisations in which more than 65 per cent of the cadres are criminals... Such is the case with my Jiye Sindh... I have learnt that you have committed various crimes. You are all criminals.' Many of the leading Jiye Sindh activists present in the meeting later confessed their complicity in criminal activities ranging from robberies, extortions and kidnappings.
218. S. Ahmed, 'Centralization, Authoritarianism and the Mismanagement of Ethnic Relations', p. 115.
219. M. Waseem, 'Ethnic Conflict in Pakistan', p. 14.
220. See *The Herald*, February 1992; *The Muslim*, 20 May 1993.
221. *Newsline*, February 1992, p. 39.
222. ibid.

223. *The Herald*, February 1992.

224. ibid. p. 26.

225. ibid.

226. *Newsline*, February 1992, p. 46.

227. N. Hoodbhoy, 'The Rise of the Sindhi Press', *The Herald*, June 1995. Among the leading Sindhi newspapers are *Kawish, Awami Awaz, Jago Barsat* and *Pukar*.

228. *Foreign Broadcast Information Service* (Hereafter *FBIS*) NES-92-131, 8 July 1992; *The Dawn* (Karachi), 11 June 1992.

229. *Newsline*, December 1991.

230. H. Mujtaba, 'Night Without End', *Newsline*, August 1991.

231. M. Lodhi, *Pakistan's Encounter with Democracy* (Lahore: 1994).

232. A. Azam Ali, 'Sindh: A Point of No Return', *The Herald*, July 1990.

233. In 1990 the MQM became the second largest party in Sindh, having won 15 National Assembly seats from Karachi and Hyderabad and 30 constituencies in the Provincial Assembly. See *The Friday Times* 25 June–1 July 1992, p. 3.

234. T. Aslam, 'MQM: Trial Begins', *The Herald*, February 1988; A. Hasan, 'Power and Powerlessness', *The Herald*, February 1988.

235. B. Ali, 'Political Forces in Sindh' in S.A. Zaidid. *Regional Imbalances*; M. Mirza, *Aaj Ka Sindh* (Lahore: 1986); Tanvir A. Tahir, 'Political Dynamics of Sindh 1947–71,' unpublished M.Phil thesis, University of Karachi, 1990, cited in S. Akbar Zaidi, 'Sindhi vs Muhajir'; T.P. Wright, 'Centre-Periphery Relations and Ethnic Conflict in Pakistan: Sindhis, Muhajirs and Punjabis', *Comparative Politics*, spring 1991. Also see M. Ahmer, 'Ethnicity and State Power in Pakistan', for ethnic riots between Muhajirs and Pathans.

236. S.A. Zaidi, 'Sindhi vs Muhajir', p. 338.

237. A.A. Ali, 'Sindh'; Ameenah Azam Ali, 'No Business as Usual', *The Herald* March 1987; A. Hasan, 'A Generation Comes of Age', *The Herald* October 1987; A. Hasan, 'A Decade of Urban Decay', *The Herald*, January 1990; see K. Bahadur, 'National Integration In Pakistan: The Case of Muhajir Qawmi Movement (MQM), *Journal of Peace Studies*, vol. II, Issues 12–13, September–December 1995.

238. A.A. Ali, 'Sindh'.

239. *The Dawn*, 25 May 1993.

240. *Newsline*, September 1994. See also the interview by Altaf Hussain, *India Today*, 15 July 1995.

241. Rahul Bux Palejo, cited in K. Bahadur, 'National Integration in Pakistan'.

242. *The Statesman*, 1 January 1995.

243. Z. Abbas, 'Words of Violence', *The Herald*, July 1990.

244. The Sindhis fear Biharis would join Muhajirs and create further politico-economic rivalry in the province. See *FBIS*-NES-93-021, 3 February 1993.

245. M. Mirza, 'Altaf Hussain Conspires to Stage Comeback', *The Friday Times* 28 June–3 July 1993, p. 3.

246. 'Sweeping the dust under carpets', *The Telegraph*, 11 January 1995.

247. *The Statesman*, 3 August 1995.

248. A. Rashid and F. Shaheed, *Pakistan: Ethno-Politics*, p. 34.

249. *The Telegraph*, 1 October 1990.

250. This is the finding of research commissioned by the Karachi Chambers of Commerce and Industries. Cited in M. Ahmar, 'Ethnicity and State Power in Pakistan', p. 6. According to one estimate quoted by Ahmar 34 working days were lost in 1995 due to strikes organized by the MQM.

251. According to an estimate the octroi collection in Hyderabad, for instance, declined

from Rs. 240,000 per day in 1988 to Rs. 120,000 per day in 1990. See *The Friday Times*, 7–13 January 1993.

252. MQM Constitutional Petition before the Supreme Court of Pakistan (Boston: 1994) Part I, pp. 62–86.

253. M.G. Chitkara, *Muhajir's Pakistan*, p. 48.

254. ibid., p. 65. In December 1998 the MQM also wrote to the UN Secretary-General Kofi Annan for intervention, *POT*, vol. XXVI, no. 317, p. 4142.

255. *Asian Age*, 4 August 1995.

256. K. Mumtaz, 'The Gender Dimension in Sindh's Ethnic Conflict'.

257. Mumtaz Nizamani, one-time President of the organization, comes from thepeasantry.

258. The commitment of these women to MQM leadership is testified to by the following comment of a woman speaker in a 1988 rally: 'When our children are in the firing line, and our men are so committed, how can we stay away?', cited in K. Mumtaz, 'The Gender Dimension in Sindh's Ethnic Conflict', p. 157.

259. M. Abbas, 'The New Vanguard', *The Star*, 28 July 1988 cited in K. Mumtaz, 'The Gender Dimension in Sindh's Ethnic Conflict'.

260. *The Frontier Post*, 25 July 1991, cited in K. Mumtaz, 'The Gender Dimension in Sindh's Ethnic Conflict'.

261. K. Mumtaz, 'The Gender Dimension in Sindh's Ethnic Conflict', p. 160.

262. K. Mumtaz and F. Shaheed, *Women of Pakistan: Two Steps Forward One Step Back* (London: 1987).

263. When Dr Motilal Jotwani met Syed at Kanishka Hotel in New Delhi on 13 July 1987 the latter categorically told him that the Two-Nation Theory was 'misconceived'. Cited in M.G. Chitkara, *Muhajir's Pakistan*, p. 165.

264. For Syed's views on this issue see his following works: *The Past, Present and Future of Sindh Sindhu Desh; What and Why and Consciousness of Sindh*, cited in K.R. Malkani, *The Sindh Story*.

265. T. Anwar, *Langage and Politics in Pakistan*, p. 120. Also see Syed's interview to *The Herald* of August 1989.

266. Interview with G.M. Syed, *The Tribune*, 20 July 1987, cited in K.R. Khoray 'Separatism In South Asia', p. 243.

267. See H. Mujtaba's review of Syed's book in *Newsline*, February 1994.

268. K.R. Malkani, *The Sindh Story*, p. 145.

269. ibid. p. 135.

270. A.A. Kazi, 'Ethnic Nationalism', p. 16.

271. ibid. p. 9. The same view was reiterated in my interview with Aftab A. Kazi in Washington in June 1992. Also see *Amrita Bazar Patrika*, 12 April 1988 and *The Hindustan Times*, 11 April 1988.

272. K.R. Malkani, The Sindh Story, op. cit., p. 97.

273. Cited in T. Amin, *Ethno-National Movements of Pakistan*, p. 100.

274. *The Dawn*, 28 August 1983.

275. The proceedings of the World Sindhi Congress in Delhi were widely reported in the Indian press.

276. *The Morning News*, 26 August 1983.

277. M.J. Akbar's interview with Syed. See M.J. Akbar, *India: The Siege Within*, p. 65.

278. Submission of Aziz Ahmed Khan, Director General for South Asia, Pakistan Ministry of Foreign Affairs, 18 May 1989, cited in K.R. Khoray 'Separatism In South Asia' p. 244.

279. This is admitted by the protagonists of Sindhi nationalism currently resident in the USA.

280. *The Dawn*, 31 May 1972.
281. *FBIS*-NES 31 May 1972.
282. The Al-Zulfiqar group was founded by Murtaza Bhutto.
283. S. Mahmood, *Sindh Report*, p. 58.
284. *FBIS*-NES-90-024, p. 59.
285. *The Times*, 8 May 1990.
286. *FBIS*-NES-92-101, 26 May 1992, p. 55.
287. *FBIS*-NES-93-053, 22 March 1993, p. 68.
288. ibid. 13 October 1995.
289. I. Ahmed, *State, Nation and Ethnicity*, p. 208.
290. *The Telegraph*, 15 March 1998.
291. ibid.
292. A. Mir, 'The RAW Factor', *Newsline*, April 1998, pp. 41–4.
293. *The Telegraph*, 8 June 1998; *The Asian Age*, 8 June 1998.
294. *The Asian Age*, 10 September 1998.
295. ibid.; Public Opinion Trends (hereafter POT), 8 November 1998, p. 3518.
296. *The Asian Age*, 5 August 1995.
297. ibid.; POT, 8 November 1998, vol. XXVI, no. 272.
298. *The Telegraph*, 15 July 1995.
299. *The Dawn*, 16 July 1995.
300. *The Hindu*, 26 August 1986.
301. Interview with G.M. Syed, *The Herald*, August 1989.
302. This view was confidentially confirmed in my discussion with retired Indian Police officers.
303. Interview with Ejaz Jatoi cited in K.R. Khoray, p. 243.
304. M.G. Chitkara, *Muhajir's Pakistan*, p. 62.
305. Z. Hussein, 'Sindh: Day of the Nationalist', *The Herald*, June 1988. One may recall the fanfare with which Syeed had unfurled the flag of Sindhu Desh at a 1988 Sindh National Alliance rally, *The Friday Times*, 23–9 July 1992, p. 7.
306. *The Herald* (Karachi), February 1992.
307. This section amongst the Sindhis has acquired a major financial stake even in Karachi. See S. Akbar Zaidi, 'Sindhi vs Muhajir'.
308. H. Mujtaba, 'Sindhi Separatism: Myth or Reality?', *Newsline*, February 1992, p. 39.
309. Interview with G.M. Syed, *Pakistan Times*, 5 June 1986.
310. Cited in *Newsline*, February 1992, p. 41.
311. *Newsline*, February 1992, p. 42.
312. F. Ahmed, *Ethnicity and Politics*, p. 57.
313. *Newsline*, February 1992, p. 31.
314. S. Harrison, 'Ethnicity and Political Stalemate in Pakistan'.
315. ibid. The Pir of Pagro especially lent a helping hand to Islamabad.
316. M.G. Chitkara, *Muhajre's Pakistan*, p. 147.
317. S.A. Zaidi, 'Sindhi vs Muhajir', op.cit., p. 1297.
318. I. Bakhtiar, 'Estranged Bedfellows', *The Herald*, March 1997, pp. 41–2.
319. S. Ahmed, 'Centralisation, Authoritarianism and the Mismanagement of Ethnic Relations, pp. 121–2.
320. At one point between December 1986 and January 1987 clashes between Muhajirs and Pathans became more frequent than between Muhajirs and Sindhis. See *The Viewpoint* 18 and 25 December 1986; *The Herald*, vol. 18, 1987.
321. B. Ali, 'Political Forces in Sindh'.
322. See *The Viewpoint* 18 and 25 December 1986; *The Herald*, vol. 18, 1987. The

Pakhtuns who practically control the transport sector in Karachi play a major role in the arms and drug trades. Punjabis and Pakhtuns settled in Karachi formed the Punjabi-Pakhtun Itehad (PPI) to counteract Muhajir violence.

323. *The Telegraph*, 13 February 1998.
324. Oskar Verkaaik, *A People of Migrants*, p. 71.
325. 'The Rule of the Poor' (MQM Urdu document) cited in ibid., p. 11.
326. See *The Telegraph*, 19 December 1994, for accounts of recent MQM factional clashes. Also see *The Herald*, July 1994 and January 1995.
327. I. Bakhtiar, 'The MQM: Dead or Alive', *The Herald*, December 1992.
328. S. Ahmed, 'Pakistan at Fifty: A Tenuous Democracy', *Current History*, December 1997, pp. 419–24.
329. *The Telegraph*, 26 March 1998.
330. G. Hasnain, 'Carnage City', *Newsline* July 1998, p. 57.
331. *The Telegraph*, 26 March 1998.
332. *Newsline*, July 1998, p. 60.
333. G. Hassain, 'Carnage City', p. 60.
334. *The Statesman*, 27 February 1995. Pakistan's population comprises 80 per cent Sunnis and 18 per cent Shias. Many Shia-Sunni clashes are essentially Muhajir-Sindhi confrontations, the former being mostly Shias.
335. *The Friday Times*, 10–16 September 1992, p. 5.
336. *Newsline*, March 1994.
337. ibid.
338. ibid.
339. *The Telegraph*, 5 October 1998. In what came to be called the 'Islamabad Declaration', the Conference condemned the Punjabi leadership as: '…myopic rulers, [who] have constantly used force and applied instruments like martial laws and doctrine of necessity and slogans of Pakistan nation, brotherhood and Muslim *ummah* to swindle, rob and deny the people of the federating units of their political economic, cultural and human rights'.
340. H. Alavi, 'Nationhood and Communal Violence'.
341. M.B. Tonyo, 'Ethnicity in Sindh and National Cohesion', *Sindh Quarterly*, vol. XIX, no. 1, 1991, pp. 30–31.
342. S. Ahmed, 'Centralisation, Authoritarianism and the Mismanagement of Ethnic Relations', p. 118.
343. This theme is explicated in all of Alavi's major writings on the ethnic question in Pakistan.
344. See S. Das and B. De, 'Ethnic Revivalism: Problems in the Indian Union' in K.S. Singh ed., *Ethnicity, Caste and People: India and the Soviet Union* (Delhi: 1992).
345. R.B. Rais, 'Building State & Nation In Pakistan'.
346. ibid.
347. Cited in G.M. Mehkri, 'The Common Man In Sindh', *Sindh Quarterly*, vol. XIII, no. 1, 1985.
348. S. Ahmed, 'Pakistan at Fifty', p. 419. It is not without significance that Pakistan imposed emergency immediately after exploding her nuclear devices in May 1998, although in India no tampering was done with its democratic apparatus after nuclear explosions were carried out in the same month. In fact, during the parliamentary debates in New Delhi a significant dissenting voice was recorded against the Vajpayee government's nuclear policy.
349. H. Alavi, 'Nationhood and Communal Violence', p. 153.

350. A. Rashid, *Private Industrial Investment in Pakistan 1960–70* (Cambridge: 1982); V. Ahmed and R. Amjad, *The Management of Pakistan's Economy 1947–82* (Karachi: 1984); O. Noman, *The Political Economy of Pakistan*.

351. B. Ali, 'Pakistan's Decade of Generals', *EPW*, 22, 28, 1987; S.A. Zaidi, 'How the Bourgeoisie Views Pakistan', *EPW*, 23, 48, 1988.

352. D. Reetz, 'National Consolidation or Fragmentation of Pakistan: The Dilemma of General Zia-ul-Haq (1977–1988)' in D. Weidemann ed., *Nationalism, Ethnicity and Political Development: South Asian Perspective* (Delhi: 1991). Also see A.H. Syed in 'Political Parties and the Nationality Question in Pakistan', *Journal of South Asian and Middle Eastern Studies*, vol. XII, no. 1, autumn 1988, and A.S. Ahmed in *Pakistan Society* (Karachi: 1984) for inherent ethnic pluralism in Pakistani society.

353. Quoted in K.R. Malkani, *The Sindh Story*, p. 133.

354. B. Anderson, *Imagined Communities* (London: 1983).

355. A. Rashid and F. Shaheed, *Pakistan: Ethno-Politics*, p. 10.

356. D. Khan, 'A Sindhi View,' *Sindh Quarterly*, vol. XVII, no. 4, 1989.

357. *Communalism Combat*, 29 January 1997.

358. S.G. Mustafa Shah, 'Sindhi Society and Sindh Tomorrow', p. 6.

359. S. Ahmed, 'Centralisation, Authoritarianism and the Mismanagement of Ethnic Relations' p. 124.

360. T. Ali, *Pakistan: Military Rule or People's Power* (London: 1970); S. Harrison, *In Afghanistan's Shadow*; I. Baloch, 'The Baluch Question in Pakistan and the Right of Self-Determination' in W. Zingle, *Pakistan in the 80s: Law and Constitution* (Lahore: 1985); L. Ziring, *Pakistan: The Enigma of Political Development*. (Folkstone: 1980)

361. Cited in S. Ahmed, 'Pakistan at Fifty', p. 419.

362. *Newsline*, July 1998, p. 28.

363. Sharif's 11 June remark on the Kalabagh project is worth quoting: 'We surprised the world on May 28 by exploding nuclear devices. Now we will conquer another battlefield by constructing the Kalabagh dam', cited in ibid., p. 42.

364. ibid. p. 41.

365. *Times of India*, 4 September 1999.

366. Reposing faith in the resolution of the Sindh question, a commentator rises to the height of political idealism: 'The basic foundation for social contract lies in the fact that, based on our religious and cultural heritage, all Pakistanis – including the minorities – should consider and treat each other as members of their own family in terms of striving to advance their welfare and protection of their extended family. East Pakistanis should be free to follow... [their] own dreams, and advance to the extent... [they] can. However, they should treat each other as members of their own family in terms of striving to advance their welfare and protection of their rights.' A.N. Memon, 'Sindhis in Pakistan: The Case for Social Contract', *Journal of Peace Studies*, II, 12–13, September–December 1995.

367. F. Ahmed, 'Transformation of Agrarian Structures in Pakistan' in N.M. Lan ed., *Unreal Growth: Critical Studies in Asian Development* (New Delhi: 1984), vol. II, pp. 606–31. Also see his 'Agrarian Change and Class Formation in Sindh', *EPW*, vol. XIX, no. 9, 29 September 1984.

368. For such positive developments in the realm of civil society in Pakistan see I.H. Malik, 'Continuity or Change in Contemporary Pakistan? State, Ideological Polarisation, and Ethnic Pluralism' in S.K. Mitra and R.A. Lewis eds., *Subnational Movements in South Asia* (Boulder: 1996). Also see his 'The Politics of Ethnic

Conflict in Sindh'. It is not without significance that fundamentalist forces did not secure more than 8 per cent of the total votes in the last parliamentary elections in Pakistan. Even during the recent Kargil crisis which involved armed confrontations between India and Pakistan on the issue of Pak-sponsored infiltration into Jammu and Kashmir a section of the press in Pakistan adopted a critical stance towards the Islamabad regime. See for instance, F.S. Aijazuddin, 'India Came with an Olive Branch, Pakistan Replied with Kargil', *The Dawn*, reproduced in *The Asian Age*, 18 July 1999.

Conclusion

The foregoing analysis has identified the roots of the Kashmir and Sindh Questions in the distorted nation-building strategies adopted respectively in India and Pakistan. Both the Kashmir and Sindh imbroglios confirm the broader theoretical premise with which the present work began. First, they demonstrate that a nation-building strategy cannot easily redefine political or imagined communities if the constituent elements perceive the process to be inimical to their interests and aspirations. Secondly, the two issues indicate that in situations where ethnic and state boundaries do not converge the members of disaffected ethnic communities tend to purge their imposed national identities and engage in ethnic assertions in conjunction with their compatriots across artificial national boundaries. In such circumstances the concerned political actors identify themselves – at least temporarily – with activists and affairs outside their own state borders, thus blurring the distinction between domestic and foreign affairs. Such a tendency can be clearly noticed in Kashmir, while the potential or some signs of this trend are present in the case of Sindh.

Western scholars have traditionally considered subcontinental ethnic assertions – as in Kashmir, Punjab and the North-East in India or in Sindh and North-West Frontier Provinces in Pakistan – to be secessionist politics that would ultimately lead to the dissolution of national unity in the two countries.[1] The secession of East Pakistan leading to the formation of Bangladesh in 1971 is cited as an evidence of this thesis. Some have seen ethnic politics in South Asia as an instance of nationalism yielding place to nationism.[2] While nationalism is viewed as the desire of a nation to have a state of its own, nationism may be defined as the desire of a state to have a nation of its own. It has been argued that ethnic, religious, linguistic and other forms of communal loyalties – strengthened by an uneven distribution of scarce resources – pose a challenge to the pluralist societies of India and Pakistan, creating a space for the transmutation of nationalism to nationism.[3]

I, however, consider the hypothesis of the inevitability of the breakdown of the Indian Union due to ethnic assertions as untenable. In the aftermath of her independence India had rejected cultural, religious and ethnic homogeneity as a determinant of her body polity. Instead of

173

proclaiming India as a Hindu state, the national ruling classes accepted diversity as the enduring site of the country's national politics.[4] Ethnic pluralism cannot thus be considered as potentially anti-Indian nation-state. Ethnic assertions in the country do not generally question the legitimacy of the Indian state in their initial stages. But the continuing centrist and negative postures of the Indian government usually drive sections of the actors involved in ethnic politics into fissiparous and separatist channels. The situation in Kashmir, as indicated in the present study, is amply illustrative of this process. Systematic infringement of Kashmiriyat through New Delhi's centralizing drive, the undermining of democratic institutions in Jammu and Kashmir by New Delhi's manoeuvring politics, and frustration of the Kashmiri youth caused by an absence of planned economic development more than anything else have generated secessionist politics in Kashmir. During the first 49 years of Indian independence Jammu and Kashmir had the opportunity of tasting only 12 years of representative government. As Jayaprakash Narayan, one of the most perceptive critics of the Indian polity, noted as early as 1966: 'We profess democracy, but rule by force in Kashmir… We profess secularism but let Hindu nationalism stampede us [in Kashmir]… the [Kashmir] problem exists not because Pakistan wants to grab Kashmir, but because there is deep and widespread discontent among people.'[5] But it was not before the late 1980s – particularly after the fateful 1987 elections – that a dominant trend within Kashmiri ethnic politics challenged the sanctity of the Indian state and transferred its loyalty to Pakistan. In the Punjab, too, the Sikh movement did not initially betray secessionist tendencies. This is best testified to by the Anandpur Sahib resolution of 1987 – the first concrete expression of Sikh demand – which hardly challenged the continuation of the Indian Union. Instead, nine-tenths of the resolution was concerned with such issues as the conversion of Chandigarh to the capital city of the Punjab, a greater share for the Punjab of river water flowing through the province and a redemarcation of the boundaries of the Punjab to incorporate within it the contiguous Punjabi-speaking areas. Unfortunately for India, the ruling party in Delhi refused to appreciate this as democratic demands of the Sikhs and chose to interpret the Anandpur Sahib resolution in separatist terms. What followed was 'ethnicization in reverse' of a secular regional movement.[6] Operation Bluestar of June 1984, the tragic assassination of Indira

Gandhi by her Sikh bodyguards, Rajiv Gandhi's success in rallying popular support around the Congress against Sikh sectarianism – all these strengthened the process of reverse ethnicization. The crisis was further aggravated when Rajiv Gandhi signed an accord with the Akalis in August 1985, only to keep it in deliberate cold storage. The Sikh moderate politicians now felt humiliated, and extremism received a boost in the Punjab. In the same way, in North-East India ethnic politics has been primarily fuelled by the centrist drive of the Indian state and acute regional economic imbalances.[7]

Although Pakistan opted for a political system quite different from India, she shared with her neighbour one experience – the centrist posture of the state. Like India, Pakistan is a multi-ethnic and multi-lingual state. But instead of ethnic tightrope-walking, the Pakistani ruling class adopted a nation-building strategy that was overtly centrist and distinctly biased in favour of the Punjabis, the country's majority community. An ethos based on Urdu culture and a particular version of Islam were projected as symbols of Pakistani national identity at the expense of hopes and aspirations of a number of minority ethnic groups whose tradition did not fall within that matrix. This policy of governance constituted the prelude to a series of ethnic assertions that rocked the province of Sindh and the north-western part of the country. But even this identity politics did not initially question the legitimacy of the Pakistan state. For example, in 1949 when G.M. Syed, the doyen of Sindhi ethno-nationalism, was still eager to work within the Pakistani polity he elucidated concrete proposals for an accommodation of Sindhi identity within the national mainstream.[8] The ruling power in Pakistan not only cold-shouldered those suggestions but also proceeded to subordinate Sindhi identity to the dictates of an Urduized pan-Pakistanism. This set the scene of the Sindh imbroglio, which, as the present work indicates, is tending to acquire South Asian regional dimensions. Even the Bangladesh movement of 1971 – widely viewed as an instance of successful ethnic secessionism in the subcontinent – was the upshot of the mishandling by Pakistan's central government of legitimate East Bengali ethnic aspirations. Mujib-ur-Rahman-led Awami League agitation intially demanded autonomy for the erstwhile East Pakistan within the Pakistani federal structure. It was only after Islamabad's military junta refused to acknowledge the popular mandate of East Pakistanis in favour of the

Awami League and resorted to strong-arm methods to stifle the ethnic voice of the Bengalis that the force of secessionism gained in strength, ending in the formation of Bangladesh. As in the case of Kashmir or Punjab in India, in Pakistan, too, the character of ethnic assertions thus depends largely on the response of the state itself. Ethnic diversity is not ipso facto destructive of either India or Pakistan. Instead, ethnic assertions have tended to assume a separatist character in both these countries because, to use Karl Marx's words in *On the Jewish Question*, of 'a defective statecraft'. The trend of the transfer of loyalty from imposed state frontiers in Kashmir, and threats of the same in Sindh, needs to be viewed in this context.

What then is the solution for the present impasse in Kashmir or Sindh? I find no answer in the generalist subaltern recipe that every ethnic group in a multi-ethnic state could be a nation, that every ethnic group should have a nation of its own. Subversion of democratic rights of an ethnic group within a federal polity due to a distorted nation-building process – as in the case of the Kashmiris in India and Sindhis and Muhajirs in Pakistan – need not lead one to rationalize the Kashmir or Sindh question in terms of the dictum of the right of self-determination.[9] For such a discourse in the international context implies a fragmentation of the present world into a hundred thousand nation-states, since so many ethnic groups have been identified in the 160-odd nation-states.[10] Moreover, ethnic separatist politics in a pluralist country like India or Pakistan is unlikely to solve the issue of the exploitation of minority ethnic groups. After all, as soon as minorities become majorities new minorities appear whose rights do not automatically stand guaranteed in the new situation. Take for instance the case for Khalistan, the proposed independent state for the Sikhs. Although the Sikhs constitute only 1.9 per cent of the total Indian populace, they form about 60 per cent of the people in the Punjab. The question therefore remains: would the new state of Khalistan ensure the rights of its 40 per cent odd minority ethnic groups? Similarly, the militants' blueprint for either an independent Kashmir or Kashmir as a part of Islamic Pakistan would contain a sizeable Hindu Pundit community whose safety or even survival could be at stake. Likewise, an independent Sindhu Pradesh could be tolerant towards such non-Sindhi ethnic groups as Muhajirs, Baluchs or Pathans. To quote a perceptive comment:

The paradox here lies in the fact that the only efficient (ethnic) reaction against nationalism seems to consist in the promotion of a different nationalism. Once victorious, this nationalism may victimize minorities – just as its own members were once victimized by a different nationalism before achieving sovereignty.[11]

Resolution of the Kashmir or Sindh impasse has thus to be found in appropriate methods of nation-building. If ethnic assertions sometimes represent centrifugal tendencies in both India and Pakistan, there also exist in the two countries – as indicated in the present study – strong centripetal forces, which need to be enriched. Commenting on the 'centripetal power of India's nation-state consciousness', Dipankar Gupta aptly remarks: 'Not religion, not language, not rational economic calculation, but an intangible tangle of sentiments arising out of multiple factors, some cultural, some civilizational, some historical, that provide the binding force to India's popular self-awareness as a nation-state.'[12]

The democratic necessity for the two post-colonial successor states in South Asia is 'Diversity in Unity', which implies undoing of the lower social status traditionally accorded to regional, ethnic, local, religious and linguistic specificities. Subnational or regional identities have to be granted legitimacy within the federal structure of India and Pakistan. The following quote that highlights the crux of the Kashmir question is also applicable for the Sindh issue: 'The bonds between a region and nation can be built on stronger grounds within a political cult which is sensitive to democratic aspirations of people of different regions... when national and regional interests were presented as incompatible, the nation itself appeared opposed to the region.'[13] Fortunately for India, the substitution of one-party hegemony by coalition politics at the centre has provided regional political formations with deterministic voices in the national polity. We should not thus any longer think either of representing India from Delhi, and of Pakistan from Islamabad, or of Mumbai and Lahore being alternatives respectively to Delhi and Islamabad. Instead, India has to be represented in Calcutta, Chennai, Vishakapatnam, Amritsar and Srinagar, just as Pakistan should be represented in Lahore, Karachi and Peshawar.

In the case of India, a possible political panacea for the ethnic imbroglio has been recently found in the splitting up of existing linguistic-based provinces into smaller federal units. But I have serious doubts as to the viability of this idea.

First, there is not much evidence to show that smaller provinces in India are either administratively well governed or remain more accountable to the people. A number of states were curved out in the North-East from what was once the province of Assam. This has not necessarily ensured better government in the region. Instead, bigger states with substantial decentralization of power and local participation in administration – as in West Bengal, Kerala and Tripura – have experienced newer and more effective forms of governance. The issue, therefore, is not about the size of the state. What is crucial is the nature of political leadership and particular class interests the ruling party seeks to serve.

Secondly, suspicion has been voiced that smaller federal units might strengthen the already existing centralizing posture of Indian federalism. Smaller states would inevitably be in a weak bargaining position in their relations with the federal government. Constant dependence on the central government by smaller units would strengthen the long arm of New Delhi. Besides, tampering with the existing structure of federal polity is likely to fuel separatist and fissiparous tendencies.

Thirdly, the politics of small states fails to identify the two main distortions in India's body polity – regional imbalance and class polarization. One doubts if the creation of smaller states would undo these processes. Under the present bourgeois-landlord dominated state structure new administrative boundaries or a few administrative jobs in non-productive sectors cannot by themselves solve any of the basic problems of nation-building in India. Until poverty is alleviated, intra-state migrations in search of livelihood will continue; so long as resources remain scarce and unequally distributed, national identity will tend to be fragmented. In such circumstances, the politics of small states diverts popular attention from broad-based left and democratic movements that alone can guarantee the strengthening of a pluralist polity in India.

What India actually requires is a provision for regional autonomy within the existing provinces. This calls for a restructuring of centre-state relations and creation of autonomous districts within federal units to take care of localist and ethnic aspirations. The formations of Boro Autonomous Council, the autonomous district councils in Tripura, and the Gorkhaland Hill Council were thus steps in the right direction. The

Indian government should provide these councils with enough financial and administrative resources to make them effective administrative units. Regional autonomy would on the one hand protect the language, culture and social identity of minority groups, and on the other devolve administrative power to the grass-roots level to meet the special needs of the localities. At the same time the people from these autonomous regions would have access to administrative jobs and educational opportunities all over the province. This would benefit all sections of Kashmiris, the Jharkhandis in Bihar, the hill people in the Uttarkhand region of Uttar Pradesh and the Nepali-speaking people of the Darjeeling hill areas.

The present analysis of Kashmir and Sindh has also highlighted the regional dimension of the two issues. A resolution of these questions requires normalization of Indo-Pakistani relations. Fortunately – despite recent tensions – some positive signs can be deciphered in this realm. During the last parliamentary elections in Pakistan the Kashmir issue was not a selling proposition. Pressure groups within the civil societies of both states are increasingly realising that co-operative methods are more worth pursuing than fighting wars.[14] The process of normalization did suffer a setback from the nuclear race initiated in the subcontinent in May 1998. But the regimes in neither Islamabad nor New Delhi could ignore growing popular pressures for peace. The Indian premier Vajpayee's historic bus trip to Lahore and signing of the Lahore declaration in February 1999, increasing exchange of cultural and business delegations and recent discussions for the supply of electricity from Pakistan to India are indicative of this truth. While armed forces clashed in the Kargil sector along the Line of Control in May–June 1999, the residents living close to either sides of the border prayed for peace. 'We do not want any more wars', exclaimed Sukhjinder Singh, a farmer.[15] Another agriculturist, Balwinder Singh, whose land is located across the barbed wire fence right on the Indo-Pak border in the Punjab, asserted that war was the last thing the villagers wanted. 'It not only exposes us to [the] horrible spectre of death, but also throws our entire life out of gear', he remarked.[16] When Balwinder regretted that they could never build *pucca* houses for fear of another war breaking out and urged both countries to strive for peace he was voicing the concern of a significant segment of subcontinental society. The Kargil tensions failed also to disrupt the Delhi-Lahore bus service. Almost all passengers coming from Pakistan regretted the escalating tensions. An elderly woman expressed the feelings of her fellow travellers: 'Why cannot they remain in peace and let the people on both sides meet. We do not want war again.'[17] In Pakistan there has also been the emergence of a 'dissenting voice' against the state policy of fomenting tension in Kargil.[18] A constructive Indo-Pak bilateralism would undoubtedly create possibilities of resolving the Kashmir and Sindh issues within the national polities of the two countries. We can then think of developing cultural alternatives to the present centrist bias in the state structures of India and Pakistan by emphasizing all that is democratic in our national cultures, stressing not centrality but diversity in our pre-colonial and colonial past. The need of the hour in both countries is to preserve cultural and ethnic diversities without endangering national identities. Recent studies[19] have discounted the prospect of an imminent demise of ethnicity either due to globalization or subsumation of fragmented identities by broader civic concerns of a liberal-democratic order.[20] Instead, current trends of world politics indicate the persistence of ethno-nationalism as a viable force within nation-states for upholding equal rights for all members of a pluralist society. Ethno-nationalism seeks, in the words of a commentator, 'new channels of representation, access for excluded interests to the political systems, and the reform of the decision-making processes and the rules of the political game'.[21]

In such circumstances, both New Delhi and Islamabad have to abandon their traditional policy of considering ethnic assertions as mere law and order issues and trying to confront them with such legislation with a colonial flavour as the Terrorist and Disruptive Activities Prevention Act in India, or the Anti-Terrorism (Amendment) Ordinance of 1999 in Pakistan. Neither the Indian rhetoric that the purpose of Indo-Pak talk is only to ensure 'vacation of Azad Kashmir',[22] nor Islamabad's attempt to silence such leading journalists of the country as Najam Sethi on the pretext of his 'RAW connections' are constructive gestures. Equally disturbing was the BJP's decision to celebrate the birthday of Shyamaprasad Mookherjee on 23 June 1999 as 'Kashmir Day' when the Hindu Mahasabha leader's martydom for the cause of Jammu and Kashmir's integration with the Indian Union was to be recalled with full glory and respect. Instead, the Indian and Pakistani governments should search for political settlements in both

Kashmir and Sindh. Even General Shankar Ray Chaudhuri, the former Indian Chief of Army Staff and a member of the Indian Parliament, himself admitted 'sheer force could not solve insurgency – a process of positive dialogue had to be initiated'.[23] What we require is not the much-trumpeted call for national integration propagated by the ruling authorities in the two countries, but an enrichment of common Indian and Pakistani nationhood based on an extension of democracy to the grass roots, abolition of socio-economic discriminations and creation of an equitable political order. 'Nation-state sentiments' and 'sub-regional identifications' in both India and Pakistan have to be harmonized. Only then will nation-building strategies in the two successor states of South Asia cease becoming nation-destroying strategies, and ethnic pluralism may then become a source of sustenance and not of dissidence for the two federations.

NOTES

1. A classic exposure of this view is found in S. Harrison, *India: The Most Dangerous Decades*. (Princeton: 1960)
2. See for instance M. Yapp, 'Language, religion and political identity: a general framework' in D. Taylor and M. Yapp eds., *Political Identity in South Asia* (London: 1979).
3. R. Ghosh ed., *Protest Movements in South and South-East India: Traditional and Modern Idioms of Expression* (Hong Kong, 1987).
4. D. Gupta, 'The Indispensable Center: Ethnicity and Politics in the Indian State', *Journal of Contemporary Asia*, vol. 20, no. 4, 1990.
5. Cited in M.J. Akbar, *India: The Siege Within* (Harmondsworth: 1985), p. 267.
6. D. Gupta, 'The Indispensable Center: Ethnicity and Politics in the Indian State'.
7. This is the hypothesis of my current research on 'Ethnic Politics in North-East India'.
8. Cited in *Sindh Quarterly*, vol. XII, no. 1, 1984. Also see *The Friday Times* 13–19 August 1992, p. 13.
9. S. Bose, for instance tends to present the Kashmiri ethnic assertion as a movement for self-determination. See his *The Challenge in Kashmir: Democracy, Self-Determination and a Just Peace* (New Delhi: 1997).
10. T.H. Eriksen, 'Ethnicity and Nationalism: Definitions and Critical Reflections', *Bulletin of Peace Proposals*, vol. 23 (2) 1992, pp. 219–24.
11. ibid. p. 224.
12. D. Gupta, *The Context of Ethnicity: Sikh Identity in a Comparative Perspective* (Delhi: 1997), p. 17.
13. N. Bhattacharya's Preface to Balraj Puri, *Kashmir Towards Insurgency* (Tracts For The Times/4, New Delhi: 1995 ed.), p. vii.
14. See S. Ahmed and S. Das, 'Movements of People, Ideas, Trade and Technology:

Towards a Peaceful Coexistence of India and Pakistan' (CMC Occasional Paper, Albuquerque March 1998); S. Das, 'Regional Security through Constructive Bilateralism: Prospects for South Asian Stability', *Economic and Political Weekly*, vol. XXXV, no. 49, 2–8 December 2000. Also see N. Kamal, 'Pakistani Perceptions and Prospects of Reducing the Nuclear Danger in South Asia' (CMC Occasional Paper, Albuquerque, January 1999).

15. *Times of India*, 29 May 1999.
16. ibid.
17. *Times of India*, 30 May 1999.
18. S. Das, 'Regional Security through Constructive Bilateralism'.
19. See A. Melucci, *Nomads of the Present* (London: 1989); K. Yoshino, *Cultural Nationalism in Contemporary Japan: A Sociological Enquiry* (London: 1994); J. Hutchinson, *Modern Nationalism* (London: 1994); W.H. McNeill, *Polyethnicity and National Unity in World History* (Toronto: 1986); A.D. Smith, *Nations and Nationalism in a Global Era* (Cambridge: 1996 ed.).
20. For the literature on the imminent dissolution of ethnic identities see R. Breton, 'From ethnic to civic nationalism', *Ethnic and Racial Studies*, III (1998); E. Hobsbawn, *Nations and Nationalism since 1780* (Cambridge: 1990); S. Castles, et al., *Mistaken Identity* (Sydney: 1992); E. Gellner, *Nations and Nationalism* (Oxford: 1983); M. Featherstone ed., *Global Culture: Nationalism, Globalisation and Modernity* (London: 1990); A. Giddens, *The Consequences of Modernity* (Cambridge, 1991).
21. See J. Hutchinson and Anthony D. Smith eds., *Ethnicity* (Oxford: 1996), p. 369.
22. *The Nation*, 20 November 1998.
23. Cited in H.K. Barpujari, 'North-East India: The Problems and Policies since 1947', General President's Address, Indian History Congress, Calcutta, 1995.

Select Bibliography

A: BOOKS & ARTICLES

Abbas, Zaffar 'Words of violence', *The Herald*, July 1990.
—— 'Sindh: Falling Apart?', *The Herald*, May 1989.
Abdullah, Farooq, *My Dismissal* (Delhi: 1985).
Ahmar, Moonis, 'Security Perception in the Indo-Pakistan Relationship', *Pakistan Horizon Quarterly*, vol. XXXVII, no. 1, 1984.
—— 'Ethnicity and State Power in Pakistan: A case study of the Karachi crisis', unpublished paper, 30 May 1996.
Ahmed, Akbar S., *Pakistan Society* (Karachi: 1984).
Ahmed, Eqbal, 'Zia's Hand in Sindh's Agony', *The Friday Times*, 28 July–1 August.
—— 'The Challenge in Sindh', *The Dawn*, 21 June 1992.
—— 'Behind the crisis in Sindh', *The Friday Times*, 19–25 July 1990.
Ahmed, Feroz, 'The Rise of Muhajir Separatism', *South Asia Bulletin*, vol. 8, 1988.
—— 'Sindh: Another Bangladesh', *Pakistan Democratic Forum*, November 1983.
—— *Pakistan's Problem: Ethnicity and Politics in Pakistan* (Karachi: 1998).
—— *Ethnicity and Politics in Pakistan* (Lahore: 1998).
—— 'The Language Question in Sindh', in S. Akbar Zaidi ed., *Regional Imbalances and The National Question in Pakistan* (Lahore 1992).
—— 'Agrarian change and class formation in Sindh', *Economic & Political Weekly* (hereafter *EPW*), vol. 19, no. 39.
—— 'Ethnicity and Politics: The Rise of Muhajir Separatism', *South Asia Bulletin*, vol. and nos. 1 and 2, 1988.
—— 'Pakistan's problem of national integration', in Mohammad Asghar Khan ed., *Islam, Politics and the state: The Pakistan Experience* (London: 1985).
—— 'Agrarian change and class formation in Sindh', *EPW*, vol. XIX, no. 39, 29 September 1984.
—— 'Transformation of agrarian structure in Pakistan' in Ngo Manh Lan ed., *Unreal growth: Critical Studies in Asian Development*, vol. II. (New Delhi: 1984).
Ahmed, Ishtiaq, *Nation and Ethnicity in Contemporary South Asia* (London and New York: 1998).
Ahmed, Samina, 'Centralization, Authoritarianism and the Mismanagement of Ethnic Relations in Pakistan', in Michael E. Brown and Sumit Ganguly eds., *Government Policies and Ethnic Relations in Asia and the Pacific* (Massachusetts: 1996).
—— 'Pakistan at Fifty: A tenuous Democracy', *Current History*, December 1997.
Ahmed, Samina and Das, Suranjan, 'Movements of people, ideas, trade and technology: towards a peaceful coexistence of India and Pakistan' (CMC Occasional Paper, Albuquerque: March 1998).
Ahmed, Viqar and Amjad, Rashid, *The Management of Pakistan's Economy 1947–82* (Karachi: 1984).
Akbar, M.J., *The Siege Within: Challenges To A Nation's Unity* (Harmondsworth: 1985).
—— *Kashmir: Behind the Vale* (New Delhi: 1991).
Akhtar, Shaeen, 'Uprising in India-held Jammu and Kashmir', *Regional Studies*, vol. IX, no. 2, 1991.

—— 'Human Rights Violations in IHK', *Regional Studies*, vol. IX, no. 2 Spring 1993.

Alavi, Hamza, 'The State in Post-Colonial Societies: Pakistan and Bangladesh', *New Left Review*, July/August 1974.

—— 'Class and State in Pakistan', in Gerdezi et al. eds., *Pakistan: The Roots of Dictatorship* (London: 1983).

—— 'Nationhood and Nationalities in Pakistan', *EPW*, 24, 27, 1989.

—— 'Nationhood and communal violence in Pakistan', *Journal of Contemporary Asia*, vol. 21, 2, 1991.

Ali, Ameenth Azam, 'No business as usual', *The Herald*, March 1987.

—— 'Sindh: A Point of No Return', *The Herald*, July 1990.

Ali, Babar, 'Political forces in Sind' in S. Akbar Zaidi ed., *Regional Imbalances and the National Question in Pakistan* (Lahore: 1992).

—— 'The National Question in Pakistan', *EPW*, vol. 21, no. 43.

—— 'Sindh and Struggle for Liberation', *EPW*, vol. 22, no. 10.

—— 'Pakistan's Decade of Generals', *EPW*, 22, 28, 1987.

Ali, Mubarak, 'In the shadow of History' (Lahore: 1993), *The Herald*, July 1986.

Ali, Salamat, 'Trouble in Kashmir', *Far Eastern Economic Review*, 18 May 1989.

—— 'Line of control', *Far Eastern Economic Review*, 10 May 1990.

Ali, Tariq, *Pakistan: Military Rule or People's Power* (London: 1970).

Amin, Tabir and Bijwa, Nisar, *Kashmir Report* (Institute of Policy studies, Islamabad: June 1990).

Amin, Tahir, *Ethno-National Movements of Pakistan: domestic and international factors* (Islamabad: 1988).

Amjad, Rashid, *Private Industrial Investment in Pakistan 1960–70* (Cambridge: 1982).

Anderson, B., *Imagined Communities: Reflections on the Origin and Spread of Nationalism* (London: 1983).

Ardener, E., *The Voice of Prophecy and other Essays* (Oxford: 1989).

Arnold, David, *Police Power and Colonial Rule: Madras 1859–1947* (New Delhi: 1986).

Aslam, Talat, 'MQM: The Trial Begins', *The Herald*, February 1988.

Ayoob, Mohammed ed., *Regional Security in the Third World: Case Studies from South East Asia and the Middle East* (Kent: 1996).

Azar, Edward E. and Chung-in Moon eds., *National Security in the Third World: the management of internal and external threats* (Aldershot: 1988).

Azmi, Ahmed A., *Kashmir: An Unparalleled Curfew* (Karachi: 1990).

Bagchi, Amiya Kumar, 'Public Sector Industry and Quest for Self-reliance in India', *EPW*, 17, 14–16 April 1982.

Bahadur, Kalim, 'National Integration in Pakistan: The case of Muhajir Qawmi Movement (MQM)', *Journal of Peace Studies*, vol. II, Issues 12–13 September–December 1995.

Bajpai, Kanti et al., *Jammu and Kashmir: An agenda for the future* (Delhi Policy Group, Delhi: March 1999)

Bakhtiar, Idrees, 'Estranged Bedfellows', *The Herald*, March 1997.

——'The MQM: Dead or Alive', *The Herald*, December 1992.

Ballard, Roger, 'Kashmir Crisis View from Mirpur', *EPW*, vol. XXVII, 90 and 91, 2–9 March 1991.

Baloch, Inayatullah, 'The Baluch Question in Pakistan and the Right of Self-Determination' in W. Zingle, *Pakistan in the 80s: Law and constitution* (Lahore: 1985)

Banton, Michael, 'Modelling Ethnic and National Relations', *Ethnic and Racial Studies*, 17 January 1994.

Banuazizi, Ali and Weiner Myron eds., *The State, Religion and Ethnic Politics in Pakistan, Iran and Afghanistan* (Lahore: 1987).

Bardhan, Pranab, 'Dominant Proprietary Classes and Indian Democracy' in Atul Kohli ed., *India's Democracy: an analysis of changing state-society relations* (Princeton: 1990).

Barpujari, H.K., 'North East India: The Problem and Policies since 1947', General President's Address, Indian History Congress, Calcutta, 1995.

Barth, F. ed., *Ethnic Groups and Boundaries: The Social Organization of Cultural Difference* (London 1969).

Basu, Subho and Das, Suranjan eds., *Electoral Politics in South Asia* (Calcutta: 2000).

Bazaz, Prem Nath, *The History of Struggle for Freedom in Kashmir* (1976).

——*The shape of things in Kashmir* (New Delhi: 1965).

——*Kashmir in crucible* (New Delhi: 1967).

Beg, Aziz, *Captive Kashmir* (Lahore: 1957).

Beg, Mahammad Afzal, *Sheikh Abdullah defended* (Srinagar: 1961).

Bettleheim, C., *India Independent* (tr. W.A. Caswell, London: 1968).

Bhatia, Prem, 'The Kashmiri Muslims' psyche', *Amrita Bazar Patrika* (Calcutta), 3 September 1988.

Bhattacharya, Ajit, *Kashmir: The Wounded Valley* (New Delhi: 1994).

Bose, Jyoti et al. eds., *People's Power in Practice: 20 years of Left Front in West Bengal* (Calcutta: 1997).

Bose, N.K., 'Social and Cultural Life in Calcutta', *Geographical Review of India*, 20 December 1958.

Bose, Sumantra, *The Challenge in Kashmir: Democracy, Self-Determination and a Just Peace* (New Delhi: 1997).

Brass, Paul, *The Politics of India after Independence, New Cambridge History of India*, vol. IV: 1 (Cambridge: 1990).

——*Ethnicity and Nationalism* (New Delhi: 1991).

Breton, Reymond, 'From ethnic to civic nationalism', *Ethnic and Racial Studies* II: 1.

Brines, Russell, *The Indo-Pakistani Conflict* (London: 1968).

Brecher, Michael, *The Struggle for Kashmir* (New York: 1953).

Burke, S.M., *Pakistani Foreign Policy: A Historical Analysis* (London: 1973).

Burki, Shahid J., 'Twenty Years of the Civil Service of Pakistan: A Re-evaluation', *Asian Survey*, vol. 9, no. 4, April 1969.

——*Pakistan: The continuing search for Nationhood* (Boulder: 1991).

Buzan, Barry, Regional Security (I), *Arbejdsprirer no. 28* (Copenhagen: 1989).

——*People, States and Fear; the national security problem in international relations* (Sussex: 1983).

Callard, Keith, *Pakistan: A Political Study* (London: 1977).

Castles, Stephen et al., *Mistaken Identity* (Sydney: 1992).

Chadda, Maya, *Ethnicity, Security and Separatism in India* (Columbia: 1997).

Chagla M.C., *Kashmir 1947–1985* (New Delhi: 1965).

Chakrabarti, Shyamal, *Kashmir: Atit, Bartaman, Bhabishyat* (in Bengali; Calcutta: 2000).

Chandra, Nirmal K., 'Role of Foreign Capital in India', *Social Scientist*, no. 57, 1977.

Chatterjee, Rakhahari, 'Ethnicity and Confict in South Asia: A Sudy of Two Cases', in Kanti Bajpai et al. eds., *Essays in Honour of A P. Rana* (Baroda: 1989).

Chaudhuri, Asim, *Private Economic Power in India: A Study in Genesis and Concentration* (Delhi: 1975).

Chitkara, M.G., *Muhajir's Pakistan* (New Delhi: 1996).

Chopra, V.D., *Genesis of Indo-Pakistan Conflict* (New Delhi: 1990).

185

Kashmir and Sindh

Clad, James and Ali, Salamat, 'Will words lead to war?', *Far Eastern Economic Review*, 26 April 1990.
Cohen, Stephen P., 'Kashmir: The Roads Ahead', in Stephen P. Cohen and Kanti Bajpai eds., *South Asia after the Cold War: International Perspectives* (Boulder: 1993).
Committee For Initiative on Kashmir, *India's Kashmir War* (New Delhi: 1990).
Cronin, Richard P. and Lepoer, Barbara Leitch, *South Asia: US Interests and Policy Issues* (Congressional Research Service, Library of Congress, Washington DC: 12 February 1993).
——*The Kashmir Dispute: Historical Background to the Current Struggle* (Congressional Research Service, Library of Congress, Washington DC: 19 July 1991).
Das, Suranjan, 'The Indian National Congress and the Dynamics of Nation-Building: Aspects of Continuity and Change', in T.V. Sathyamurthy ed., *State and Nation in the Context of Social Change*, vol. I (Delhi: 1994).
——'Regional Security through Constructive Bilateralism: Prospects for South Asian Stability', *EPW*, vol. XXXV, no. 49, 2–8 December 2000.
Das Gupta, Jyoti Bhusan, *Jammu and Kashmir* (The Hague: 1968).
De, Barun and Das, Suranjan, 'Ethnic Revivalism: Problems in the Indian Union' in K.S. Singh ed., *Ethnicity, Caste and People: India and the Soviet Union* (New Delhi: 1990).
Desmond, Edward, 'The insurgency in Kashmir', *Contemporary South Asia*, 1985, 4(1), March 1995.
Devos, George A., and Romanucci, L Ross eds., *Ethnic Identity: Cultural Continuities and Change* (Chicago: 1982).
Dhar, Somanth, *Jammu and Kashmir* (New Delhi: 1977).
Dixit, Jyotinder N., *My South Block Years: Memoirs of a Foreign Secretary* (New Delhi: 1998).
Dole, N.Y., 'Kashmir: A Deep-Rrooted Alienation', *EPW*, 5–12 May 1990, XXV, 18 and 19.
Douglass, A. William, 'A Critique of Recent Trends in the Analysis of Ethnonationalism', *Ethnic and Recial Studies*, vol. III, no. 2, April 1988.
Dua, B.P., *The Indian National Congress and Indian Society 1885–1985: ideology, social structure and political dominance* (Delhi: 1989).
Edward, John, *Languages, Society and Identity* (Oxford: 1985).
Embree, T. Ainslie, 'Pluralism and National Integration: The Indian Experience', *Journal of International Affairs*, vol. 27, no. 1, 1973.
Enloe, Cynthia, 'Religion and Ethnicity' in P. Sugar ed., *Ethnic Diversity and Conflicts in Eastern Europe* (Santa Barbara: 1980).
Engineer, Asghar Ali, *Secular crown on fire: The Kashmir Problem* (Delhi: 1991).
Eriksen, Thomas. H., 'Ethnicity and Nationalism: Definitions and Critical Reflections', *Bulletin of Peace Proposals*, vol. 23 (2), 1992.
——*Ethnicity and Nationalism* (London: 1993).
Esposito, John L., 'Islam: Ideology and Politics in Pakistan' in Ali Banuazizi and Myron Weiner, *The state, religion, and ethnic politics: Pakistan, Iran and Afghanistan* (Lahore: 1987).
Featherstone, Mike, *Global Culture: Nationalism, Globalisation and Modernity* (London: 1990).
Fernandes George, 'India's Policies in Kashmir: An Assessment and Discourse', in Raju G.C. Thomas ed., *Perspectives on Kashmir: The roots of conflict in South Asia* (Boulder: 1992).
Ganar, Jabbar Abdul, *Kashmir and National Conference Politics 1975–1981* (Srinagar: 1984).
Ganguly, Sumit, *The Crisis in Kashmir: Portents of War, Hopes of Peace* (Cambridge: 1997).

——'The Prospects of War and Peace in Kashmir' in Raju G.C. Thomas ed., *Perspectives on Kashmir: The roots of conflict in South Asia* (Boulder: 1992).

Geertz, Clifford, 'The New Integration Revolution: Primordialist Sentiments and Civil Politics in New States' in Cliford Geertz ed., *Old Societies and New States* (Glencow: 1988).

Gellner, Ernest, *Nations and Nationalism* (Oxford: 1983).

Ghosh, Rajeswari ed., *Protest Movements in South and South-East India: Traditional and Modern Idioms of Expression* (Hong Kong: 1987).

Giddens, Anthony, *The Consequences of Modernity* (Cambridge: 1991).

Glazer, N. and Moynihan, D.P., *Ethnicity* (Harvard: 1975).

Gopal, Sarvapalli, *Jawaharlal Nehru: A Biography 1947–56* vol. II (New Delhi: 1979).

——*Jawaharlal Nehru: A Biography*, vol. III (Delhi: 1985).

Gossman, Patricia, 'An International Human Rights Perspective' in Robert G. Wrising ed., *Kashmir: Resolving Regional Confiict. A symposium* (Meerut: 1998).

Gough, K. and Sharma, H.P. eds., *Imperialism and Revolution in South Asia* (New York: 1973).

Gramsci, Antonio, *Selections from the Prison Notebooks*, ed. and tr. Quintin Hoare and Geoffrey Nowell Smith (London: 1990).

Gupta, Dipankar, *The Context of Ethnicity: Sikh Identity in a Comparative Perspective* (Delhi: 1997).

——'The Indispensable Center: Ethnicity and Politics in the Indian State', *Journal of Contemporary Asia*, vol. 20, no. 4, 1990.

Gupta, Sisir, *Kashmir: A Study in Indo-Pakistan Relations* (Bombay: 1967).

Gurmani, M.A., 'The Pakistan Minister for Kashmir Affairs', *Pakistan Times*, 14 Jan 1949.

Haq, Zia-ul-, 'Islamic Processes: Realities and Trends', *South Asia Bulletin*, 8, 1988.

Harrison, Selig S., *India: the most dangerous decades* (Princeton: 1960).

——*In Afghanistan's Shadow: Baluch Nationalism and Soviet Temptations* (New York: 1981).

——'Ethnicity and Political Stalemate in Pakistan' in A. Banuzzui et al. eds., *The State, Religion and Ethnic Politics* (Lahore: 1987).

——'Ethnicity and Political Stalemate in Pakistan' in S. Akbar Zaidi ed., *Regional Imbalances and the National Question in Pakistan* (Lahore: 1982).

Hasan, Arif, 'Power and Powerlessness', *The Herald*, February 1988.

——'A Generation comes of Age', *The Herald*, October 1987.

——'A Decade of Urban Decay', *The Herald*, January 1990.

Hasan, S. et al., *Kashmir, Imprisoned: A Report* (Delhi: 1990).

Hashmi, Bilal, 'Dragon Seed: Military in the State' in Hasan Gandezi and Jamil Rashid eds., *Pakistan: the Roots of Dictatorship: the political economy of a praetorian state* (Delhi: 1986).

Hasnain, Ghulam, 'Carnage city', *Newsline*, July 1998.

Hassan, Arif, 'The MQM factor', *The Herald*, March 1987.

Hayes, Louis D., 'The impact of US policies on Kashmir conflict', *International Studies*, no. 2.

Heisler, Martin O., 'Ethnic and Ethnic Relations in the Modern West', in Joseph Montville ed., *Conflict and Peace-Making in Multiethnic Societies* (Lexington: 1990).

Hewitt, Vernon, *Reclaiming the Past: The Search for Political and Cultural Unity in Contemporary Kashmir* (London: 1995).

Hobsbawm, Eric, *Nations and Nationalism since 1780* (Cambridge: 1999).

Hoodbhoy, Nafisa, 'The rise of the Sindhi Press', *The Herald*, June 1995.

187

Horowitz, Donald, *Ethnic Groups in Conflict* (Berkeley: 1985).
——'Making Moderation Pay: The comparative politics of ethnic conflict management', in Joseph V. Montville ed., *Conflict and Peace-Making in Multiethnic Societies* (Lexington: 1990).
——'Ethnic conflict management for policymakers' in Joseph V. Montville ed., *Conflict and Peace-making in Multiethnic Societies* (Lexington: 1990).
Hussain, Altaf, *Safr-e-Zindagi and the Journey of Life* (Autobiographical Account of Altaf Hussain) (Lahore: 1988).
——*MQM constitutional petition in the Supreme Court of Pakistan* Part 1 (Boston: 1994).
Hussain, Karar, 'Sindh: The Rise and Growth of Nationalism', *Sindh Quarterly*, vol. XVI, no. 3, 1988.
Hussain, Mushahid and Hussain, Akmal, *Pakistan: Problems of Governance* (New Delhi: 1993).
Hussain, Zahid, 'Sindh: A Province Held to Ransom', *Newsline*, August 1998.
—— 'Sindh: Day of the Nationalist', *The Herald*, June 1998.
Hutchinson, John, *Modern Nationalism* (London: 1994).
Hutchinson, John and Smith, Anthony D. eds., *Ethnicity* (Oxford: 1996).
Islam, Rounaq, *Pakistan: Failure in National Integration*. (Dhaka: 1977 ed.).
Ispahani, Mahanaz, 'Pakistan: Dimensions of Insecurity', *Adelphi papers*, no. 246, Winter 1989/90.
Issacs, Harold, *Deas of the Tribe* (New York: 1975).
Jagmohan, *My Frozen Turbulence* (New Delhi: 1991).
Jain, Ajit Prasad, *Kashmir: What really happened* (Bombay: 1972).
Jalal, Ayesha, *The State of Martial Rule: the Origins of Pakistan's Political Economy of Defence* (Cambridge: 1990).
—— *The Sole Spokesman: Jinnah, the Muslim League and the Demand for Pakistan* (Cambridge: 1985).
—— *Democracy and Authoritarianism in South Asia: A comparative and historical perspective* (Cambridge: 1995).
—— 'Kashmir Scars', *New Republic*, July 23 1990.
Jamal, Yusuf, 'Terror in the valley', *The Telegraph*, 6 November 1988.
Jha, Prem Shankar, *Kashmir 1947: rival versions of history* (Delhi: 1998).
Kak, B.L., *Kashmir: The Untold Story of Men and Masters* (Jammu: 1974).
Kamal, Najir, 'Pakistani Perceptions and Prospects of Reducing the Nuclear Danger in South Asia', *Times of India*, 29 May 1999.
Kandar, Sahid, *The Political Economy of Pakistan* (Lahore: 1987).
Kaul, R.N., *Sheikh Mohammad Abdullah: A Political Phoenix* (Delhi: 1985).
Kaul, Santosh, *Freedom struggle in Jammu and Kashmir* (Delhi: 1990).
Kazi, Aftab 'Ethnic Nationalities, Education and Problems of National Integration in Pakistan', *Sindh Quarterly*, no. 1, 1989.
—— 'Ethnic Nationalism and Super-Powers in South Asia: Sindhis and Baluchis', *Journal of Asian and African Affairs*, vol. 1, July 1989.
Kennedy, Charles H., 'The Politics of Ehnicity in Sindh', *Asian Survey*, vol. XXXI, no. 10, Oct 1991.
—— 'Managing Ethnic Conflict: The case of Pakistan', *Regional Politics and Policy*, vol. 3, no. 1, spring 1983.
Khan, Hayat S.S., *The Nation that Lost its Soul: Memoirs of Sirdar Shaukat Hayat Khan* (Lahore: 1995).
Khan, Akbar, *Raiders in Kashmir* (Islamabad: 1970).

Khan, Asghar ed., *Islam, Politics and the State: The Pakistan Experience* (London: 1985).

Khan, Ayub, *Friends not Masters: A Political Autobiography* (Oxford: 1967).

Khan, Darya. 'A Sindhi view', *Sindh Quarterly*, vol. XVII, no. 4, 1989.

Khan, H. Mahamood, *Underdevelopment and Agrarian Structure in Pakistan* (Boulder: 1981).

Khan, Hafeez R., 'The Kashmir Intifada', *Pakistan Horizon*, vol. 23, no. 2, April 1990.

Khan, I., *Fresh Perspectives on India and Pakistan* (Oxford: 1985).

Khan, Ibrahim M.S., *The Kashmir Saga* (Lahore: 1985).

Khan, M. Shafi, *Focus on Kashmir*, September 1989, February 1990 (Institute of Policy Studies, Islamabad: 1989).

Khan, Mohammad Asgar, 'Thoughts on Sindh', *Sindh Quarterly*, vol. XII, no. 2, 1984.

Khan, Mohammad Ishaq, 'Reflections on Kashmiri Nationalism', paper presented in the seminar on 'Towards understanding the Kashmir crisis', Jamia Milla Islamia, New Delhi, 13–15 November 2000.

Khan, Omar A., 'Political and Economic Aspects of Islamisation' in Asghar Khan ed., *Islam, Politics and the State: The Pakistan Experience* (London: 1980).

Khan, R.Z., 'The Kashmir Question and Struggle for Identity', paper presented at a seminar on Kashmir, University of Sweden, 11–12 April 1992.

Khan, Sairah Irshad, 'Living with violence', *Newsline*, October 1991.

Khory, Kavita, 'Separatism in South Asia: the politics of ethnic conflict and regional security' (unpublished Ph.D. thesis, University of Illinois at Urbana Champaign, 1991).

Khuhro, Hamida ed., *Sindh through centuries* (Karachi: 1993).

Kitromildes, Paschalls, 'Imagined communities and the origin of the national question in the Balkans', *European History Quarterly*, 19 February 1982.

Kohli, Atul, *The State and Poverty: The Politics of Reform* (Cambridge: 1989).

Korbel, Joseph, *Danger in Kashmir* (Princeton: 1966).

Krishna, R., 'Growth, investment and poverty in midterm appraisal of 6th plan', *EPW*, 18, 47, 19 November 1983.

Kureishi, Omar, 'The country that got derailed on its way to nationhood', *Asian Age*, 12 September 1999.

Lamb, Alastair, *Birth of A Tragedy: Kashmir 1947* (Hertingfordbury: 1994).

—— *Crisis in Kashmir 1947–1966* (London: 1966).

—— *Incomplete Partition: the genesis of the Kashmir Dispute* (Hertingfordbury: 1971).

—— *Kashmir: a disputed legacy* (Karachi: 1992 ed.).

Langhari, J.R., 'Environmental Concern: Kalabagh Dam and Sindh: Punjab Water Dispute in Pakistan', *Journal of Asian and African Affairs* vol-e, no. e, 1990.

—— 'The Kalabagh Dam and the Loss of Water to Sindh', *Sindh Quarterly*, vol. XIV, no. 4, 1981.

La Palembara, Joseph and Weiner, Myron, *Political Parties and Political Development* (Princeton: 1966).

Lieten, G., *Continuity and Change in Rural West Bengal* (New Delhi: 1992).

Lillenthal, David, 'Another Korea in the Making', *Colliers*, 4 August 1951.

Lockwood, E. David and Lepoel, Barbara L., *Kashmir: Conflict and Crisis* (Congressional Research Service, Library of Congress, Washington DC: 8 August 1991).

Lodhi, Maleeha, *Pakistan's Encounter with Democracy* (Lahore: 1994).

Maddison, A., 'The Historical Origins of Indian Poverty', *Banca Nazionale Del Lavoro Quarterly Review*, 23, 92, 1970.

Madhok, Balraj, *Jammu Kashmir and Ladakh: Problem and Solution* (Delhi: 1987).

—— *Kashmir: Centre of New Alignments* (New Delhi: 1963).

Mahmood, Sohail, *Sindh Report* (Lahore: 1989).

189

Majumder, Aunohita, 'A lost road map in J and K', *The Statesman*, 23 September 1999.
—— 'The Overbearing Past', *The Statesman*, 5 March 1998.
Malik, Bazaaz Gauri 'Genesis of Kashmir Trouble', *The Statesman*, 29 March 1990.
Malik, Iftikhar H., 'The Politics of Ethnic Sindh: Nation, Region and Community in Pakistan', in Subrata Mitra and R. Alison Lewis eds., *Subnational movements in Asia* (Westview: 1996).
—— 'The Kashmir Dispute: A Cul-de-Sac in Indo-Pakistan Relations?' in Raju G.C. Thomas ed., *Perspectives on Kashmir: The roots of conflict in South Asia* (Boulder: 1992).
Malkani, K.R., *The Sindh Story* (Delhi: 1984).
Maluka, Zulfikar Khalid, T*he Myth of Constitutionalism in Pakistan* (Karachi: 1995).
Manchanda, Rita. 'Loss of confidence', *Far Eastern Economic Review*, 3 September 1992.
—— 'Kashmir's worse-off half', *Himal South Asia*, May 1999.
Manzoor Faizili ed., *Kashmir Predilection* (Srinagar: 1988).
Maqsood, Arshad, 'New Delhi and Kashmir: Integration or Alienation?', *The Kashmir Dossier*, February 1991.
Mayer, P.B., 'Development and Deviance: The Congress as the Raj' in J. Masselos ed., *Struggling and Ruling: The Indian National Congress 1885–1985* (Delhi: 1987).
McNeill, William H., *Polyethnicity and national unity in world history* (Toronto: 1986).
Mehkri, G.M., 'Random thoughts on Sindh: some painful and ominous realities: Sindh and the immigrants from India', *Sindh Quarterly*, vol. XVI, no. 1, 1988.
—— 'The common man in Sindh', *Sindh Quarterly*, vol. XIII, no. 1, 1985.
Melucci, Alberto, *Nomads of the present* (London: 1989).
Mhaffee, De A., *Road to Kashmir* (Lahore).
Mir, Amir, 'The RAW factor', *Newsline*, April 1998.
Mirza, Mahamud, *Aaj Ka Sindh* (Lahore: 1986).
—— 'Rise and fall of the MQM', *The Friday Times*, 25 June–1 July 1992.
—— 'Altaf Hussain conspires to stage comeback', *The Friday Times*, 28 January–3 February 1993.
Montville, Joseph V., 'Epilogue: The Human Factor Revisited', in Joseph V. Montville ed., *Conflict and Peace-Making in Multiethnic Societies* (Lexington: 1990).
Morris-Jones, W.H., *Dominance and Dissent: Their interrelations in the Indian Party System* (London: 1966).
Mujtaba, Hassan, 'Sindhi, Separatism: Myth or Reality?' *Newsline*, February 1991.
—— 'Night without End', *Newsline*, August 1991.
Mukherjee, Dilip, 'Pakistan's Growing Pains: Language Riots in Sindh', *Times of India*, 17 July 1992.
Mullik, B.N. *My years with Nehru* (Bombay, New York: 1972).
Mumtaz, Khawar, 'The Gender Dimension in Sindh', in Kumar Rupesinghe and Khwar Mumtaj eds., *International Conflicts in South Asia* (New Delhi: 1996).
Mumtaz, Khawar and Shaheed, Farida, *Women of Pakistan: Two steps forward, one step back* (London: 1987).
Munshi, Surendra, 'Their Feudal Lords', *The Telegraph*, 28 June 1999.
Mustafa, Seema, 'Why Kashmir is still haunting', *The Asian Age*, 25 September 1999.
Nandurkar G.M. ed., *Sardar Patel in Tune with the Millions* (Birth Century vol. II, Ahmedabad: 1975).
—— *Sardar's letters – Mostly unknown* (Post Century vol. 1, part. 2, Ahmedabad: 1980).
Narayan, Jay Prakash, 'The Need to Re-Think', *The Hindustan Times*, 15 May 1964.
Nayar, Kuldip, 'Polls in Kashmir', *The Hindustan Times*, 31 January 1998.

Nehru, Jawaharlal, *Independence and after* (New Delhi: 1949).

Noman, Omar, *The Political Economy of Pakistan 1947–85* (London: 1988).

Noorani, A.G., 'The Betrayal of Kashmir: Pakistan's Duplicity and India's Complicity' in Raju G.C. Thomas ed., *Perspectives on Kashmir: The roots of conflict in South Asia* (Boulder: 1992).

—— 'A pattern of outrages in Kashmir', *The Statesman Weekly*, 8 May 1993.

Nossiter, T.J., *Marxist State Governments in India* (London: 1988).

Oldenburg, Philip, *India Briefing, 1990* (Boulder 1970).

Panhwar, M.H., 'The Economic Plight of Sindh under Pakistan', *Sindh Quarterly*, vol. XVIII, no. 2, 1990.

Papnek, Hanna, 'Pakistan's Big Businessmen' *Economic Development and Cultural Change* 21, 1972.

Patel, Vallabbhai, *The Tragedy of Kashmi* (New Delhi: 1975).

Phadnis, Urmila, 'Ethnic Dynamic in South Asian State', *South Asia Journal*, January–March 1990.

Poplai S.L. (ed.), *India 1947–50*, vol. 1, Internal Affairs (Oxford: 1959).

Premdas, Ralph R., *The Internationalization of Ethnic Conflict*.

Punjabi, Riyaz, 'Kashmir: The Bruised Identity', in Raju G.C. Thomas ed., *Perspectives on Kashmir: The roots of conflict in South Asia* (Boulder: 1992).

Puri, Balraj, *Jammu and Kashmir: Triumph and Tragedy of Indian Federalism* (New Delhi: 1981).

—— 'Jammu and Kashmir: Congress (I)'s Short Sighted Game', *EPW*, vol. XVIII no. 49, 3 December 1983.

—— 'The Challenge of Kashmir', *EPW*, vol. XXV, no. 4, 27 January 1990.

—— 'Why Jammu goes restive', *The Tribune*, 10 December 1990.

—— 'Kashmiriyat: the vitality of Kashmiri identity', *Contemporary South Asia*, 1995 4(1).

—— *Kashmir Towards Insurgency: Tracts For Times* 4 (New Delhi: 1995 ed.).

—— *Jammu: A Clue to Kashmir Tangle* (Delhi: 1966).

Pye, L.W., 'Party System and National Development in Asia', in Joseph La Palmobara and Myron Weiner eds., *Political Parties and Political Development* (Princeton: 1966).

Qasim, Mir, *My Life and Times* (New Delhi: 1992).

Ra'an, Uri, 'The Nation State Fallacy' in Joseph V. Montville ed., *Confict and Peacekeeping in Multiethnic Societies* (Lexington: 1990).

Rahaman, Nafisur and Soofi, A.G., *ABC of Kashmir's Bid for Freedom* (Muzaffarabad: 1956).

Rahman, Tariq, *Language and Politics in Pakistan* (Oxford: 1998 ed.).

Raina, Dina Nath, *Unhappy Kashmir: The Hidden Story* (New Delhi: 1990).

Rais, Rasul Baksh, 'Building state and nation in Pakistan', paper presented in ICES Seminar, August 1993, Colombo.

Ranadive, B.T., *National Problems and the Working Class in India* (Calcutta: 1989).

Rashdi, Mumtaz, 'Sindh Malaise', *Pakistan Illustrated Weekly*, 30 June 1991.

Rashid, Abbas and Saheed, Farida, *Pakistan: ethno-politics and contending elites* (Geneva: 1993).

Rashid, Jamal, 'Ethnic Conflicts', *The Friday Times*, 9–15 July 1992.

Raychaudhuri, Tapan, 'Historical Roots of Mass Poverty in South Asia: A hypothesis', *EPW*, 20, 18, 4 May 1985.

Reetz, Dietrich, 'National consolidation or fragmentation of Pakistan: The Dilemma of General Zia-ul-Haq (1977–1988)' in D. Weldemann, *Nationalism, Ethnicity, and Political Development: South Asian Perspective* (Delhi: 1991).

191

Kashmir and Sindh

Rizvi, Gowher, 'India, Pakistan and Kashmir Problem 1947–1972' in Raju G.C. Thomas ed., *Perspectives on Kashmir: The roots of conflict in South Asia* (Boulder: 1992).

—— 'Nehru and the Indo-Pakistan rivalry over Kashmir 1947–64' Contemporary South Asia 1995 4(1).

Rose, Leo, 'The Politics of Azad Kashmir' in Raju G.C. Thomas, *Perspectives on Kashmir: The roots of conflict in South Asia* (Boulder: 1992).

—— 'Indian Foreign Relations: Reassessing Basic Policies', in Marshall M. Boulton and Philip Oldendug eds., *India Briefing* (Boulder: 1970).

Rosen, G., *Democracy and Economic Change in India* (Berkeley: 1967).

Rotschild, Joseph, *Ethnopolitics: A Conceptional Framework* (New York: 1981).

Rudolph, Lloyd and Rudolph, Susanne, *In Pursuit of Lakshmi: the Political Economy of the Indian State* (Chicago: 1987).

Rustamji, F., 'Do we have to live with terrorism forever?', *Delhi Midday*, 23 March 1999.

Said, Abdul and Simons, R.L. ed., *Ethnicity in an international Context* (New Brunswick: 1978).

Sayed, Anwar H., 'Political parties and the Nationality Question in Pakistan', *Journal of South Asian and Middle Eastern Studies*, vol. XII no. 1, autumn 1988.

Sayeed, Khalid B., *Politics in Pakistan: The Nature and Direction of Change* (New York: 1980).

Schermerhorn, R.A., *Ethnic Plurality in India* (Arizona: 1978).

Schofield, Victoria, *Kashmir in crossfire* (London: 1996).

Shah, Mehtab Ali, 'The Kashmir Problem: a view from four provinces of Pakistan', *Contemporary South Asia*, 1995 4 (1).

—— *The Foreign Policy of Pakistan: Ethnic Impact of Diplomacy 1971–1994* (London and New York: 1997).

Shah, Sayid G. Mustafa, 'Sindhology: its meaning and scope', *Sindh Quarterly*, vol. X, no. 3, 1982.

—— 'Sindhi Literature and Sindhi Society', *Sindh Quarterly*, vol. X, no. 1, 1982.

—— 'Sindh: Conflagration of Martial Laws and its Resurrection from Ashes', *Sindh Quarterly*, vol. XV, no. 1, 1987.

—— 'Sindh Society and Sindh Tomorrow: The Resurgence and the Revolt of the Indigenous in Pakistan', *Sindh Quarterly*, vol. XV, no. 4, 1987.

—— 'Sindh: The causes of present discontent, Sindhi leadership, hopes and hazards', *Sindh Quarterly*, vol. XII, no. 1, 1984.

Shepperdson, M. and Simmons, C. eds., *The Indian National Congress and the Political Economy of India 1885–1947* (Aldershot: 1988).

Shiels, L. Fredrick ed., *Ethnic Separatism and World Politics* (New York: 1984).

Shirokov, G.K., *Industrialization of India* (Moscow: 1973).

Silva, K.M. De and May, R.J. eds., *Internationalization of Ethnic Conflict* (New York: 1982).

Singh, Karan, *Heir Apparent: An autobiography* (Delhi: 1982).

Singh, P.C., 'Muhajirs and Ethno-Nationalism in Pakistan', *Journal of Peace Studies*, vol. II, 12–13, September–December 1995.

Singh, Prakash, 'An Indian Perspective II', in Robert G. Wrising ed., *Kashmir: Resolving Regional Conflict: A Symposium* (Meerut: 1996).

Singh, Tavleen, *Kashmir: A Tragedy of Errors* (New Delhi: 1995).

Smith, Anthony D., *The Ethnic Reviva*, (Cambridge: 1981).

—— *Nations and Nationalism in a Global Era* (Cambridge: 1996 ed.).

—— 'Ethnic Myths and Ethnic Revivals', *Archives Europeens De Sociologie*, 24 March 1984.

Stack, John F. ed., *Ethnic Identities in a Transitional World* (Connecticut: 1981).

Subrahmanyam, K., 'Kashmir', *Strategic Analysis*, vol. III, no. 2, May 1990.

Suffi, G.M.D., *Kashmir*, vol. 1 (1974 ed.).

Suhrawardy, A.H., *Kashmir: The Incredible Freedom Fight* (Lahore: 1991).

Suhrke, Astri and Noble, Laela Garner eds., *Ethnic Groups in International Relations* (New York: 1977).

Surjeet, Harkishen Sing, *Kashmir and its future* (People's Publishing House: 1955).

Syed, Anwar H., 'Political Parties and the Nationality Question in Pakistan', *Journal of South Asian and Middle Eastern Studies*, vol. XXII, no. 1, autumn 1988.

Syed, G.M., *Sindhoodesh chho ain chha lai* (Ulhasnagar: 1974).

—— *Sindhudesh: A study in its separate identity through the ages* (Karachi: nd).

—— *A Case for Sindhudesh* (Bombay: 1985).

Symonds, Richard, *The Making of Pakistan* (London: 1950).

Teresa, Joseph, *Kashmir, human rights and the Indian Press: Contemporary South Asia* (2000) 9(1).

Tonyo, Mahammad Bachal, 'Ethnicity in Sindh and national cohesion', *Sindh Quarterly*, vol. XIX, no. 1, 1991.

Tremblay, Reeta Chaudhuri, 'Kashmir: The valley's political dynamics', *Contemporary South Asia*, vol. 4, no. 1, March 1995.

Thomas, Raju G.C. ed., *Perspectives on Kashmir: the roots of conflict in South Asia* (Boulder: 1992).

Varshney, Asutosh, 'Three Compromised Nationalisms: why Kashmir has been a problem' in Raju G. C. Thomas ed., *Perspectives on Kashmir: The roots of conflict in South Asia* (Boulder: 1992).

Vas, Lt. Gen. E.A. (Rtd.), *Without Baggage: A Personal Account of the Jammu and Kashmir operations October 1947–January 1949* (Dehradoon: 1987).

Verkaaik, Oskar, *A people of migrants: ethnicity, state and religion in Karachi* (Amsterdam: 1994).

Vincent, John A., 'Differentiation and Resistance: Ethnicity in Valle d' Aosta and Kashmir', *Ethnic and Racial Studies*, vol. 5, no. 3, July 1982.

Viswam, S. and Ali, Salamat, 'Vale of Tears', *Far Eastern Economic Review*, 8 February 1990.

Waseem, Mohammad, *Politics and the state in Pakistan* (Islamabad: 1994).

—— 'Ethnic conflict in Pakistan: Case of MQM', paper presented at the conference on 'Communalism and Migration: South Asians in diaspora', Edinburgh, June 1997.

Webster, N., *Panchayati Raj and the Decentralization of Development Planning in West Bengal: a case study* (Copenhagen: 1990).

Weiner, Myron, 'The Macedonian Syndrome: An Historical Model of International Relations and Political Development', *World Politics*, vol. XXIII, no. 4, July 1973.

—— *The Indian Paradox: Essays in Indian Politics* (New Delhi: 1989).

Welsh, David, "Domestic Politics and Ethnic Conflict", *Survival* vol. 35, no. 1, spring 1993.

Westergaard, K., *People's Participation, local government and rural development: the case of West Bengal* (Copenhagen 1986).

Widmalm, Sten, *Democracy and Violent Separatism in India: Kashmir in a Comparative Perspective* (Uppsala: 1997).

Wilcox, Wayne Ayers, *Pakistan: The consolidation of a nation* (New York: 1963).

Wright, P. Theodar Jr., 'Indian Muslim Refugees in the Politics of Pakistan', *Journal of Commonwealth and Comparative Politics*, July 1974.

—— 'Centre-Periphery Relations and Ethnic Conflict in Pakistan: Sindhis, Muhajirs, Punjabis', *Comparative Politics*, April 1991.

Wrising, Robert G., 'Kashmir Conflict: The new phase' in C.H. Kennedy ed., *Pakistan* (Boulder: 1983).

—— 'Ethnicity and Political Record in Pakistan', *Asian Affairs*, vol. 15 no. 2, summer 1988.

—— *India, Pakistan and the Kashmir Dispute: On Regional Conflict and Its Resolution* (New York: 1994).

—— ed., *Kashmir: resolving regional conflict: a symposium* (Meerut: 1996).

Yaap, M., 'Language, religion and political identity: a general framework' in David Taylor and M. Yapp eds., *Political Identity in South Asia* (London: 1979).

Zaidi, A.M. ed., *Congress Presidential Addresses*, vol. 5 (New Delhi: 1989).

Zaidi, S. Akbar, 'Sindh Vs Muhajir: Contradiction, conflict, compromise', in S. Akbar Zaidi ed.,*Regional Imbalances and the National Question in Pakistan* (Lahore: 1992).

—— *Regional Imbalances and the National Question in Pakistan* (London: 1992).

—— *Issues in Pakistan's Economy* (Karachi: 1999).

—— 'How the Bourgeoisie views Pakistan', *EPW*, 23, 48, 1988.

Ziring, Lawrence, 'The Rann of Kutch', in Masuma Hasan, ed., *Pakistan in a changing world: Essays in Honour of K.K. Sarwar Hasan* (Karachi: 1978).

—— *Pakistan: The Enigma of Political Development* (Folkestone: 1980).

—— 'Public Policy Dilemas and Pakistan's Nationality Problem: The Legacy of Zia-ul-Haq', *Asian Survey*, vol. XXVIII, no. 8, August 1988.

Zutshi, U.K., *Emergence of Political Awakening in Kashmir* (Delhi: 1988).

B. NEWSPAPERS, PERIODICALS AND PRESS REPORTS

Agence France Presse (Paris)
Amrita Bazar Patrika (Calcutta)
Communalism Combat (Mumbai)
Contemporary South Asia (Abingdon)
Economic and Political Weekly (Mumbai)
Far Eastern Economic Review (Hong Kong)
Foreign Broadcast Information Service (Washington DC)
Ganashakti (Calcutta)
Himal South Asia (Kathmandu)
India Today (Delhi)
New York Times (New York)
Newsline (Karachi)
Newsweek (New York)
Pakistan Horizon (Karachi)
Pakistan Observer (Dhaka)
Pakistan Times (Islamabad)
Peace Initiatives (Delhi)
People's Democracy (Delhi)
Public Opinion Trends Analysis and News Service (Delhi)
Regional Studies (Islamabad)
Reuter's Library Report

Sindh Quarterly
South Asia Journal (New Delhi)
Strategic Analysis (New Delhi)
Survival (London)
Surya India (Delhi)
The Asian Age (Calcutta)
The British Broadcasting Corporation Report (London)
The Dawn (Karachi)
The Economist (London)
The Friday Times (Karachi)
The Frontline (Chennai)
The Herald (Karachi)
The Hindu (Chennai)
The Hindustan Times (Delhi and Calcutta)
The Indian Express (Delhi)
The Kashmir Times (Jammu)
The Morning News (Karachi)
The Nation (Lahore)
The New Republic (New York)
The Organiser (Delhi)
The Patriot (Delhi)
The Pioneer (Delhi)
The Sindh Percher (London)
The Statesman (Calcutta)
The Telegraph (Calcutta)
The Times (London)
The Times of India (Delhi and Calcutta)
The Tribune (Chandigarh)
The Viewpoint (Lahore)

Index